THE GARDEN
TREES
HANDBOOK

A complete guide to
choosing, planting and caring
for garden trees

ALAN TOOGOOD

Facts On File
New York • Oxford • Sydney

Copyright © 1990 by Swallow Publishing Ltd

Facts On File, Inc.
460 Park Avenue South
New York NY 10016
USA

Toogood. Alan R.
The garden trees handbook: a complete guide to choosing, planting, and caring for garden trees / Alan Toogood.
p.   cm.
ISBN 0-8160-2275-5
1. Ornamental trees. I. Title.
SB435.T64 1990   89-48820
635.9′77--dc20   CIP

Conceived and produced by
Swallow Books
260 Pentonville Road
London N1 9JY

Project Designer: Stephen Bitti
Designers: Hilary Krag and Paul Oakley
Editor: Sam Elder
Consultant: Carol Hupping
Picture Research: Liz Eddison
Encyclopedia Illustrations: Coral Mula
Practical Illustrations: Will Giles, Gillie Newman, Sandra Pond and Michael Woods
Maps: Swanston Graphics, Derby
Studio: Del and Co
Typesetter: Goodfellow and Egan, Cambridge
Printed in Singapore by Imago

CONTENTS

1

WHY

GROW

TREES?

*T*ree populations in the wild are decreasing as they are cleared to provide
land for growing crops, for housing and for roads, and similar major
construction projects. To a great extent in the past, and to a more limited extent
today, wild trees have been felled to provide timber for building. Conversely,
however, trees are being planted on a large scale nowadays, mainly for the
production of timber. Yet these commercial plantations are generally of one
species and do little to enhance the countryside.

It is important, therefore, that private gardeners, whether their plots are large
or small, as well as owners of large estates and parks, and those responsible for
town planning should all plant a diverse range of trees, not only for the
enjoyment of people but also to help the environment. Undeniably trees
enhance their surroundings. Properly cared for they add immeasurably to the
attractive appearance of a garden. Without trees the planet Earth would be a
desert. Already there are "tree deserts" in many parts of the world with
inevitable problems of soil erosion.

*Today it is important to plant trees not only for enjoyment, but also to help
the environment.*

INTRODUCING GARDEN TREES

The usual definition of a tree is a woody plant with only one stem, known as a trunk, from which branches are produced. Shrubs are also woody plants but they differ from trees in that they produce a number of stems.

With trees, branching may start very near ground level or it may commence higher up. The branch system is also known as the crown of a tree, and this term is applied especially to those trees which have a spreading habit of growth. The crown may be rounded or dome-shaped, for instance.

HABITS, SHAPES AND SIZES

Trees vary enormously in habit or appearance, as can be seen in the Encyclopedia of Trees section (pages 110–215). Some trees are conical or cone-shaped, which makes them compact in habit and useful where there is little space for lateral spread. Many of the conifers or cone-bearing trees, including the very popular

Right: Trees naturally vary widely in shape, some growing quite formally as in the cone-shaped conifers, a good example of which, Chamaecyparis lawsoniana, *is shown here.*

Basic tree shapes: **1** *Broad columnar, with minimum lateral spread;* **2** *Conical, typical of many of the conifers;* **3** *Fastigiate, in which the branches grow upwards;* **4** *Spreading, the majority of trees are this shape; and* **5** *Weeping, with pendulous branches.*

cupressus and tsuga, are of conical habit.

Also with minimal lateral spread are the broad columnar trees, such as thuja and some ilex, whose branches grow upwards rather than outwards. This is also the case with fastigiate trees, whose branches are almost vertical, more or less in line with the trunk. These are the narrowest trees available and extremely useful where space is limited, as in small gardens. Examples of fastigiate trees are *Prunus davidiana* (ornamental peach), *Populus nigra* 'Italica' (Lombardy poplar), *Fagus sylvatica* 'Dawyck' (Dawyck beech) and *Cupressus sempervirens* (Mediterranean cypress).

The majority of trees, however, have a spreading habit with their branches held at anything from almost horizontal to an angle of about 45 degrees. They obviously take up a lot more lateral space then conical, columnar or fastigiate kinds. Also wide-spreading are

1   2   3   4   5

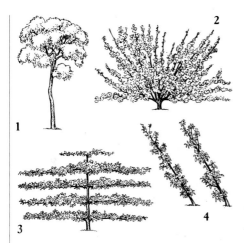

Artificial tree shapes: **1** *Standard;* **2** *Fan;*
3 *Espalier; and* **4** *Oblique cordon.*

Right: A vertical cordon, a useful form to train certain fruit trees such as apples and pears. Like the oblique cordon, it is economical in terms of space.

weeping trees whose branches are pendulous, in some species hanging right down to the ground. Examples of weeping trees are *Pyrus salicifolia* 'Pendula' (willow-leaved pear), *Salix alba* 'Tristis' (golden weeping willow) and *Fagus sylvatica* 'Pendula' (weeping beech).

Training trees

All those shapes are natural, but gardeners train trees to various other shapes, the most common being the standard tree. This has a branch-free trunk to a height of at least 1.8m (6ft) and then branching begins. It is a useful form if you want to sit or walk under the tree and is generally used for street trees. It is also used for some fruiting trees, such as apples and pears. There is also a half-standard, whose length of clear trunk is about half that of the standard. Again, it is popular for some fruiting trees.

Gardeners also produce dwarf, restricted forms of trees, often with stems or branches on one plane (such as cordons, espaliers and fans) in order to accommodate them in small gardens. This applies generally to fruiting trees such as apples and pears, although other fruit trees can be trained too. Generally, these forms do not

come within the scope of this book so specific information is not included. Furthermore, not everyone approves of such training. Gardeners interested in trained fruit trees should refer to a specialist fruit book.

Some trees are used for training into formal hedges. Among this group are *Fagus sylvatica* (European beech), *Taxus baccata* (English yew), *Chamaecyparis lawsoniana* (lawson cypress), × *Cupressocyparis leylandii* (leyland cypress), *Ilex aquifolium* (European holly) and *Carpinus betulus* (European hornbeam).

Possibly the most ancient form of tree training is bonsai, the art of dwarfing trees, which are grown in containers. Again, it is not within the scope of this book, but there are many publications available on this popular subject.

Height and spread

Trees vary enormously in size, ranging from 4.5m (15ft) in height to 91m (300ft) or more, as in *Sequoia sempervirens* (redwood). Certainly, there is something to suit every size of garden.

Height is not such a problem as spread in small gardens, but it makes sense not to choose an excessively tall tree for a small garden even

though it may have a very narrow fastigiate habit, for such a tree would be out of proportion with its surroundings. In the Encyclopedia section the listed trees have been grouped according to their height to make for easy selection.

The crown spread of spreading or weeping broad-leaved trees varies according to the tree's surroundings. In an open situation, with no other trees or buildings nearby, a tree will assume its full spread. But if surrounded or partly surrounded by other trees or buildings, the spread will be restricted. This is why spreads of trees have not been given in the Encyclopedia section. As a rough guide, sideways spread of broad-leaved trees grown in open conditions is about 40 per cent of height. This is a useful spacing guide when planting groups of trees.

The same comments apply to conifers, but spread can be approximately 20 per cent of height when trees are young and growing vigorously, and increase to around 33 per cent as they near maturity. Use the latter figure as a guide when spacing conifers. A few develop wider crowns, especially *Pinus pinea* (stone pine) and *Cedrus libani* (cedar of Lebanon), both of which become flat-topped and spreading with age.

Root spread is also variable, but you need to have some idea of this when planting so as to avoid possible damage to underground pipes and cables and the foundations of buildings. It can at least equal crown spread, but may be two or three times more. The roots of fastigiate and columnar trees will certainly spread further than the crown. Populus are known to have an extensive root spread and should be kept well away from underground services and buildings.

DECIDUOUS AND EVERGREEN

All trees are either deciduous or evergreen. Deciduous trees drop all their leaves each year, usually in the autumn. Once their leaves have fallen they become dormant or take a rest, when they are virtually inactive. Deciduous trees are mainly broad-leaved, although some conifers such as larix drop their leaves in autumn.

Trees are either deciduous or evergreen and it is a good idea to combine the two in groups. The majority of conifers are evergreen, but Larix decidua *is one that drops its leaves in autumn.*

Evergreen trees retain their leaves throughout the year. Old leaves are shed, however, and this is a continual process. If an evergreen tree suddenly loses a large amount of foliage, something is definitely wrong. Most conifers are evergreen, but there are also numerous broad-leaved evergreen trees.

Some trees are semi-evergreen, dropping most or all of their leaves in severe winter weather, but retaining their foliage during mild winters or when grown in warmer areas.

Unlike deciduous trees, evergreens do not have a dormant period. Many evergreens are more tender than deciduous trees and are best given protection from cold winter winds. Some may not succeed in very cold areas.

In any planting scheme you should aim for a mixture of deciduous and evergreen plants, which will be mainly shrubs and trees. A proportion that works well is two-thirds deciduous and one-third evergreen. If this is reversed and evergreens are dominant you will risk having a heavy, sombre scheme.

A tall screen or windbreak can consist of a mixture of evergreen and deciduous trees to avoid a solid "wall" of foliage, which can be rather claustrophobic. While evergreens are better for all-year-round wind protection, a mixed windbreak will still be effective provided it does not include too many deciduous trees.

ORIGINS OF THE TREES WE GROW

In northern Europe and North America the trees that are grown are either indigenous or come from similar climates. It is possible to grow some sub-tropical trees outdoors in these parts of the world provided they are attempted only in the milder areas. Trees from the tropics cannot be grown outdoors in these areas unless they come from high altitudes with a cool climate similar to our own.

The trees we grow originate from all over the world. There are eucalyptus and cordyline from Australia. China and Japan have given us many trees, including species of acer, cornus, malus, prunus, sorbus and magnolia. A species of aesculus comes from India, and the Himalayas have yielded species of rhododendron and betula, among others. There are species of crataegus, salix, fagus, quercus, sorbus and many more from northern Europe; and arbutus, aesculus, pinus, evergreen quercus, ficus and olea from the Mediterranean. Many trees originate from North America, including species of betula, cornus, cupressus, picea and sequoia. Native to South America are species of embothrium, araucaria and nothofagus. These few examples give some idea of the wide distribution of the trees we grow in our gardens and parks.

Many trees were introduced into cultivation in the 19th century and the early part of the 20th century, and their collection, together with many other plants, by intrepid plant hunters often risking their lives in hostile terrain, makes fascinating reading.

THE ROLE OF TREES IN THE GARDEN

Trees have many uses in gardens, from directing the eye to some particular part to providing shade for people and plants. In between they can provide colour and interest from leaves, flowers and stems. Shrubs can do all of these things, of course, but the purpose of including trees in gardens is to provide additional height to the overall scheme.

Planting schemes are often planned to form layers, such as you might find in nature. A ground-level layer can be formed of dwarf plants, including small shrubs and many hardy perennials and bulbs. A taller layer is then provided by larger shrubs and possibly some very tall perennials. Above these are trees and climbing plants. This arrangement not only allows the maximum use to be made of space, but also makes for a much more interesting scheme. For further inspiration, study the planting schemes in gardens open to the public.

FOCAL POINTS

A focal point is an object or a plant that draws the eye to a particular part of a garden to encourage people to explore that area. Many things that can be used as focal points: statues, ornate containers such as urns, seats, summer-houses, and plants like shrubs and trees.

A well-planned garden will be divided into a number of areas each hidden from the other, but there will also be vistas or long views. Focal points are generally created at the ends of vistas. They can also be created on the bends of paths or at the top of a flight of steps.

Suitable trees need to be distinctive, for they have to catch the eye. Good examples are the cone-shaped conifers, particularly those with

A group of Taxus baccata *'Fastigiata' (Irish yew) can be used to effect to create a distinctive focal point in a private garden.*

golden foliage such as *Chamaecyparis lawsoniana* 'Lane' (lawson cypress/Port Orford cedar). Due to its shape, *Juniperus virginiana* (pencil cedar) also makes an excellent focal point, as does the columnar *Taxus baccata* 'Fastigiata' (English yew). In a large garden the fastigiate *Cupressus sempervirens* (Mediterranean cypress) and the broad, columnar *Calocedrus decurrens* (Californian incense cedar) are superb.

Weeping trees are also distinctive, and for creating a focal point in a small garden consider planting *Pyrus salicifolia* 'Pendula' (willow-leaved pear) with silver-grey foliage. This colour creates a sense of distance, which is important in small gardens. For very large gardens and parks a larger weeping tree such as *Fagus sylvatica* 'Pendula' (weeping birch) is more appropriate.

Many more trees of outstanding habit and colour are included in the Encyclopedia section.

LAWN SPECIMENS

Many trees of distinctive habit are ideal for planting as single specimens in lawns. Many of those described in the Encyclopedia of Trees are recommended for this purpose. Lawn specimens can be used in both large and small gardens and, in fact, a lawn is generally one of the easiest places to plant trees. There should be no trouble digging planting holes as invariably there are few if any roots from other trees or shrubs to contend with. The trees will not be hemmed in by other plants and therefore should have optimum conditions for growth.

There are several reasons for using trees as lawn specimens. Firstly, as we have already seen, single trees can be used as focal points and often these are positioned in lawns – say at the end of a lawn to draw the eye further into the garden.

Specimen trees are also often used to "break up" a large expanse of lawn and this technique is to be seen in large gardens and estates. Trees are often included in the lawns of small gardens, however, because this is the only place for them: they have space to develop without encroaching on neighbours' gardens or overhanging the pavement or highway.

Obviously one should not have too many specimen trees in lawns, and in a small garden one would probably be sufficient. In larger gardens they can be dotted at random. Do not make the mistake of placing specimen trees in the middle of a lawn – this should be kept open to create a sense of space. Instead, position them near the edges.

Lawn specimens create the all-important height in garden design and for this reason alone are well worth considering. They also create contrast in shape, for lawn specimens should be of distinctive habit such as conical, broadly columnar, fastigiate or weeping. If you require light shade as relief from the sun, then a spreading lawn specimen will provide this.

Growing trees in isolation shows off any distinctive characteristics: for instance, attractive bark, large leaves, flowers and so on. Only trees with such features, or distinctive shape, should therefore be chosen for lawn planting.

That said, there are many trees that are suitable for growing in lawns. They include small trees like *Acer griseum* (paper-bark maple), *Betula* species (birch), *Prunus maackii* (Manchurian cherry), *Pyrus salicifolia* 'Pendula', *Salix purpurea* 'Pendula' (pendulous purple osier) and *Eucalyptus* species (gum tree). Medium and large trees include *Aesculus* species (horse chestnut), *Ailanthus altissima* (tree of heaven), *Betula* species, *Catalpa bignonioides* (Indian bean tree/ southern catalpa), *Ginkgo biloba* (maidenhair tree), *Gleditsia triacanthos* (honey locust), *Liquidambar styraciflua* (sweet gum), *Paulownia tomentosa* (royal paulownia), *Robinia pseudoacacia* (false acacia), *Araucaria araucana* (monkey puzzle), *Cedrus atlantica* (Atlas cedar) and *Eucalyptus* species.

Many other evergreen conifers are also suitable, especially cone-shaped ones, as are fruiting trees such as apples and pears.

Remember that some trees with a dense crown, like fagus and evergreen quercus, create a great deal of shade beneath them in which grass will not grow. If this is acceptable, then fine, otherwise choose trees with a very light canopy of foliage like betula species. Such trees will create dappled shade, or a pattern of shade and sunlight, and in these conditions the grass will thrive.

In any case, for the first few years of a tree's life it is highly recommended that a wide circle of bare soil is left around it to encourage optimum growth (see Chapter 3).

GROUPS OF TREES

Woodland gardening has become increasingly popular because there are so many desirable plants that thrive in cool, moist conditions with dappled shade. You do not have to live in the country to have a woodland garden – many people are creating this feature in town and city gardens where, surprisingly perhaps, they do not look out of place. Also, you don't need a large garden: the small-garden owner can create a woodland effect with two or three small trees.

If you have existing mature woodland then possibly all that needs to be done is to thin out some of the trees and maybe thin the crowns of the remainder (see page 66). Many large forest trees such as fagus and quercus have very dense crowns, creating too much shade. A certain amount of light is essential in a woodland garden; ideally there should be areas of light and shade. Few plants thrive in gloomy conditions.

If you are starting a woodland from scratch, choose trees with relatively light crowns such as betula species, many of which are valued for their white bark which contrasts well with other trees and shrubs. Examples that mix well with betula are *Sorbus aria* (whitebeam), *Sorbus aucuparia* (mountain ash), *Prunus avium* (wild cherry), *Prunus padus* (sweet cherry) and *Prunus subhirtella* (spring cherry). Evergreen trees also look good in a woodland garden and help to furnish it for the winter. Suitable examples include *Taxus baccata* and *Ilex aquifolium* (European holly).

If you simply want to plant groups of trees without necessarily creating a woodland garden you must give thought to contrast in shape, texture and colour. For instance, a group of spreading, conical and weeping trees makes a marvellous contrast in shape. Take account of foliage colour, too. There are all shades of green, there is grey and silvery foliage (particularly among the conifers), red- or purple-leaved trees, and there are trees with golden or variegated leaves. A group need not necessarily consist of only foliage trees. Consider some of those with attractive flowers (see pages 19–22).

Various trees, including betula and acer species, can be incorporated successfully into woodland.

SCREENING

In large gardens and estates tall trees can be used to good effect for screening and/or creating windbreaks. To make an aesthetically pleasing screen choose a mixture of evergreen and deciduous trees. A mix of broad-leaved and coniferous trees is pleasing, but a screen composed of one species only can look decidedly monotonous in the garden.

If you have a screen formed purely of evergreens it can create a very "heavy" or sombre appearance – a "great wall" which dominates the scene! A screen formed only of deciduous trees is not so effective at hiding things or filtering the wind, especially in the winter when the leaves have fallen. This is why a combination of evergreen and deciduous trees is more appropriate. Furthermore a mixed screen creates pleasing contrasts in shape, height, colour and texture.

Some combinations are, of course, more pleasing than others and there are many permutations to consider. For instance, why not consider a screen composed of *Chamaecyparis lawsoniana* (evergreen conifer), *Sorbus aria* (broad-leaved deciduous), *Picea abies* (evergreen conifer) and *Populus canescens* (broad-leaved deciduous). Plant these in "blocks" in the above sequence and you will have an interesting screen of variable height in green and grey shades.

A selection of trees suitable for forming screens and/or windbreaks is given in the box below and more examples will be found in the Encyclopedia.

Trees for screening can be planted as close as 1.8–2.4m (6–8ft) apart, in a single line or, if you

TREES FOR SCREENS AND WINDBREAKS

Evergreen	Colour	Mature height
Chamaecyparis lawsoniana	Deep green	30m/100ft
× *Cupressocyparis leylandii*	Grey-green	18m/60ft
Cupressus macrocarpa	Bright green	21m/70ft
Picea abies	Dark green	45m/150ft
Pinus nigra	Deep green	30m/100ft
Pinus radiata	Bright green	23m/75ft
Quercus ilex	Deep green	18m/60ft
Thuja plicata	Medium green	61m/200ft
Deciduous		
Larix decidua	Light green	45m/150ft
Populus alba	White or grey	27m/90ft
Populus canescens	Grey	30m/100ft
Populus tremula	Fresh green	27m/90ft
Quercus robur	Medium green	18-30m/60-100ft
Salix alba	Silky white	22m/75ft
Sorbus aria	Grey and white	15m/50ft
Tilia cordata	Deep green	30m/100ft

Gold or yellow is a popular foliage colour and brightens up a garden. This is a cultivar of Gleditsia triacanthos *(honey locust).*

want a really wide and dense screen, in double staggered rows. Later on it may be necessary to thin out some, but plant closely initially to give a quick effect. Sometimes a screen will become bare at the base as the lower branches of the trees naturally die off. Also, if the base of a screen is shaded by other large plants in front of it, then branches could die due to lack of light. So avoid planting anything tall that will reduce light immediately in front of a screen, in the early years at least. If the screen does become bare at the base, plant a row of tough shrubs in front of it to help filter the wind.

FOLIAGE COLOUR

Some deciduous trees have colourful foliage in the spring and summer, evergreens have colourful foliage all the year round.

One should be careful in the use of foliage colour, though, for not all colours suit all gardens. Because coloured-leaved trees are inclined to create an exotic atmosphere, be very wary of using them in natural or country gardens as they may not be in keeping with the general "atmosphere". A bright golden-leaved tree, for instance, would look distinctly out of place in a woodland-garden setting. In such situations it would be far better to use more subdued trees, perhaps opting for flowering kinds if some colour is needed. Furthermore, bear in mind that trees come in a vast array of green shades! Some grey-green or blue-green trees might be a better choice.

However, the exotic-looking coloured-foliage trees certainly have their uses and can be highly recommended for adding colour on a higher level in modern gardens or other areas. They are especially useful for associating with modern architecture and do much to enhance a "concrete jungle". Use them too in or near modern paved areas.

There are coloured-leaved trees for both large and small gardens. Often they are used as lawn specimens.

TREES FOR FOLIAGE COLOUR

Type of tree	Deciduous	Evergreen
Gold		
Acer negundo 'Auratum'	•	
Catalpa bignonioides 'Aurea'	•	
Cedrus deodara 'Aurea'		•
Chamaecyparis lawsonia cultivars		•
Chamaecyparis obtusa 'Crispii'		•
Cupressus macrocarpa cultivars		•
Fagus sylvatica 'Dawyck Gold'	•	
Gleditsia triacanthos 'Sunburst'	•	
Juniperus chinensis 'Aurea'		•
Red/purple		
Acer platanoides 'Crimson King'	•	
Fagus sylvatica 'Dawyck Purple', *purpurea*, and 'Riversii'	•	
Prunus cerasifera 'Nigra'	•	
Prunus cerasifera 'Pissardii'	•	
White-variegated		
Acer negundo 'Variegatum'	•	
Acer platanoides 'Drummondii'	•	
Ligustrum lucidum cultivars		•
Grey/silver		
Cedrus atlantica 'Glauca'		•
Chamaecyparis lawsoniana 'Elegantissima'		•
Eucalyptus gunnii		•
Picea pungens cultivars		•
Pyrus salicifolia 'Pendula'	•	
Sorbus aria		•

Giving a very bright effect are trees with yellow or gold foliage. Among the most popular here is *Gleditsia triacanthos* 'Sunburst' (honey locust). This colour helps to light up a garden, although the trees should not be grown in shade otherwise the colour will be lost – the leaves will revert to green. Yellow goes especially well with grey and, of course, with all shades of green, so there is no problem when it comes to combining plants. Some people combine yellow foliage with purple leaves, a very dramatic combination.

Trees with white-variegated foliage also help to lighten a planting scheme. A particularly popular one is *Acer negundo* 'Variegatum' (box elder). They show up especially well against a dark background, such as a group of deep green conifers. White-variegated foliage and purple leaves go well together.

Grey foliage creates a sense of distance in a garden and is therefore particularly useful in small gardens where this illusion is most welcome. A specimen tree with grey foliage, such as *Pyrus salicifolia* 'Pendula' placed at the far end of the garden would be ideal in this situation.

Red or purple foliage, such as that of *Prunus cerasifera* 'Pissardii' (purple-leaved plum/cherry plum), can be rather "heavy", but looks good when associated with white-variegated leaves, such as the variegated box elder recommended above, or even shrubs such as *Cornus alba* 'Elegantissima' (dogwood) or *Rhamnus alaterna* 'Argenteovariegata' (buckthorn).

Other colours, as well as grey, can be used to help create the illusion that a garden is longer than it really is. The pale colours like grey, silver, pale blues or pale greens can create a sense of distance because they are not seen so intensely. These can be used at the far end of a garden. The strong colours such as red and purple are more clearly seen and therefore seem to be nearer the eye. They can appear to bring parts of the garden closer and are therefore best used nearest the house.

Many deciduous trees provide glorious autumn leaf colour. Generally these need a dark background to show them off, such as a group of dark green conifers. Trees with autumn foliage also look good near water, such as a lake. If autumn leaf colour is notable, this is indicated in

TREES FOR AUTUMN LEAF COLOUR

Name	Colour	Soil
Acer	Red shades	Acid
Amelanchier	Scarlet	Acid
Cercidiphyllum	Yellow or red	Acid
Liquidambar	Scarlet and orange	Acid
Malus (some species)	Red	Acid/alkaline
Nyssa	Red or orange	Acid
Parrotia	Gold, crimson, orange	Acid
Prunus (some species)	Flame shades	Acid to neutral
Quercus (some species)	Red	Acid to neutral
Sorbus (some species)	Gold, orange, red	Alkaline

the Encyclopedia. It should be borne in mind that leaf colour is variable: it can be better in some seasons than in others. Also, soil conditions may have an influence on leaf colour: it appears that autumn colour is better on the poorer soils, such as shallow chalks and acid, sandy types.

FLOWER COLOUR

Trees that are noted for their spectacular displays of flowers are particularly popular with private gardeners. There are many suitable for small gardens just as there are numerous large trees with conspicuous flowers suitable for the larger garden, for parks and estates. In addition, there are flowering trees for every season, although the majority tend to bloom in the spring or summer.

Try to position trees so that their flowers show up well. Many trees have light yellow, white or pale pink blooms which do not show against certain backgrounds. But given a dark background, perhaps composed of dark green broad-leaved evergreen trees or conifers, they will be really conspicuous.

Flowering trees do need choosing rather carefully for some are decidedly dull when out of flower – which can be for 50 weeks of the year. Unfortunately this does apply to some of the most popular flowering trees, including laburnum and most of the prunus species. These trees are very widely planted by amateur gardeners, yet for most of the time they are dull. This is not to say that they should not be planted – they can be highly recommended where sufficient space is available to grow them as part of a collection of trees for various seasons – but in small gardens where one or perhaps two small trees are all that one can grow, choose trees that still look attractive when out of flower. The alternative is to choose trees with two seasons of interest.

Flowering trees that are attractive when flowerless include *Caragana arborescens* (Siberian pea tree), as this has pleasing pinnate foliage; *Koelreuteria paniculata* (pride of India/varnish tree), again with pinnate leaves (both small trees); *Ailanthus altissima*, pinnate foliage; and *Catalpa bignonioides*, very bold foliage (both medium to large).

There are plenty of flowering trees with two seasons of interest – such as flowers in the spring and leaf tints and/or fruits in the autumn. Some of the prunus come in this category, including the medium-sized *Prunus sargentii*, which makes a good spring display with its pink flowers and becomes ablaze in autumn with flame shades.

Above: Amelanchiers or snowy mespilus are among the most beautiful small flowering deciduous trees, creating their display in the spring.

Above: Cercis siliquastrum, *the Judas tree, is a small deciduous tree noted for purple-rose pea flowers which are produced in late spring.*

Left: The Japanese crab, Malus floribunda, *is a very popular small flowering tree that produces a profusion of pale pink blossoms, which emerge from red-pink buds in late spring.*

Many of the malus have two seasons of interest, including the small-growing *M. × purpurea* and cultivars, and so do the crataegus like *C. crus-galli* (cockspur thorn).

Trees noted for flower colour do not need any more care than other trees. Feeding will help to initiate flower buds and the element potassium plays a role here. But all trees should be fed regularly, as described in Chapter 3.

The trees do not need pruning to produce a good display of flowers, as is commonly supposed – they will do this quite naturally. With trees it is not usual to remove dead flowers and indeed in many instances one should allow the seeds or fruits to develop as these are an added attraction. Not so with rhododendrons, though. With these it is recommended that the seed heads are carefully twisted off, ensuring the buds below them are not damaged. There is no point in allowing rhododendrons to spend their energy on seed production (unless you wish to save the seeds): far better to allow this energy to be spent on growth and flower-bud initiation.

The trees listed in the box below are particularly popular, but many more noted for their flowers will be found in the Encyclopedia.

TREES WITH ATTRACTIVE FLOWERS

Name	Colour	Size: Small	Medium	to large	Spring Early	Spring Mid	Spring Late	Summer Early	Summer Mid	Summer Late
Aesculus	Pink/white		●				●	●		
Amelanchier lamarckii	White	●			●	●	●			
Arbutus	White	●	●		●	●	●			
Catalpa	White or pink		●		●	●	●	●	●	●
Cercis siliquastrum	Purple-rose	●				●	●			
Cornus species	White/pink	●	●				●	●		
Crataegus laevigata cultivars	Pink/red/white	●				●	●			
Embothrium	Scarlet	●						●	●	
Eucryphia	White	●	●					●	●	●
Koelreuteria	Yellow	●							●	
Laburnum	Yellow-green		●					●	●	●
Magnolia	White/pink/purple	●	●		●	●	●	●	●	●
Malus floribunda	Pink	●				●	●			
Paulownia	Light violet		●			●	●			
Prunus	White/pink	●	●		●	●	●			
Rhododendron	Various	●			●	●	●			
Stewartia	White		●					●	●	●

STEM COLOUR

The subject of stem (trunk) colour is often neglected by gardeners, which is a pity since the bark of many trees is both interesting and attractive. Both deciduous and evergreen trees may have stems worthy of note.

The stems of trees generally show up best in winter when leaves have fallen and few plants are in flower. Generally speaking such trees need a suitable background if the stems are to show to advantage. Often they are used as lawn specimens because white or red-brown stems, for example, show up well against a background of grass. White stems especially, such as those of many species of betula, really show up well when given a dark background such as a group, hedge or screen of dark green conifers, or featured in a woodland garden.

The bark of Acer capillipes, *one of the striking snake-bark maples.*

TREES WITH ATTRACTIVE STEMS

Name	Colour/texture	Size: Small	Size: Medium to large
Acer species (many)	White, often striped	•	
Arbutus (some species)	Orange-red	•	•
Betula species (many)	Often white, patchwork	•	•
Cryptomeria japonica	Orange-brown, shredding		•
Eucalyptus	White, grey, patchwork	•	•
Metasequoia glyptostroboides	Red-brown, flaking		•
Platanus × acerifolia	Cream, brown, flaking		•
Prunus maackii	Brown, glossy, flaking	•	
Salix alba cultivars	Red, yellow, coloured twigs		•
Sequoia sempervirens	Red-brown, thick, fibrous		•
Sequoiadendron giganteum	Red-brown, thick, fibrous		•
Taxodium distichum	Red-brown, thick, fibrous		•
Thuja species	Brown shades, peeling		•
Trachycarpus fortunei	Brown, thick, fibrous	•	

Left: Eucalyptus or gum trees usually have attractive bark. E. niphophila, *the alpine snow gum, which has patchwork bark of several colours is one of the smallest eucalyptus and is therefore recommended for small gardens.*

Right: Many of the birches are noted for their white or silvery bark. This species, Betula ermanii, *is one of the best, a large tree with conspicuous peeling bark, which starts orange-brown, but later turns to cream-white.*

Below: Metasequoia glyptostroboides, *the dawn redwood, is a large coniferous tree with very attractive, flaking, reddish-brown bark. It makes a superb lawn specimen and looks especially good near water. The tree is deciduous with fresh green leaves in spring which turn gold in autumn.*

TREES TO PROVIDE SHADE

The best trees for providing shade are the spreading and weeping kinds; fastigiate, broad columnar and conical trees produce very much less. Including shade-giving trees in a scheme enhances the pleasure to be derived from the garden, not only aesthetically but in practical ways as well. Trees that give shade will allow you to sit on the lawn in comfort on a bright, hot day. Positioned alongside a patio or terrace, a shady tree will perform the same function in this outdoor-living area.

Shading, of course, is essential for many different plants. They prefer dappled shade – a pattern of shade and sunlight – and this is provided by deciduous trees with a light canopy of foliage such as betula, sorbus, crataegus, malus, pyrus and prunus, to name a few examples.

The majority of shade-loving plants will not grow under trees with a dense canopy of foliage and which cast really deep shade, such as fagus, evergreen quercus, and taxus. These dense trees provide ideal shade for people, but if only

light shade is required, particularly in a small garden, choose trees with a light canopy of foliage such as those recommended above.

FRUITS

Some trees carry crops of colourful ornamental fruits and are grown mainly for this purpose. Many are at their best in autumn. One point to note with such trees, particularly in country gardens, is that the fruits are quickly stripped by birds. Generally this is not such a problem in town and city gardens.

TREES WITH ORNAMENTAL FRUITS

Name (fruit description)	Small	Medium to large
Arbutus (large fruits)	●	
Cotoneaster frigidus (small berry fruits)	●	
Crataegus species (small berry fruits)	●	
Idesia polycarpa (small berry fruits)		●
Ilex (small berry fruits)	●	
Magnolia (some species, large, red)		●
Malus (mainly large fruits)	●	
Photinia (small berry fruits)	●	
Sorbus (small berry fruits)	●	

Before buying trees noted for ornamental fruits, take a look around your neighbourhood and make a note of those whose fruits persist for a long period. They are probably the ones that the birds do not relish and therefore leave alone. Birds seem to go for the small berry fruits such as those of sorbus, crataegus and ilex. Larger fruits, like those of most malus, generally tend to be left alone.

Do not underestimate the ornamental value of trees that bear edible fruits. Most are attractive when in flower and are extremely handsome when laden with crops of ripening fruits. Apple trees, for instance, make very attractive lawn specimens. See pages 205–15 for a descriptive list of trees with edible fruits.

In general, spreading trees, such as Crataegus × prunifolia, *are the best to choose if you want areas of shade in your garden.*

Fruiting trees are not suitable for street planting as falling fruits can make a mess of pavements. Home gardeners, too, should make sure fruiting trees do not overhang the highway nor, indeed, neighbours' gardens. Some fruits, particularly those of mulberries, can stain paving, so keep such kinds well away from patios or other paved areas.

Left: Sorbus vilmorinii *produces globular rose-pink berries in the autumn. This is a small tree suitable for planting in lawns and borders.*

Right: The black mulberry, Morus nigra, *produces sharp yet sweet fruits. A small tree, it makes a fine lawn specimen and is a good shade tree.*

Below: Crab apples often provide colourful autumn fruits and these are edible, generally being used for preserves. They are small trees which are frequently planted as specimens in lawns.

PLANT ASSOCIATIONS

In a garden, trees are not grown alone but take their place with many other plants. Even established lawn specimens may have diminutive plants growing around them, especially bulbs. In this section we will consider growing plants in groups that include trees as well as shrubs and perennials. You can create some very pleasing "pictures" by grouping plants well and this makes for a more interesting and aesthetically balanced garden.

All plants in any one group must, of course, require the same conditions, otherwise the scheme will not work. As an example of what to avoid, moisture-loving plants cannot be grown successfully with those that require very well-drained, dryish soils. And you cannot realistically grow sun-loving and shade-loving plants together.

You can create groups for different seasons of the year, and this type of arrangement is most pleasing. It is not difficult to achieve striking contrasts in flower and foliage colour and shape with such schemes.

The alternative is to group plants that "perform" in succession so that there is something of interest all the year round. This type of scheme is very easily planned provided you know the flowering seasons of the subjects you want to include.

When grouping plants always try to make sure that each variety helps to enhance the beauty of the others rather than dominating or clashing with them. The following examples of plant associations are intended to provide some practical ideas that will give much pleasure.

WOODLAND GARDEN

Betula species with white stems look superb in a woodland garden and, provided the soil is acid, contrast dramatically with red-flowered rhododendrons. Camellias, with pink or red flowers, also look good with birches, their deep green shiny foliage contrasting pleasantly with the white bark. These also need acid soil.

In a group of birches and rhododendrons, or camellias, you might like to include various perennials for contrast. Try an underplanting of hostas (plantain lilies) with large, bold foliage; and some drifts of candelabra primulas and *Meconopsis betonicifolia* (Himalayan blue poppy).

HEATHER GARDEN

A heather garden is nowadays a popular feature for it is labour-saving – the ground being densely covered by the heathers and therefore requiring neither weeding nor cultivation – and creates interest all the year round from flowers and coloured foliage.

Suitable trees to include in a heather garden, or as a background to heather beds, are again betula species with white bark. Also include pinus species as these are the natural companions of some heathers. Bear in mind that heathers should not be planted under trees.

Ulex or gorse is another natural companion for heathers and could be included in such a garden. *Ulex europaeus* can be recommended, but even better is the double-flowered 'Plenus'. The flowers of these spiny shrubs are yellow and appear mainly between early and late spring.

WET AREAS

There are several trees suitable for planting in wet areas, including alongside lakes and in bog gardens. One that is particularly recommended is *Taxodium distichum* (swamp cypress/bald cypress) with fibrous red-brown bark and deciduous bright green leaves that turn red-brown in autumn. There are numerous shrubs and perennials that enjoy these conditions to group with the taxodium. Coloured-stemmed cornus can be especially recommended; *Cornus alba* 'Sibirica' has bright crimson stems and *C. stolonifera* 'Flaviramea' has yellow shoots. These stems show up well in the winter when the leaves have fallen. Young shoots are the most brightly coloured, so for a good crop cut down the old stems to within a few centimetres of the ground each year in mid-spring.

The same technique can be used for several coloured-stemmed willows, so that they are grown as shrubs. Examples include *Salix alba* 'Chermesina' (scarlet willow) with orange-red young shoots, and *S. a.* 'Vitellina' (golden willow) whose young stems are bright yellow.

Moisture-loving perennials to include in this group if desired are *Osmunda regalis*, the 1.2m (4ft) high royal fern; and *Lysichiton americanum* (skunk cabbage) with huge yellow spathes in spring followed by large "cabbagy" foliage.

For planting at the edge of a lake or stream there is no moisture-loving tree to beat a weeping willow, like Salix alba *'Tristis'.*

LAWN SPECIMENS

Specimen trees in lawns may be accompanied by drifts of small spring-flowering bulbs beneath them, if you wish – not right up to the trunk, as you should allow a circle of bare soil around the tree, at least in the early years, but certainly in the grass below the branches.

Among the most popular small spring-flowering bulbs are crocuses, especially the large-flowered Dutch hybrids. There are various attractive species, too, such as *C. tomasinianus*, *C. vernus* and *C. aureus*. Other spring bulbs that look attractive in short grass are fritillarias (fritillaries). The most popular is *F. meleagris* (snake's-head fritillary/ checkered lily) with bell-shaped purple and white checkered flowers.

Left: Of the many trees suitable for planting in heather gardens birches with white stems are among the most attractive.

Obviously the bulbs should not be grown in dense shade, so this idea is suitable only for trees having light canopies that allow plenty of sun to reach the ground below the branches. Furthermore, you must be prepared to let the grass grow longer where the bulbs are planted for it should not be mown until the bulbs' foliage has completely died down. Cutting off green leaves will result in poor or no flowering the following year.

TREES FOR LAWNS
Acer griseum
Catalpa bignonioides
Gingko biloba
Pyrus salicifolia 'Pendula'

Pyrus salicifolia *'Pendula' is an excellent choice for lawn planting as it is distinctive.*

MIXED BORDER

In a mixed border you might well include for spring colour the small tree *Malus × purpurea* (purple crabapple) or a cultivar such as 'Eleyi' or 'Lemoinei', with purple-flushed young foliage and purple flowers. Adjacent to this try growing a cultivar of *Syringa vulgaris* (lilac), preferably one with white flowers. If the season allows them to flower together, you have a pleasing picture. If not, you will still have the foliage of the malus contrasting well with the white syringa.

Spring bulbs can be drifted around the malus and syringa. Late-flowering daffodils and *Muscari armeniacum* (grape hyacinth) with blue poker flowers are just two suggestions that work well. Plant them in really bold drifts for maximum impact.

Also for spring you might like to plant a *Magnolia salicifolia*, which produces its white blooms on bare branches in the middle of the season. Those fond of white and yellow schemes may wish to choose a yellow forsythia such as *F. viridissima* to go with this magnolia. Complete the picture with an underplanting of blue muscari as described above.

A very striking summer group could feature *Pyrus salicifolia* 'Pendula' (willow-leaved pear), a pendulous tree with silvery-grey foliage, surrounded by bold drifts of *Euphorbia griffithii* 'Fireglow'. This hardy perennial spurge has brilliant red-orange bracts that contrast beautifully with the grey pyrus, which creates an excellent foil. For something more subdued with the pyrus, plant *Philadelphus coronarius* 'Aureus', a mock orange with soft-gold foliage and scented white flowers in early summer. Another idea is to include pink or red shrub roses with the pyrus and to punctuate this group with blue or purple delphiniums.

There is no shortage of plants to choose from for autumn schemes. Firstly, select your tree for autumn leaf colour. This might be *Crataegus × prunifolia*, an acer or *Prunus sargentii* (Sargent cherry). Next choose some autumn-colouring shrubs such as *Rhus typhina* (stag's horn sumach) or *Cotinus coggygria* (smoke tree) to

A mixed border should contain trees and shrubs for each season with a good balance of both evergreen and deciduous.

plant around the tree. Shrubs with autumn berries would be suitable, too, such as *Euonymus europaeus* cultivars, or cotoneasters. Then, for dramatic contrast, plant some clumps of pampas grass, *Cortaderia selloana*, with its fountain of arching foliage and, in autumn, tall plumes of silvery silky flowers.

Contrary to popular belief, winter need not be a dull time in the garden: there are countless suitable plants for winter schemes. Not only do many plants flower in winter, but there are numerous others noted for colourful bark.

A winter-flowering tree that immediately springs to mind is *Prunus subhirtella* 'Autumnalis' (autumn cherry), which produces its semi-double white blossoms between mid-autumn and early spring. Or you might prefer the cultivar *P. s.* 'Autumnalis Rosea' with palest pink flowers. Some attractive shrubs to plant with this prunus include *Hamamelis mollis* cultivars (Chinese witch hazel), with spidery yellow flowers on bare branches; *Mahonia japonica*, an evergreen with large compound leaves and fountains of fragrant yellow flowers in mid-winter through to early spring; and, if the soil is acid or lime-free, *Rhododendron mucronulatum* with rose-purple blooms in the period mid-winter to early spring.

TREES IN CONTAINERS

Possibly never before has the growing of plants in ornamental containers been more popular than it is today. Undoubtedly the reason is that modern gardens are much smaller than was once common and containers are a convenient means of providing more growing space. Indeed, containers are often grouped on the patio – an important feature of the modern-day garden. However, the idea of growing plants in containers is far from new. Hundreds of years ago, for instance, gardeners in cool-temperate climates grew citrus fruits in large tubs so that they could move them under cover for protection during the winter.

WHAT TO GROW

Various ornamental trees grow well in containers. *Caragana arborescens pendula* (Siberian pea tree) is an attractive small weeping tree. Small cultivars of *Chamaecyparis lawsoniana* (lawson false cypress/Port Orford cedar) are recommended if you want the formal effect created by their neat cone shapes.

Cordyline australis (cabbage palm), with its palm-like habit, gives a sub-tropical touch to a patio, as does *Trachycarpus fortunei* (chusan palm/fan palm). *Crataegus laevigata* (*C. oxyacantha*) (hawthorn) cultivars are suitable small flowering trees for tubs.

Cultivars of *Ilex* × *altaclarensis* are useful evergreens for creating a formal effect as they are broadly columnar in habit. They can be trimmed if desired for even more formality. *Taxus baccata* 'Fastigiata' (Irish yew/English yew) has a neat columnar habit of growth and is also recommended where formality is required.

Very popular as a clipped tub specimen is *Laurus nobilis* (sweet bay/bay laurel/Grecian laurel). It can be trained into a pyramid or a mop-headed standard, and should be regularly trimmed to maintain a neat formal shape.

Some of the crabapples make good tub specimens, including the pale pink late spring-flowering *Malus floribunda* (Japanese crab/floribunda crabapple). Three excellent small weeping trees for tub-growing are *Pyrus salicifolia* 'Pendula' (willow-leaved pear), *Salix caprea* 'Pendula' (Kilmarnock willow) and *S. purpurea* 'Pendula' (pendulous purple osier).

Of the fruits, citrus are very amenable to container cultivation. Popular for the purpose are *Citrus limon* (lemon), *C. aurantium* (Seville orange/bitter orange) and *C. sinensis* (sweet orange). Grow as bush trees or dwarf pyramids.

Figs grown as bush trees fruit well in tubs because of root restriction. Less exotic fruits can be grown too, including apples and cherries (grow as dwarf bush or dwarf pyramid trees on dwarfing rootstocks); pears (dwarf bush or dwarf pyramid); plums (dwarf bush or dwarf pyramid on dwarfing rootstocks); and peaches and nectarines (bush trees). If you are interested in growing dwarf trained forms you will need to consult a specialist fruit book for details of training and pruning.

CONTAINERS AND COMPOSTS

Final containers at least 60cm (24in) in diameter and depth are needed for small trees, but young newly purchased trees should be started off in 30cm (12in) pots, then 45cm (18in) containers before being planted in the final size.

Large, square, wooden tubs in the classical style are attractive. Or you might prefer round half-barrels. Some trees look good in large terracotta containers (especially classical styles). Cordyline, laurus and citrus seem suited to these. Don't despise large concrete containers in a modern setting – some of the better-quality ones are extremely pleasing to the eye.

A soil-based potting compost is recommended because, being heavier than peat-based or soil-less, it is better able to support the tree. Also, the additional weight means that the tree is less liable to be blown over in high winds.

Laurus nobilis, *the sweet bay, is a popular choice for containers and looks good on terraces and patios. It is a tree that is often trained to various shapes, such as mop-headed.*

ROUTINE CARE

Young trees will need potting on regularly into larger containers until they reach the final size, at which stage repotting will be needed every two years to give the trees a fresh supply of compost. Both should be carried out in early spring.

Drainage must be good in a container, so to assist this a layer of coarse material such as broken clay flower pots, stones or gravel, 2.5–5cm (1–2in) in depth according to the size of container, should be placed in the bottom, and topped with a thin layer of coarse peat or

Citrus fruits, including oranges, are ideal for growing in containers such as Versailles tubs, since they can be moved under glass in winter if necessary.

leafmould. Remember to leave a space of at least 2.5cm (1in) between compost surface and rim of container for watering.

Two people may be required to repot a tree in a large container. First insert a long blade all around the inside to cut the rootball away from the container. Then lay the container on its side. One person should hold the tree at its base and gently pull it, while the other person firmly taps the rim of the container with a block of wood. The rootball should soon slide out.

The rootball is reduced in size by teasing away about 5cm (2in) of compost all round, including top and bottom. Roots can be pruned back if necessary, then replant the tree in its container, using fresh potting compost. The compost must be worked right down to the bottom of the container; do not leave air spaces.

You will need to check regularly that the tree has enough water – as frequently as every day during warm weather. Apply sufficient water so that it runs out of the bottom of the container; you will then know that the entire volume of compost has been moistened.

Regular watering quickly leaches plant foods out of the compost, so frequent feeding is recommended during the growing season. Feed every two weeks, or even weekly for fruits. Apply a liquid fertilizer that is well balanced in nitrogen, phosphorus and potash. A high-potash fertilizer can be used for fruit trees as this element helps to form and ripen flowers and fruits.

In the autumn any tender trees can be moved under glass in areas subjected to hard winters. Those remaining outside can have their containers insulated to prevent the compost freezing solid. An effective method is to wrap them with thick wads of straw, bracken or even newspapers, held in place with wire netting.

REPOTTING A CONTAINERIZED TREE

*T*rees in final containers will need repotting every two years to give them a fresh supply of compost, as it quickly deteriorates. This is best carried out in early spring before the trees start into growth.

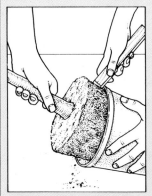 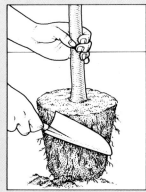 

1 *The rootball should slide out of the container if it is first loosened with a long blade, then gently pulled. At the same time another person should firmly tap the rim of the container with a piece of wood to ease removal.*

2 *Reduce the rootball in size by teasing away about 5cm (2in) of compost all round, including the top and bottom. This can be done with a hand fork or a hand trowel. If necessary, prune back the roots as well.*

3 *Thoroughly wash out the container and allow it to dry completely. Then replant the tree in its container using fresh compost and working it right down to the bottom. Do not leave any air spaces.*

2
BUYING
AND
PLANTING

*T*he proliferation of garden centres has revolutionized the buying of plants, including trees. Now you can buy specimens in containers and plant all the year round provided the ground is not very wet or frozen. However, this is a rather sweeping generalization and for best results you should pay careful attention to timing, especially for evergreens.

It is still possible to buy non-containerized, field-grown trees from nurserymen. Deciduous kinds are supplied bare root, with no soil around the roots. Field-grown evergreens, including conifers, are supplied root balled, with roots having a ball of soil around them that is tightly wrapped with hessian or burlap, or a similar material, to keep it in place.

It is also possible to buy trees from mail-order nurserymen and these will be supplied potted, root balled or bare root. For obvious reasons mail-order trees are generally small, but this is no bad thing for many trees since small specimens often establish themselves faster than larger ones.

One of the advantages of buying from a reliable mail-order catalogue is that the available range of plants is generally wider than you will find at a garden centre and you are more likely to be able to buy less-common plants from a mail-order nurseryman than from a local garden centre.

When planting trees, pay careful attention to timing, especially for evergreens including conifers.

WHEN AND WHAT TO BUY

Your first consideration in buying a tree is the time of year – you may be able to buy a specimen at any time, but you should consider the condition of the soil before planting. In addition, choosing a suitable tree for your garden, that is in good condition, is vital if it is to thrive.

TIME OF YEAR

Best results are achieved by buying and planting at the optimum time.

Let us start with deciduous trees. If these are bought in containers from a garden centre they can in theory be planted at any time of the year. Many people like to buy trees when they are in leaf or in full flower so that they can see what they are buying – and of course their instant effect is often an important consideration.

However, you must be realistic when it comes to planting container-grown deciduous trees. Do not plant when the ground is very wet or frozen. You will never make a good job of planting in these conditions and there is a high risk that the tree may never become established.

Conversely it is not a good idea to plant during very dry or drought conditions. At such times it is unlikely you will be able to supply enough water to get the tree established.

Apart from these considerations, year-round planting of container-grown deciduous trees is a possibility. It all depends on prevailing local conditions.

You are much more restricted with bare-root deciduous trees. These must be planted while they are completely dormant or resting, which is between late autumn and late winter/early spring. If you have a choice, late-autumn planting is preferable as the ground will still be comparatively warm and, hopefully, not too wet.

Evergreen trees, including conifers, if they are container-grown, can in theory be planted the

Conifers, such as Picea pungens *'Koster', will establish rapidly if planted into soil which is warm and not too wet.*

year round provided soil conditions are suitable. Bear in mind, however, that evergreens do not have a dormant period – they grow throughout the year. Therefore, planting into very cold soil during the winter is likely to give them a severe shock and it could be some time before they start making new roots. In the meantime they could well expire.

It is far better to plant evergreens into soil that is warm and moist but not wet. In these conditions they will very soon put new roots into the soil, when they are said to be established. The faster establishment occurs, the less risk there is of a tree expiring.

Optimum soil conditions for the planting of evergreens are found in mid- to late spring, when the soil is warming up, and in late summer/early autumn when the ground is still warm. Evergreens can also be planted in the summer provided the soil is not too dry and there is little risk of a drought. In a wet summer, evergreen trees will establish well. Tender trees are best planted in spring.

You may be faced with the problem of holding or storing plants until soil conditions are suitable. If they are in containers this is not a problem since they can be kept in a sheltered part of the garden until conditions improve. But never allow the rootballs to become frozen solid for long periods. In the event of hard frosts keep the plants under cover in cool, light, airy conditions. Make sure the compost never dries out as this could be fatal, for conifers especially.

If you cannot plant bare-root or root-balled trees immediately then they can be held for up to a week in a shed or garage, provided the roots are kept covered to prevent them drying out. If longer storage is necessary the trees will have to be planted temporarily or "heeled in" on a spare piece of ground in a sheltered spot (see below). When soil conditions improve heeled in trees can be lifted and planted permanently.

WHAT TO BUY

One of the advantages of buying from a garden centre or from a local nurseryman is that you can see what you are buying. It is possible, for instance, to avoid any plants that are infected with pests or diseases. If the foliage of conifers is turning brown from the base upwards it indicates they are suffering from a serious and fatal disease, phytophthora. If the foliage is browning and dropping this is a sign that at some time the rootballs have dried out.

HEELING IN TREES

*I*f soil conditions are unsuitable for planting, trees have to be stored. Bare-root trees are stored by heeling in on a spare piece of ground, in a sheltered spot. They can be held in this way for several months.

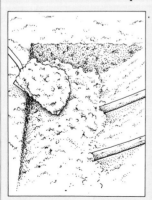 

1 *Lay the trees in a trench at an angle of about 30 degrees to the ground and then completely cover the roots with soil. The trees can be placed quite close together and their roots can be touching.*

2 *There is no need to firm this soil too much: a light treading will be sufficient for this temporary planting because, since they are lying at an angle, there is little likelihood of the trees being blown about by the wind.*

Avoid any trees with sickly looking foliage, perhaps unnaturally tinged with red or yellow, which indicates a nutrient deficiency. Also avoid trees that are loose in their containers. This indicates they are not yet established. In fact, they may have recently been lifted from the ground and planted in containers, rather than grown in them all their lives (which is much to be preferred). Also avoid trees whose roots are growing out of the bottom of the containers for this indicates that the containers are packed with roots. The roots may be spiralling tightly around the inside of the container. Trees with such a root system may fail to root strongly into the soil when planted and growth could be poor.

It is very important to make sure you buy a well-shaped tree. It should have a good strong central leader (the continuation of the main trunk) and the trunk itself should be straight. A crooked trunk will never straighten out. The tree should be symmetrical, not lop-sided with more branches growing on one side than on another. It is especially important that weeping

When buying trees make sure they are well shaped and symmetrical – a poorly shaped specimen will never develop its proper habit.

trees are symmetrical. If trees are being sold as standards or half-standards they should have a trunk free from shoots or branches to at least 1.8m (6ft) for standards and about half this for half-standards.

SIZES TO BUY

Some trees establish much more quickly and satisfactorily if small specimens are planted. This applies to a number of evergreens, including various conifers.

Examples are abies, araucaria, cedrus, cryptomeria, cupressus, eucalyptus, ilex, picea, pinus, pseudotsuga, sciadopitys, sequoia, sequoiadendron and tsuga. Recommended heights to buy vary according to subject but range from 30 to 60cm (1–2ft). Further details are given in the Encyclopedia.

It is possible to buy fairly large specimens of some subjects, including the conifers × cupressocyparis and chamaecyparis. You can safely buy large specimens of rhododendrons too, as these establish well at virtually any size.

Many deciduous trees are supplied as quite large specimens, in the region of 2.4m (8ft) in height. These include malus, prunus, sorbus, pyrus, salix, tilia, populus, betula and fagus. Such trees will be about four years old.

Always remember that young trees consisting of a single stem without side shoots or branches (known as whips) establish very quickly and could eventually catch up with larger specimens. They would of course be much cheaper in price and for this reason alone are well worth considering if a large number of trees is to be planted, perhaps for a tall screen or windbreak.

Remember, too, that small specimens are unlikely to need staking after planting, unlike larger specimens which should have some kind of support until they have rooted into the soil.

So far semi-mature trees have not been considered. These are very large trees and consequently extremely expensive. They provide immediate effect and are ideal for giving a semi-mature atmosphere to a new garden. Such trees are often planted in public places as they are more vandal-proof than smaller specimens. Some growers specialize in their production and, since special equipment is required, will also transport and plant them.

THE QUESTION OF SPACE

Before you buy, ask yourself if you have sufficient space for a tree. Guidelines on tree size and spread have been given (see pages 9–11) together with recommendations for spacing. Root spread has also been covered there, and heights are given for all the trees described in the Encyclopedia.

It is not advisable to allow tree branches to overhang neighbours' gardens or the highway, so take this into account when choosing sites. Never plant trees close to buildings as the roots could damage foundations and underground services such as drains, sewers and water supplies. Populus, for instance, which has a wide root spread, should never be planted within at least 18m (60ft) of any building, and preferably much more.

Do not plant a tree where it will eventually grow up through overhead cables.

CHOOSING AND PREPARING THE SITE

To thrive, a tree must be planted in conditions that suit it. These include sufficient sun or shade, shelter from wind and a satisfactory soil. The climate must be suitable and this is covered in the Encyclopedia by means of the plant hardiness zone system.

SUN

Many trees need to be grown in positions that receive full sun and this applies to many of the flowering kinds such as cercis, cornus, koelreuteria and sophora. Golden or yellow

Many trees need to be grown in positions which receive full sun, including many of the flowering kinds such as Sophora tetraptera.

Many magnolias like dappled shade. This is
Magnolia campbellii *'Lanarth'.*

broad-leaved and coniferous trees, in particular,
need plenty of sun if they are to produce really
good foliage colour.

Many trees will, however, thrive in partial
shade, which means that they receive full sun for
only part of the day.

If sun-loving trees do not obtain sufficient sun
they will become weak and spindly and their
foliage colour will be pale.

SHADE

Few trees will succeed in total shade, although
some do like the conditions of dappled shade
created by woodland, such as *Ptelea trifoliata*
(this will take full shade), ilex, magnolias and
rhododendrons. Some should not be subjected
to early morning sun in areas prone to frosts, as
frozen flower buds thawed out rapidly by the sun
will be killed. This applies especially to trees
that flower early in the year or whose flower
buds are already formed, such as magnolias and
rhododendrons.

SHELTER

Many trees appreciate a site sheltered from strong prevailing winds. Such a position will ensure stronger growth and greater height. The trees will also flower and fruit better. It is especially important to give fruiting trees a sheltered site to ensure pollinating insects do their work. Insects do not like working in windy conditions and are liable to neglect fruit trees in windy gardens.

It is a well-known fact that constant strong winds have a dwarfing influence on trees. They will also create mis-shapen trees that lean away from the direction of the wind and have lop-sided crowns. Such specimens are a common sight in coastal areas, which are subjected to strong winds straight off the sea. Also in coastal areas salt-laden winds in summer can result in browned foliage on the side facing the sea, or in severe cases in leaves being stripped off altogether.

Some trees should not be planted in frost pockets – low-lying areas, such as valleys, where cold air rolls down the slopes and collects in the bottom. This applies especially to trees that are noted for their early flowers, which could be damaged or killed by spring frosts. Fruiting trees like apples, pears, plums and cherries should never be planted in frost pockets as their blossoms are very prone to late spring frosts and if killed no fruits will be forthcoming.

Some trees can actually provide shelter and are planted close together to form windbreaks or screens (see page 16).

SOILS AND PREPARATION

The majority of trees are very adaptable and will thrive in acid (lime-free) or alkaline soils (those containing lime or chalk). But some definitely will not tolerate alkaline conditions; these include rhododendrons, some magnolias, arbutus, embothrium and halesia. If these are planted in limy soils their leaves will turn yellow, growth will be stunted (a condition known as lime-induced chlorosis), and they are quite likely to die.

Soil is easily tested for lime content with a soil-testing kit, following the instructions provided. The degree of acidity or alkalinity is measured on a logarithmic scale known as the pH scale. On this scale 7.0 is neutral. Numbers below this indicate increasing acidity (the lower the number, the more acid the soil) and higher figures indicate increasing akalinity (the higher the number, the more limy the soil).

Generally the type of soil is not important for most trees provided it is well drained and not prone to lying very wet or becoming water-logged. Sandy and chalky soils are usually naturally well drained. In some, the drainage may be excessive so that they suffer from water shortage in summer. Ideally the soil should be well drained yet able to hold sufficient water for the needs of plants; it is then said to be moisture retentive.

Clay and loamy soils are able to hold on to larger volumes of water than sandy or chalky soils, and are classed as moisture retentive. Clay soils can lie very wet or even become waterlogged in winter. Peat soils are also moisture retentive and can become quite wet.

The ability to hold on to water depends on the humus content of the soil. Humus is decomposed organic matter which retains moisture by acting like a sponge. Sandy and chalky soils are very low in organic matter. Clays and loams contain larger amounts while peaty soils are very high in humus.

Trees that relish a high humus content include alnus, azara, betula, calocedrus, cercidiphyllum, embothrium, ginkgo, halesia, magnolia, mespilus, photinia, pseudopanax, pterocarya, rhododendron, sciadopitys, stewartia and styrax. It is easy to raise the humus content by adding bulky organic matter to the soil as described below.

A deep soil is necessary for optimum growth of many trees, especially large kinds such as aesculus, fraxinus, liriodendron, pseudotsuga, quercus, sequoia and sequoiadendron. In thin soils overlying rock the trees may not grow to their maximum size.

If you have a wet soil and are not able to improve drainage then choose trees that will tolerate these conditions, such as alnus, salix, tilia, populus and taxodium.

Before planting, the site should be thoroughly prepared and the soil improved, if necessary. For specimen trees, prepare a site about 90cm (3ft) square. If you are planting in a lawn remove a circle of grass of this diameter – this looks more attractive than a square.

Firstly it is important to eradicate any perennial weeds by spraying them when in full growth with a translocated herbicide. This can also be used to kill off a circle of grass in a lawn. Grass is best killed off rather than dug out, as you will never be able to remove all the roots and it could well reappear again.

Then the site should be dug to two depths of the spade blade, known as double digging. This will break up any hard layer in the subsoil and allow the tree to root easily and deeply.

When digging deeply keep the topsoil and the subsoil in their proper places – on no account bring the subsoil up to the surface. Double digging is described and illustrated below.

During digging take the opportunity to incorporate bulky organic matter which will raise the humus content. This is beneficial to all soils, helping well-drained types like sand or chalk to retain moisture and improving the drainage of clays and other poorly drained types.

There is, however, no point in adding bulky organic matter to peaty soils since these are already rich in humus.

Bulky organic matter can be mixed into the subsoil and topsoil. Suitable materials include well-rotted garden compost, well-rotted manure, peat, and chipped or shredded bark. The last two are especially recommended when preparing sites in woodland gardens. Peat is especially relished by rhododendrons.

To help improve drainage, incorporate coarse sand or grit during digging, particularly if the soil is peaty. Ideally several months should then elapse after digging before the tree is planted to allow the ground to settle. Deeply dug soil can settle by as much as 15cm (6in).

About a week to ten days before planting apply a compound fertilizer, either organic or inorganic according to preference, containing the major elements nitrogen, phosphorus and potassium. Mix this well into the topsoil and then firm the ground well by treading.

The site is now ready for planting.

DOUBLE DIGGING

*T*he site for a tree should be thoroughly prepared by digging the soil deeply – known as double digging – to break up the hard lower soil.

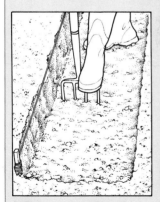

1 *Remove a reasonably wide trench, say about 60cm (2ft), the depth of the spade blade, then dig over the bottom of the trench to the depth of a fork.*

2 *Add bulky organic matter such as well-rotted manure, garden compost, peat or bark. It is a good idea to fork this into the bottom of the trench.*

3 *Take out a second trench behind, and the same size as, the first, and throw the soil from the second forward so that it fills the first one.*

PLANTING TECHNIQUES

The most important consideration to bear in mind when planting bare-root trees is that the roots must not dry out, so keep them covered until you are ready to plant the tree.

Remove a hole sufficiently wide to take the roots when they are spread out to their full extent. On no account should the ends of roots curl upwards against the side of the hole. The hole should be sufficiently deep to ensure that, after planting, the tree is at the same depth that it was in the nurseryman's field. This is indicated by a soil mark at the base of the stem. The planting depth is the top of the soil mark.

Next insert a stake if one is required. Further details of staking are given on pages 52–3.

The tree should now be positioned in the hole with the trunk about 2.5cm (1in) away from the stake (if a single central stake has been used). The roots should be spread out to their full extent. If any have damaged ends cut them off with a pair of sharp secateurs or pruning shears.

Spade a layer of fine topsoil over the roots and then, gripping the tree by the trunk, gently shake it up and down to work the soil well between the roots. Next firm the soil by treading it, placing the weight on your heels. Add a further layer of soil and firm this also. Continue in this way until the hole has been filled to the surrounding soil level. If applicable, complete the job by tying the tree to the stake.

Container-grown and root-balled trees are planted in a similar way except that the rootball must not be disturbed. Water them a few hours before planting.

It is best to remove the container after the tree has been positioned in the hole. If possible cut it and peel it away. This is the method for flexible plastic containers and root-wraps. However, if the tree is in a rigid pot then this will need to be removed by holding the tree by the trunk just above the soil and sharply tapping the top of the pot, when it should fall away.

Plant in a hole about 30cm (1ft) wider all round than the rootball. To give an idea of planting depth, the top of the rootball should be slightly below soil level after planting, that is 12–25mm (½-1in). Return some fine soil in the space between the rootball and the sides of the hole and firm it well. Continue to add soil, firming it as you proceed, until you reach ground level. Again, if applicable, after planting tie the tree to a stake.

Different trees relish different soil conditions. Some, including the embothriums illustrated here, appreciate plenty of humus in the soil.

PLANTING BARE-ROOT TREES

*B*are-root deciduous trees are planted while they are completely dormant or resting which is between late autumn and late winter/early spring. If there is a choice, late-autumn planting is preferable.

1 *To avoid roots drying out keep them well covered with a sheet of plastic or burlap until you are ready to plant the tree. Dry roots must be avoided since they may mean the tree fails to become established.*

2 *The soil mark at the base of the stem indicates the original planting depth of the tree so bear this in mind when removing the planting hole. A spade laid across the hole you have dug acts as a guide to depth.*

3 *After digging out the hole insert a stout wooden stake if one is required. A stake 5–8cm (2–3in) in diameter is recommended for trees. Be sure to hammer it well down into the ground until it is really firm.*

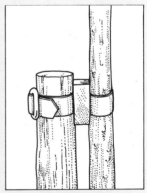

4 *Position the tree in the hole close to the stake and then spread out the roots to their full extent. The roots should lie flat – on no account must the ends start to turn upwards.*

5 *Return the fine topsoil to the hole, working it between the roots and firming well with your heels as you proceed. Initially work the soil between the roots by gently shaking the tree.*

6 *After planting, tie the tree to the stake if applicable, using plastic buckle-type ties complete with plastic buffer. The ties should be firm but not so tight that the bark is damaged.*

STAKING TREES

Unless you are planting very small specimens, trees will need to be provided with a stake for the first two or three years until they are well established in the soil. If a single vertical stake is used (the normal method of support) it should be inserted in the planting hole before the tree is positioned, to avoid root damage. Generally stakes are positioned on the windward side of trees, but this is not absolutely essential.

Timber stakes 5–8cm (2–3in) in diameter are suitable. They should be inserted at least 60cm (2ft) into the ground for stability. If using a single vertical stake, its top should be just below the lowest branch of a standard or half-standard. If the tree is well branched virtually to ground level, ensure about 1.8m (6ft) of stake is protruding above ground. Therefore, fairly long stakes are needed – at least 2.4m (8ft) in length for standard and other tall trees.

After planting tie the tree to the stake, using plastic buckle-type tree ties, complete with a buffer placed between trunk and stake. The buffer prevents the tree from rubbing against the stake, which can severely damage the bark. The ties can be slackened as the trunk thickens and should be inspected at least once a year to make sure they are not too tight.

The alternative to buying ties is to make your own from thick string or twine, creating a buffer with a slice of rubber hose or something similar,

provided it is soft and does not damage the bark of the tree.

When using a single vertical stake place one tree tie about 2.5cm (1in) below the top of the stake and another approximately 30cm (1ft) above the ground.

That is the traditional method of staking a tree. However, the trend nowadays is for a single short stake, the top of which is only 30cm (1ft) above ground level. Once again it should be inserted deeply before the tree is planted. The theory behind the short stake is that it anchors the roots but allows the top part of the tree to move in the wind, which encourages rapid growth of new roots. The idea has not yet been generally accepted, but you may care to try it. It possibly represents an easier way of staking very bushy trees, such as some conifers, for example, and other trees with very low branches.

When planting a container-grown or a root-balled tree you will not be able to use a single stake if the size of the rootball prevents positioning the stake close to the trunk. A large tree may well have quite a wide rootball. In this instance, instead of using a single tall stake use double stakes with a wooden cross-bar at the top. The trunk of the tree is tied to this cross-bar, using one tie.

Yet another alternative is to use an oblique stake, inserted at an angle of approximately 45 degrees and ideally pointing in the direction of

An oblique stake facing the wind can be used for trees with large rootballs.

A double stake with a crossbar of timber is an alternative for large root-balled trees.

the wind. This should be inserted well into the soil, again at least 60cm (2ft). The oblique stake can be put in place after the tree has been planted, as it will be inserted some distance from the rootball with no risk of damaging the roots. The top of the stake should again be just below the lowest branch and the trunk secured to it with a single tie.

Very large or semi-mature trees need far more substantial supports and are almost always secured with guy ropes or wires. This system is also useful for trees that have been loosened by the wind.

Three ropes or wires are positioned in a triangular formation around the tree. The tops are looped around the lower branches. If wires are used each loop should be covered with a length of rubber hose to prevent the wires cutting into the tree. The ends of the ropes or wires nearest the ground should be secured to lengths of angle iron driven well down into the soil and angled away from the tree.

The three ropes or wires should be quite tight, preventing the tree from moving. If a supplier is planting a semi-mature tree for you, supports will also be provided.

If tree ties are not checked regularly and loosened if necessary, they can become extremely tight and cut into the bark, causing the permanent damage that is shown here.

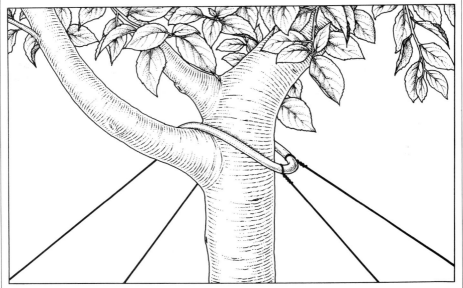

For very large or semi-mature trees that still need staking, guy ropes or wires are the best method of ensuring adequate support.

3

CARING

FOR

TREES

*T*rees are not objects that can be planted and forgotten, although invariably they are. As with any other cultivated plant they respond well to regular care and attention. Many people do not always realize that trees, like other garden plants, need feeding, watering, weeding and so on, and that such tasks are particularly important for young specimens.

Although many garden trees do not need routine pruning, there are circumstances when it is desirable, particularly with fruit trees. More common are "one-off" tasks like removing a dead branch, or thinning the crown to reduce the shade provided by the tree's foliage. Similarly, you may need to know how to treat accidental damage to a tree in such a way as to ensure that its effect on the aesthetic impact of the tree is kept to a minimum.

With all these tasks, care and attention, together with the right tools in good condition, will produce good results.

Like any other cultivated plant, trees respond to regular care and attention, especially in their early years.

ROUTINE MAINTENANCE

These are the tasks that should be frequently undertaken, perhaps on an annual basis or at intervals throughout the year. Do not be daunted by the list, which does not amount to a great deal of work. Indeed, trees are regarded as labour-saving plants.

PROTECTION

Some young trees in particular may need protecting from the weather and from animals such as rabbits and deer.

If there is any possibility of animals such as rabbits, hares, deer and rodents gnawing the bark of a young tree, a fairly frequent occurrence in rural and semi-rural areas, then tree guards of some kind should be used to protect the trunk. They should be put into place immediately the tree is planted.

It is advisable to protect the whole trunk, for deer can reach very high, and it is remarkable just how far up a tree rabbits and hares will reach when they are hungry.

There are various designs of tree guard that you can buy. Alternatively, guards can be made at home from welded, galvanized steel mesh formed into a cylinder around the trunk. Wire netting can also be used in the same way.

Inspect tree guards regularly to make sure they are still in place and no gaps have appeared in them. Most damage is done by animals during the winter when other food is more scarce. Once the trees have become established and the bark has toughened and become more woody, the guards can be dispensed with.

Some young trees, particularly tender ever-greens, may need protection from cold, drying winds during the winter, which can cause foliage to turn brown and die. Once they are well established and growing strongly this temporary protection can be removed.

A tree can be protected with a screen of plastic windbreak netting placed on the windward side or, if considered necessary, used to surround it completely. The screen should be

Plastic tree guards will prevent animals such as rabbits, deer and rodents from gnawing the bark.

56

higher than the tree and at least 60cm (2ft) away. The netting can be supported by means of several wooden stakes driven into the ground.

Although such screens are not particularly attractive, and they hide the trees for the winter, it makes sense to give vulnerable specimens every chance of survival.

OTHER WEATHER PROBLEMS

An unstaked young tree can be whipped around by winter gales, resulting in a hole being formed in the soil around the trunk. This hole can get filled with water and could lead to the death of the tree. Therefore fill the hole with soil and firm it thoroughly by treading with your heels. If necessary provide a stake for the tree.

Hard frosts can raise and loosen the soil and young trees could be partly lifted out of the ground. As soon as the ground has thawed out the soil must be made firm again.

Snow can cause a lot of damage to young trees, particularly evergreens, including conifers. The sheer weight of a build-up of snow can cause branches to break. In addition, upright branches of fastigiate or columnar trees can be pushed apart by snow and they may never regain their original shape. It is therefore advisable to use a long pole and gently knock snow off the branches as soon as a build-up starts. Pay particular attention to evergreens as these tend to hold on to far more snow than deciduous trees.

TREES FOR WARM AND COOL CLIMATES

Name	Shape/habit	Warm	Cool	Deciduous	Evergreen
Acer saccharinum	Spreading		•	•	
Azara microphylla	Spreading	•			•
Betula pendula	Weeping		•	•	
Caragana arborescens	Spreading		•	•	
Citrus species	Spreading	•			•
Cordyline australis	Broad columnar	•			•
Eucalyptus species	Broad columnar	•			•
Ficus carica	Spreading	•		•	
Larix decidua	Conical		•	•	
Malus baccata	Spreading		•	•	
Metrosideros	Spreading	•			•
Olea europea	Spreading	•			•
Picea pungens	Conical		•		•
Populus balsamifera	Broad columnar		•	•	
Salix alba	Broad columnar		•	•	

Above: The white spruce Picea glauca *is often grown in colder regions. This one has a broom top – not a desirable feature for the garden tree.*

Left: Olea europaea, *the olive, is a tree for warm climates, withstanding drought and fierce sun. Olives are often grown in groves, and have edible fruits.*

59

CHECKING SUPPORTS

Stakes and tree ties should be checked regularly – at least twice a year and certainly before the onset of winter. Make sure the stake is not rotting through at the base and that it has not become loose in the soil.

Tree ties must never be allowed to become so tight that they start cutting into the bark. The buckle-type ties are easily and quickly slackened. Home-made ties will probably have to be renewed. Do not go to the extreme and make ties so loose that the tree moves around. It is then likely to rub against the stake, which results in damage to the bark. Ties should hold the tree firmly yet not cut into it.

Generally, after two or three years, most trees are sufficiently well established for the supports to be removed.

THE IMPORTANCE OF BARE SOIL

It is extremely important to have an area of bare soil around young trees. If grass or weeds grow right up to the trunks the growth of the trees will be severely retarded.

Trees planted in lawns should have a circle of bare soil around them. This can be about 90cm (3ft) in diameter. Do not be tempted to plant anything in it and do not allow any weeds to grow there.

It is not difficult to control weeds around trees. Seedling weeds can be hoed out on any warm, breezy day when the soil surface is dry. The weeds will then quickly shrivel and die. On a small scale, of course, weeds can be pulled out by hand.

Weeds can be killed by spraying with a suitable weedkiller (herbicide). For crops of annual weeds a contact weedkiller containing paraquat can be used. If perennial broad-leaved weeds such as ground elder and stinging nettles are the problem, spray them with a translocated herbicide containing glyphosate. Perennial grasses such as couch grass can also be killed with a translocated herbicide, this time containing alloxydim sodium.

Never allow weedkillers to come into contact with a lawn or they will kill it, and always follow the manufacturer's instructions on how to use them to the letter.

WATERING

Possibly more young trees die through lack of water than for any other reason. It seems odd that many people should think that trees, unlike other plants, do not need to be watered during dry conditions. They will copiously water their lawns to keep them green, yet neglect recently planted trees.

After several years, when they are really well established and have put down deep roots, trees are better able to cope with dry or even drought conditions, as they find moisture in the lower layers of soil. But newly planted specimens take their moisture from the upper layer of soil, which can dry out quickly in spring and summer.

So how does one water a young tree? Many gardeners like to place a hose on the soil near the trunk and leave it running gently for about an hour. Trees can also be watered along with other plants and the lawn by means of an oscillating or rotary sprinkler. This is the most efficient way to water since all the water penetrates the soil. With a hose alone some will run off. Furthermore, a sprinkler applies the water evenly.

It is important to apply sufficient water for it to penetrate to a depth of at least 15cm (6in). This means applying the equivalent of 2.5cm (1in) of rain or about 27 litres of water per m^2 (4¾ gallons per square yard).

When using a sprinkler you can check the amount of water being applied by placing a number of empty tin cans or other containers over the site. When 2.5cm (1in) of water has collected in the bottom you know that sufficient has been applied. About an hour after watering it is a good idea also to check that water has penetrated sufficiently deeply. Simply dig a small hole at least 15cm (6in) deep with a hand trowel. If the soil in the bottom is moist then sufficient water has been applied. If dry, apply more water.

Water may run off rather than penetrate soil that has dried out and become hard on the surface. If this seems likely spike the soil to a depth of about 15cm (6in) using a garden fork before applying water.

It is difficult to say how often trees need watering during dry conditions as it all depends on the soil and how rapidly moisture is evaporating. However, a thorough watering as explained above should last plants for about a week. On the other hand, during extremely hot and/or dry weather plants may need watering several times a week.

MULCHING

Mulching is a technique whereby a layer of material such as bulky organic matter is placed over the soil surface around plants. It is highly recommended, especially for newly planted and young trees, as it helps to encourage optimum growth. The greatest benefit of a mulch is that it prevents the rapid evaporation of moisture from the soil during hot weather. Mulched plants are therefore unlikely to become suddenly short of moisture. A mulch also helps to keep the surface of the soil cool.

In addition, mulching has the advantage that it prevents the germination of weed seeds in the soil (although seeds that drop or are blown on to the surface of a mulch are likely to grow). So, mulching can largely prevent the need for weeding, which is always a time-consuming business.

Various materials can be used for mulching. Well-rotted manure and garden compost both supply some plant foods, while peat or chipped or shredded bark, though suitable, have no nutrient value. In a woodland garden the most appropriate material is chipped or shredded bark. Peat is a good alternative and is much relished by rhododendrons. Of all the mulching materials bark is the longest lasting.

A mulch should be applied immediately after planting and thereafter in spring. If necessary top it up annually. The soil should be moist when you apply a mulch and must be completely free from weeds. It has been found through experience that a suitable depth for a mulch is about 8cm (3in), although 5cm (2in) may be sufficient if you are using a bark mulch. When mulching a single tree the mulch can be placed in a circle around the trunk varying from 90 to 150cm (3–5ft) in diameter.

Other materials that can be used for mulching include sheets of black polythene or plastic and other synthetic materials, but these cannot really be recommended for the ornamental garden as they are not particularly attractive. Gravel and shingle are effective materials that are sometimes used in the ornamental garden; both also have the advantage of being permanent. A mulch of either of these need be only 2.5cm (1in) deep.

WAYS TO MULCH

*Y*oung trees especially benefit from mulching as it prevents the soil drying out rapidly, and prevents the germination of weed seeds.

Far left: Bulky organic matter such as garden compost or well-rotted manure is widely used for mulching. A depth of 8cm (3in) is recommended.

Left: Black plastic sheeting or other synthetic materials are best used in utility areas of the garden only, since they are not the most attractive mulches.

FEEDING

Young as well as older trees benefit greatly from annual feeding in the spring, preferably with an organic compound fertilizer which supplies the major elements nitrogen, phosphorus and potassium. If it also contains some trace elements such as magnesium and manganese, then so much the better. Organic fertilizers break down slowly and release their nutrients steadily throughout the growing season. Inorganic fertilizers can also be used, of course, if preferred. Their main advantage is that they tend to be quicker acting, but this is really of no great benefit for trees.

For small trees the fertilizer can be sprinkled in a circle around each one at least as far as the branch spread, but slightly more for fastigiate specimens. Apply strictly according to the manufacturer's instructions as over-application can be harmful. Then hoe or lightly fork it into the soil surface. If the tree is mulched you will first have to scrape the material away before applying the fertilizer.

For medium to large semi-mature or mature trees, a good way of feeding is to place the fertilizer in 15cm (6in) deep holes spaced about 1.5m (5ft) apart under the crown of the tree. The holes can extend as far as the branch spread. Up to 225g (8oz) of fertilizer can be placed in each hole. It is not absolutely vital to feed semi-mature and mature trees, so dispense with this operation if you wish.

For young fruit trees, latest research shows frequent liquid feeding during the growing season to be more beneficial than a dressing of dry fertilizer in spring. Weekly applications of high-nitrogen fertilizer between late spring and late summer are recommended. It has been found that such feeding results in young trees making 45 to 80 per cent more growth than if fed in the normal way and they start producing fruit a year earlier.

It is also worth trying this technique on young ornamental trees as it seems likely that it will improve their growth as well.

Most trees need no pruning but some fruiting trees need regular attention to avoid too much vegetative growth at the expense of cropping. This apple has been pruned to a natural shape.

PRUNING

The majority of trees need no pruning apart from the removal of dead or damaged branches as necessary. Sometimes young trees produce two central leaders (the continuation of the main

trunk) and one of these should be removed. But otherwise most garden trees do not need further attention.

Some fruiting trees need regular pruning in order to avoid too much vegetative growth at the expense of cropping. But even with these, satisfactory results (albeit lighter crops) are possible if you do not want to or cannot prune.

Where pruning is required specific details have been given under the appropriate entries in the Encyclopedia section. More general aspects of pruning are discussed here.

GENERAL CONSIDERATIONS

It is important to use really sharp pruning tools to ensure clean cuts, which heal much better

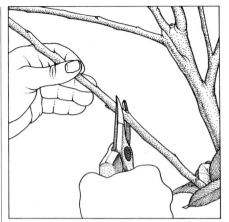

When pruning thin shoots such as those of fruit trees, cut back to just above a growth bud, ensuring the cut slopes away from the bud.

than ragged wounds. A good-quality pruning saw will be needed and, for light pruning such as that required by fruit trees, a pair of secateurs or pruning shears of the parrot-bill design. For tall fruit trees you may find a long-handled pruner useful. Handles are available in various lengths from about 1.8m (6ft) to 3.6m (12ft). A curved saw can also be used on thicker branches.

Generally speaking, pruning can be carried out in late autumn or winter for deciduous trees. Dead wood can be removed in summer, when it is most easily seen. Conifers can be pruned in early autumn and broad-leaved evergreens in late spring.

When pruning thin shoots, such as those of fruit trees, it is important to cut back to just above a growth bud. The cut should slope away from the bud so that rainwater drains away from it. If a long length of stem is left above a bud, this will simply die back to it and may even result in the death of the bud. If the cut is made too near a bud there is a chance of damage being caused.

Fungicidal compounds are available for sealing pruning cuts to prevent the entry of diseases. It is impractical to treat all small cuts so concentrate on those with a diameter of 2.5cm (1in) and more. These compounds are rather like paint and are applied with a paint brush. Large cuts made with a saw should first be smoothed off with a pruning knife as this encourages them to heal quicker and better. Although one school of thought does not recommend the use of sealing compounds, believing that cuts heal better on their own, the reduced risk of fungal infection if they *are* used makes them worth while.

REMOVING LARGE BRANCHES

When removing a large branch, whether it is dead or alive, a great amount of care is needed to avoid damaging the rest of the tree. One of the most common forms of damage is tearing the bark.

If you are faced with the removal of a large branch from fairly high up in a tall tree, seek the services of a qualified and skilled tree surgeon. It may be possible to do it yourself if the branch is low and easily accessible, but always take great care to avoid injuring yourself. Also make sure the branch will not damage plants below, or fences, walls and property when it is being removed.

It is best to remove the branch in sections, as this is more manageable. Before sawing through, tie a rope to each section to support it and prevent it from crashing to the ground. Throw the rope over a higher branch and let the other end reach the ground, where an assistant can hold it tight and then lower the branch to the ground when it has been cut through. By using this technique you will not damage lower branches or plants and objects below the tree. When cutting a branch, first cut part way through on the underside, then cut through from above, just beyond the undercut. This will prevent the bark from being torn.

Cut back the branch to within about 30cm (1ft) of the trunk. This section must be removed flush with the trunk. Never leave a snag or part of the branch, as this will die back to the trunk and may result in a cavity forming (see below). To remove the final 30cm (1ft) of branch, first make a cut underneath it flush with the trunk, then cut through from the top to meet the first cut. This technique will prevent bark being ripped from the trunk. Finally smooth off the wound with a pruning knife and "paint" it with a fungicidal pruning compound.

REMOVING A LARGE BRANCH

*I*f carelessly undertaken, the removal of a large branch can easily result in bark being torn from the tree. Large branches which are high up should be removed by professional tree surgeons.

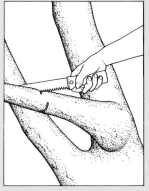

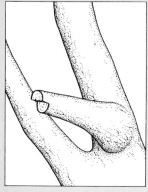

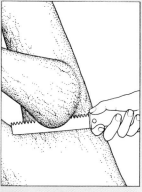

1 *Cut part way through on the underside of the branch to be removed then cut right the way through from above, just beyond the undercut. Use a really sharp pruning saw.*

2 *By removing sections of branch by staggered cutting in this way you will prevent the weight of the branch tearing the bark. Torn bark takes a long time to heal and can lead to infection.*

3 *Remove the final section flush with the trunk. First make an undercut with the pruning saw as close to the trunk of the tree as possible and about halfway through the branch.*

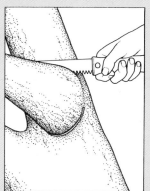

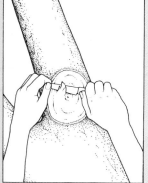

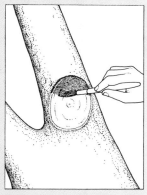

4 *Complete the removal of the final section of branch by cutting right the way through from above. If this cut is close to the trunk, you should meet up exactly with the undercut.*

5 *Smooth off any pieces of branch remaining round the wound with a pruning knife as this assists in the healing process. A rough, ragged cut may not heal over properly.*

6 *Paint the wound with a fungicidal pruning compound to prevent diseases entering and then damaging the tree. These compounds are like paint and applied with a brush.*

CROWN THINNING

Crown thinning is generally undertaken only with large, mature trees. It is usually restricted to deciduous kinds as it is not necessary or advisable to thin conifers and broad-leaved evergreens.

Invariably thinning is required to prevent trees from casting dense shade. Crown thinning, for instance, may be needed when a woodland garden is being developed under mature trees. In this situation dappled shade, as opposed to heavy, dense shade where nothing will grow, is required. It may also be needed to prevent the rest of the garden or buildings from being shaded too much.

Crown thinning reduces wind resistance, which might be necessary with trees that have a weak system of branches. It also reduces the weight of the crown and can prevent the possibility of heavy limbs falling. Alternatively, thinning may be needed to improve the shape of the crown.

Obviously crown thinning is a highly skilled operation and should only be undertaken by a qualified and knowledgeable tree surgeon who will be able to advise you exactly what is required. A well-thinned tree can be a beautiful sight, a badly thinned one a monstrosity.

The job involves the removal of branches that are dead or dying (often as a result of lack of light), badly shaped, are rubbing and crossing, and those with a narrow crotch angle. Remaining branches are then thinned according to the judgement of the tree surgeon. All cuts must be flush with the trunk or other branches. The timing of the operation is also best decided by the tree surgeon. Trees that bleed excessively such as acer, betula, carpinus and those in the *Leguminosae* family should not be pruned in late winter or spring.

CROWN REDUCTION

This may be required not only by mature trees but also by young and semi-mature specimens. With thinning, as outlined above, the actual size of the crown is not reduced; in fact it remains the same size and shape. Crown reduction, however, does reduce the crown's size, particularly its spread.

The branches are shortened with this technique. It is not carried out indiscriminately but rather the leading branches are cut back to lateral branches which take their place. Again this is a highly skilled operation best left to a qualified tree surgeon. If it has been done well you should not be able to detect that the crown has been reduced.

Removing lower branches is a form of crown reduction and may be necessary if they are overhanging a neighbour's garden or spreading out over the highway. It may also be desirable to remove some lower branches if you wish to sit or walk under the tree, or perhaps to create a planting scheme beneath it.

A good time to remove the lower branches of deciduous trees is in late summer, when they are heavy with foliage. At this stage they will be lower than when they have shed their leaves. You will then have a better idea of how many lower branches to remove.

The branches should be removed flush with the trunk of the tree as outlined under Removing large branches on pages 64–5. You should ensure the tree remains well balanced. If it is necessary to remove a branch on one side, it may be advisable to take off another on the opposite side to prevent a lop-sided appearance. Once again, with large trees the work should be undertaken by a qualified tree surgeon.

LOPPING

With lopping the main branches are cut back, often severely, to reduce height and spread. Unfortunately the technique has been (and still is to some extent) widely used for street trees which, of course, mutilates them so that they end up looking like green lollipops.

If a tree has been chosen correctly and is suitable for the site there should be no need for lopping. Should you inherit a tree that is too large for the site it would be better to consider crown reduction. If this is not sufficient you should seriously consider removing the tree and replacing it with something more suitable. However, do make sure it does not have a preservation order on it. In many areas, you are liable to be fined if you cut down a protected tree.

The dense crown of a large mature tree like this oak may need thinning to cast dappled, not deep, shade.

Always remember that a lopped tree can produce an excessive amount of new wood that can become large and very dense, even dangerous, for such wood is inclined to break away easily during gales – making further pruning necessary.

Lopping, therefore, is not a recommended practice. It is far better to plant a suitable tree initially or to replace an unsuitable one.

SUCKERS
AND WATER SHOOTS

Suckers are shoots that grow from below ground level. They come from the root system and are often produced by budded or grafted trees such as plums and cherries (prunus). Suckers should be removed as soon as noticed for if left they will grow vigorously and compete with the tree.

Ideally the soil should be scraped away to expose their point of origin and then the suckers wrenched out. Cutting them off with a pair of secateurs or pruning shears stimulates dormant buds into action and they will grow again.

If digging down to their point of origin is out of the question, suckers can be killed by spraying them when in leaf with the contact non-selective weedkiller paraquat. Make sure it does not come into contact with the tree's foliage or with any other plants nearby.

Shoots may grow direct from the trunk and main branches and these are known as epicormic or water shoots. They are vigorous and generally come from dormant buds that have been stimulated into growth by pruning.

Cutting back epicormic shoots results in more being produced, yet there is no other way for the amateur gardener. It is a case of annual pruning in the winter. Cut them back flush with the trunk or branch. If you leave them they will grow strongly and smother the crown of the tree, causing branches to die through lack of light.

Shoots may also occasionally grow from the trunks of standard and half-standard trees, even if no pruning has recently been carried out. Again, these should be pruned off as close as possible to the trunk.

Water shoots grow direct from the trunk and main branches and are extremely vigorous. They should be removed by cutting them out.

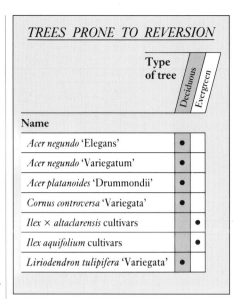

TREES PRONE TO REVERSION

Name	Type of tree: Deciduous	Evergreen
Acer negundo 'Elegans'	•	
Acer negundo 'Variegatum'	•	
Acer platanoides 'Drummondii'	•	
Cornus controversa 'Variegata'	•	
Ilex × *altaclarensis* cultivars		•
Ilex aquifolium cultivars		•
Liriodendron tulipifera 'Variegata'	•	

REVERSION OF VARIEGATED TREES

Cultivars of trees that have variegated foliage sometimes produce shoots that have all-green leaves. These shoots are said to have reverted. They should be cut out completely as soon as noticed, for they are very vigorous and could soon take over the crown of the tree.

SURFACE WOUNDS AND CAVITIES

Sometimes the bark of a tree can be accidentally damaged, as when a lawnmower collides with it. Such damage should be repaired as soon as possible after it has happened. This will ensure it heals rapidly and reduces the likelihood of infection from disease.

The damaged bark can be cut away with a sharp pruning knife and the edges of the wound made smooth. Then the wound should be sealed with a fungicidal sealing compound.

If a branch breaks off during a gale it should be cut back to the trunk or main branch as outlined under Removing large branches on pages 64–5. That basic technique can actually be applied to branches of any size.

If wounds are not treated so that they heal quickly diseases may enter the tree, infect the wood and cause decay. Also, if stumps are left after branch removal, these will die back to the trunk or main branch, diseases will again enter and decay take place. As the wood rots away so holes or cavities form in the trunk or branches.

Provided they are accessible, cavities can be treated by the amateur gardener to prevent further rotting. A tree surgery company will also undertake the work.

The technique involves removing all the decaying wood from the cavity and cutting back until healthy wood is reached. Then the healthy wood can be treated with a fungicide to kill any remaining fungal diseases, or the inside of the cavity can be charred with a blow torch.

The cavity can then be filled with a material that is harmless to the tree. The material should be flexible so that it moves with the tree rather than cracking away from the cavity. Professional tree surgeons generally use synthetic foam products, which are injected into the cavity where they harden. The amateur gardener could make up a mixture of sawdust and bitumen. Some people use mortar for filling cavities, but as it is not flexible it eventually cracks away from the cavity so that rainwater and diseases can enter and the process of decay begins all over again.

The surface of the filling material should be textured to resemble the bark of the tree and, when set, "painted" with a sealing compound. New tissue will slowly be produced around the edges of the wound and it is possible that eventually this tissue will grow over the entire surface of the repair.

Some people do not believe in filling cavities but simply char the inside with a blow torch and provide a drainage hole in the bottom so that rainwater does not collect. A length of rigid plastic pipe could be inserted to drain off the water. Cavity filling is preferable for aesthetic reasons, although charring reduces the risk of further rotting and makes subsequent trouble more noticeable. It really does come down to personal choice, though.

BRANCH SPLITTING

Sometimes branches split away from the trunk under their own weight. If action is taken before they part completely with the tree, they can often be saved by providing artificial support.

The technique involves bracing the branch to the trunk using woven steel-wire cables. The cables are secured at each end by special fixings which do not damage the tree. It is a skilled operation best undertaken by a tree surgeon, but it is useful to know what can be achieved. A splitting branch may not have to be removed.

STUMPS

This book is about planting and caring for trees, not felling them. Nevertheless, a tree needs to be felled if it becomes dangerous, as when loosened in a gale for instance. Trees can also be killed, particularly by honey fungus disease. And, of course, trees die naturally when they reach a certain age. Tree felling should be left to a qualified tree surgeon.

Whether or not the remaining stump is to be removed should be decided before the tree is felled. It may be useful to leave about 90cm (3ft) to assist with the removal of the stump.

One way of removing a stump is to excavate the soil from around it to expose the roots, which are then cut through. The stump itself can be rocked back and forth like a lever to loosen it. When all the roots have been cut through, lift the stump out of the hole. A very large stump may need to be winched out.

If you do not want to go to all this trouble and expense you could get the tree fellers to saw off the stump level with the ground.

The modern method of stump removal is to use a stump grinder to reduce it to a pile of chippings. When seeking quotations for felling, ask whether the company has a stump grinder.

A tree stump can be hidden by using it to support hanging baskets.

4

PROBLEMS

AND

REMEDIES

*U*nlike some other plants, ornamental trees suffer from comparatively few
pests and diseases so do not require regular spraying with pesticides. On
the other hand, some fruit trees such as apples and pears seem to have more
than their fair share of problems and may need routine preventative spraying
each year, assuming that the trees are small enough to be sprayed. Advice on
spraying, and on types of insecticides, are given at the end of the chapter. Pest or
disease control of large specimens is completely out of the question for
amateur gardeners.

The following are the important pests, diseases and disorders that may be
encountered on the trees described in the Encyclopedia, together with advice on
prevention and control. No tree will be attacked by all of them.

*Unlike fruit trees such as apples, ornamental trees suffer from comparatively few
pests and diseases.*

PESTS

In the list that follows, the major pests that you are likely to come across are given, along with the symptoms that suggest their presence, the trees that are most prone to infestation, and methods of prevention and/or control.

ADELGIDS

The adelgids are relations of the aphids and have a similar appearance. They are found on conifers, where they suck the sap from shoot tips, leaves and stems, which weakens the plants. They exude a white waxy wool which makes them conspicuous. Some species cause galls to be formed on the shoots.

Control

Spray as soon as noticed with an insecticide containing malathion, or a systemic one such as dimethoate.

APHIDS

These are small plant bugs about the size of a pin head which rapidly form colonies and suck the sap from shoot tips, leaves and soft stems. This weakens the plants and distorts growth. They may be green, black or brown according to species.

Control

Spray as soon as noticed with an insecticide containing malathion, or a systemic one such as dimethoate. Kill overwintering eggs by spraying dormant deciduous trees with a tar-acid formulation.

Adelgids are found on coniferous trees where they suck the sap from soft tissues.

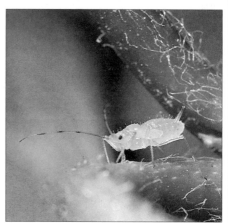

Aphids are among the most common of the sap-sucking insects which attack trees.

APHIDS, WOOLLY

Woolly aphids are found on several species, including malus. These small bugs covered in white wool form colonies on shoots, where they suck the sap. Galls form eventually.

Control
Spray trees with a systemic insecticide such as one containing dimethoate.

Woolly aphids are particularly fond of malus species, including apple trees.

Their sap-sucking activities can eventually result in galls forming on shoots.

BEETLE, ELM BARK

This is the beetle responsible for the spread of Dutch elm disease. The adults are tiny brown beetles and the larvae small white grubs with brown heads. Both tunnel underneath the bark of elm trees.

Control
It is impractical to try to eradicate bark beetles – one has to let them take their toll. If they introduce Dutch elm disease, the trees will have to be felled, and the stumps removed.

The larva of the elm-bark beetle, which feeds by tunnelling under the bark of elm trees.

BIRDS

Birds can strip trees of berries and feed on edible fruits, which ruins them. They may also peck and damage dormant buds on fruit and certain ornamental trees.

Control

In reality, there is little that can be done to protect trees from birds. Various scaring devices can be tried, although there is no guarantee they will work. Some people hang strips of silver foil in the trees to produce bright flashes when the light catches them and a crackling noise when blown by the wind, both of which may scare off birds for a time. Also available is a special nylon line which makes a humming noise when stretched above the ground and vibrated by the wind. This is reasonably effective in scaring off birds, at least for a short period of time, although it is, of course, slightly unsightly in the ornamental garden.

There is also on the market a nylon webbing which is draped over trees, mainly to protect the flower buds of fruit trees. This too looks quite unsightly and cannot really be recommended for trees in the ornamental parts of gardens. The webbing prevents birds from alighting on the trees. There are also liquid bird deterrents which are sprayed on to the trees, mainly to protect dormant winter buds. These are, however, soon washed off by rain.

CAPSID BUGS

These active green plant bugs, about 6mm (¼in) in length, have a long proboscis and pierce plant tissue to suck the sap. They feed on young foliage and shoots. The result is perforated, ragged and distorted leaves.

Control

As soon as noticed spray with a systemic insecticide such as dimethoate.

The common green capsid bug, clearly showing its long proboscis which it uses for feeding.

Capsids pierce plant tissue and suck the sap. They feed on young foliage and shoots.

Birds damage fruits by pecking holes in them.

76

CATERPILLARS

Caterpillars or moth larvae of various kinds feed on the leaves of trees. Severe infestations can result in partial or complete defoliation. Most attacks are minor.

Control

Birds will devour some caterpillars. Spray trees with an insecticide such as fenitrothion.

The larvae of the buff-tip moth feeding on the leaves of oak. A common pest of trees.

A large infestation of caterpillars is capable of completely defoliating a tree.

CODLING MOTH

This is a serious pest of apples and, to a lesser extent, some other fruits. The caterpillars are small white grubs and tunnel into the fruits during summer.

Control

To prevent trouble, spray trees with fenitrothion 28 days after flowering and again 21 days later. Hessian or burlap bands tied around the trunk and main branches in mid-summer will trap caterpillars as they leave the fruits to pupate. In winter the bands are removed and burnt.

Grubs of the codling moth tunnel into the fruits of apples during the summer.

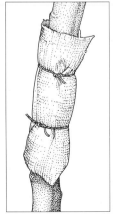

In mid-summer tie bands of hessian or burlap around the trunk and main branches to trap codling-moth caterpillars.

JUNIPER WEBBER MOTH

The caterpillars of this tiny moth are found on junipers, where they feed on the foliage after spinning it together with silky webbing. They are light brown with a red-brown head. Foliage turns brown and dies.

Control

As soon as their activity is noticed dust with an insecticide containing carbaryl. With minor attacks cut off and burn webbed foliage.

Caterpillars of the juniper webber moth spin the foliage together into clumps.

Left: Juniperus communis *'Hibernica', the Irish juniper, as well as other junipers, are prone to attack by the juniper webber moth. The feeding habit causes foliage to turn brown and die.*

LEAF MINER

Leaf miners are the larvae of flies and moths which tunnel into leaves, devouring the tissues. The tunnels appear as silvery lines or blisters. The various species have different host plants. The holly leaf miner favours ilex (holly). Attacks are not usually serious but damage is unsightly.

Control
At the first sign of leaf miners spray with a systemic insecticide such as dimethoate.

Leaf miners are the larvae of various flies and moths which tunnel inside leaves.

The holly leaf miner is very common and results in blister-like mines in holly leaves.

MEALY BUGS

The tropical and sub-tropical mealy bugs attack many woody plants including citrus and ficus (figs). Covered in a white waxy substance, these soft brown bugs move very little, congregating on the stems, where they suck the sap.

Control
As soon as noticed spray with an insecticide containing malathion.

Mealy bugs are soft brown bugs covered in a white waxy substance. They suck plant sap.

Many woody plants are attacked by mealy bugs, including citrus fruits and figs.

MITES, GALL

Mites are almost microscopic creatures. The gall mites suck plant sap, which results in galls being formed on the leaves.

Control

This is difficult, but spraying in spring with malathion, the systemic dimethoate or pirimiphos-methyl may control the problem.

These red galls are a common sight on Acer campestre, *the field maple.*

Galls produced by gall mites come in various shapes and colours. These are on willow.

MITES, RED SPIDER

There are various types of red spider mites, some of which attack fruit and ornamental trees and others which are found on plants under glass. They are minute creatures, barely visible with the naked eye. Their feeding habits result in fine pale mottling on leaves, or a bronzing of foliage. Leaves fall prematurely. In severe attacks very fine webbing is produced.

Control

Spray with dimethoate, malathion or pirimiphos-methyl (with fruit trees, after they have flowered).

Red spider mites are barely visible to the naked eye, yet the feeding habits of a large colony can cause defoliation of plants.

SAWFLIES

These minute flies are hardly noticeable but their larvae feed on leaves and can cause much damage. Apple sawflies feed inside immature fruits as do plum sawflies.

Control
Spray as soon as noticed with malathion, permethrin or the systemic dimethoate (after petal fall with fruit trees).

SCALE INSECTS

These immobile creatures look, as the name implies, like scales. They may be brown or grey according to species and congregate on shoots of many woody plants, where they suck the sap.

Control
Spray as soon as noticed with malathion or the systemic dimethoate.

Brown scale insects on cornus. These pests congregate on the shoots of many woody plants where they suck the sap.

Although adult sawflies are minute and do no damage, their larvae cause trouble.

The larvae of sawflies feed on the leaves of various trees and can cause much damage.

Right: Apple trees are very prone to attacks by apple sawfly. The larvae feed inside the immature fruits, rendering them unfit for consumption. Routine spraying is generally the only way to prevent this serious pest from attacking.

SQUIRRELS

These mammals, of which the grey is most common, feed off nuts (especially hazelnuts) and fruits. They can cause a great loss of crops.

Control
Shooting is the only method of control.

The grey squirrel (above) is a common mammal and some areas have very large populations. It is very fond of nuts (especially hazelnuts) but will also feed off conifer cones (below).

THRIPS

These minute flies feed on the undersides of leaves by scraping the tissues and sucking up the exuding sap. It results in light yellow or silver mottling discoloration. Defoliation can occur.

Control
As soon as noticed spray with malathion or a systemic insecticide such as dimethoate.

Thrips are minute yet the feeding habits of a colony cause much damage.

WEEVILS

These are beetle-like creatures, black or brown, with an elongated snout. The larvae are white with brown heads and feed off roots. The adults attack foliage, nibbling away at leaf edges.

Control
Spray plants at first signs of attack with an insecticide containing pirimiphos-methyl or permethrin.

WHITEFLY

This tiny white fly colonizes the undersides of leaves and sucks the sap which has a weakening effect on the plant. Many plants are prone to attack, including citrus.

Control
Spray as soon as noticed with an insecticide containing the systemic dimethoate, permethrin, malathion or pirimiphos-methyl.

The pine weevil eats the bark of young pines but is more of a problem in plantations than the garden.

Adult glasshouse whiteflies suck the sap from the undersides of the leaves.

Attelabus nitens, *the oak-roller weevil, as its name implies, rolls the leaves of oak trees.*

DISEASES

Some fungal and bacterial diseases can be prevented by spraying, or treated by cutting back the affected parts of the tree. For some diseases, such as fireblight or Dutch elm disease however, there is no cure: the tree has to be felled.

ANTHRACNOSE, WILLOW

A severe attack of this fungus, which is most prevalent in wet weather, can cause almost complete defoliation of willows. Cankers develop on the shoots.

Control

If possible, spray at bud burst in spring with a copper fungicide and repeat in summer.

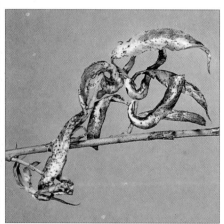

Willow anthracnose is a fungal disease which can result in severe leaf drop.

CANKER

Various fungal and bacterial diseases cause cankers or wounds on branches and shoots. The bark generally splits, resulting in rotting. Wounds are often sunken, but bark may be swollen. If a canker girdles a shoot or branch, die-back will occur beyond the canker. Apple canker is very common. The equally prevalent bacterial canker affects various prunus species.

Control

Cankers can be cut out and the wounds treated with a liquid pruning compound containing cresylic acid: Also treat pruning cuts with this. Spray trees with copper fungicide several times in late summer/early autumn.

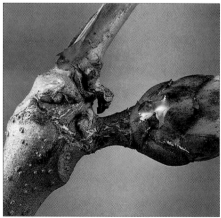

Canker on horse chestnut. Various fungal and bacterial diseases cause cankers.

Right: Willows like this Salix matsudana *'Tortuosa' are prone to the fungal disease anthracnose, which is most prevalent in wet weather.*

CORAL SPOT

This disease appears as rounded red pustules on both dead and live shoots, resulting in shoots dying back.

Control
Cut back shoots beyond the affected area as soon as noticed.

Coral spot appears as rounded red pustules on both dead and live shoots.

DIE-BACK

Various fungi, including coral spot and cankers, cause die-back of growth. There is a serious die-back disease of conifers.

Control
Cut back dead growth to healthy live wood and seal pruning cuts.

DUTCH ELM DISEASE

This very serious fungal disease of elms rapidly causes die-back of branches and then the death of the tree. It has wiped out the English elm in Britain. The disease is spread by elm bark beetles.

Control
No cure. Diseased and dead trees are felled. The stumps should also be removed, either with a stump grinder, or by winching them out.

The brown adult beetle tunnels beneath the bark of elm trees.

Damage caused by elm bark beetles.

FIREBLIGHT

This is a serious bacterial disease affecting trees in the family *Rosaceae*. Leaves turn brown and die, looking as though scorched by fire. The trees can be quickly killed.

Control
Fell and burn affected trees.

Fireblight attacks and kills trees in the rose family, causing leaves to turn brown and die.

HONEY FUNGUS

This is one of the most serious diseases of trees and shrubs. It can rapidly kill even large trees. Honey-coloured toadstools appear at the base of trunks. White fungal threads grow under the bark from the roots upwards. The fungus spreads underground from plant to plant by means of black string-like rhizomorphs. Infection is through the roots. Indications of infection are slowing down of growth, poorly coloured foliage, withering shoots and few or no leaves on shoots or branches.

Control
At the first signs of trouble drench the soil around the tree with a phenolic emulsion formulated for the purpose. If toadstools have appeared it is too late to treat the tree. Dying trees should be felled and roots removed.

LEAF SPOTS

Various fungi and bacteria cause brown spots to appear on leaves.

Control
Spray in spring with a fungicide containing copper or mancozeb.

PEACH LEAF CURL

This fungal disease attacks peaches and some other prunus species causing the leaves to curl, become swollen and turn red.

Control
Spray in late winter, repeat 14 days later and just before leaf fall with a fungicide containing benomyl or copper.

Peach leaf curl causes leaves of peaches and some other trees to curl, swell and turn red.

POWDERY MILDEW

These are fungal diseases that show as a white powdery coating on leaves and shoots. Apple mildew is a powdery type and very common.

Control
Spray in spring and summer with a fungicide containing benomyl or thiophanate-methyl.

RUST

This fungal disease appears as spots on leaves in various shades of brown, according to species. The overall effect is a rust-coloured coating, hence the name.

Control

As soon as noticed spray at fortnightly intervals until under control with a fungicide containing dithane, propiconazole or myclobutanil.

SCAB

This is a fungal disease affecting apples and pears. Symptoms: fruits, often deformed, have brown scabs; dark green patches on leaves; premature leaf fall; reduced crops of fruits; cracked and scabby bark.

Control

Clear and burn fallen leaves in autumn. Prune out shoots with diseased bark. Spray with fungicide containing benomyl or thiophanate-methyl when buds open and repeat fortnightly until mid-summer.

SILVER LEAF

A fungal disease, silver leaf is particularly common on plums and other prunus species. Leaves have a silvery appearance. Branches die back. The entire tree can be killed. Bracket fungi develop on dead branches. Diseased branches are stained purple within.

Control

Cut back diseased branches to healthy wood. Treat pruning cuts with fungicidal sealant. Dig out and burn dead trees.

TAR SPOT

This fungal disease affects acers. It appears as black spots or blotches on foliage.

Control

Clear and burn fallen leaves in autumn. Spray young foliage in spring with a fungicide containing copper.

Tar spot disease attacks acers and appears as black spots or blotches on leaves.

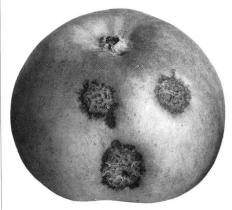

Apple scab is a fungal disease that results in brown scabs forming on the fruits.

Scab is one of the most serious fungal diseases of pears, best prevented by routine spraying.

DISORDERS

The most common disorders found in trees are due either to the weather, or to unsuitable soil conditions. In both cases, prevention is possible by choosing suitable trees for the dominant conditions in your area.

CHLOROSIS, LIME-INDUCED

This occurs if lime-hating (calcifuge) trees like rhododendrons are planted in alkaline soil. The leaves turn yellow, growth becomes stunted and plants eventually die.

Control

Plant calcifuge trees only in lime-free or chalk-free soil.

FROSTS

Spring frosts can kill the flower buds of some trees, especially fruits, resulting in no crops. Young foliage of various trees can also be damaged or killed.

Control

Especially with fruits, avoid planting in frost pockets, those low-lying areas or hollows into which cold air drains. Plant in sheltered parts of the garden. Avoid sites subjected to early morning sun. It is best to avoid susceptible (early flowering) fruits or other trees if frost is a real problem in the area.

WIND SCORCH

Cold, drying winds can scorch the foliage of some trees, particularly certain evergreens, including conifers. The leaves turn brown either at the edges or all over. Foliage may be killed. Salt-laden winds off the sea can scorch foliage, but trees suited to maritime climates can withstand these conditions.

Control

Choose a sheltered site for susceptible trees. Young trees can be protected in winter by surrounding them with a screen of windbreak netting. Often, as they develop, they become tougher and more resistant to wind.

Frosts have browned the foliage of this orange tree, but the tree should survive.

PREVENTING PROBLEMS

METHODS OF CONTROL

It is, of course, sensible to make every effort to prevent the potential problems discussed on pages 74–92 from occurring in the first place. When buying trees in garden centres and nurseries make sure they are absolutely free from pests and diseases. There are enough potential hazards around without actually buying in more! There is no cure for viruses and die-back disease of conifers, for example, so at all costs make sure you do not buy trees with these problems.

Similarly, it is important to avoid buying any trees that are particularly prone to serious diseases (such as fireblight, die-back of conifers and Dutch elm disease) if you know these conditions are prevalent in your area.

Good cultivation practice in the garden is equally important. Plant in well-prepared soil, feed regularly and water your plants when required. Trees that are healthy and growing well are better able to withstand attacks by pests and diseases, while those that are ailing or under stress are less able to cope with further problems.

Hygienic conditions in the garden (and under glass if applicable) will also help to minimize the risk of infection. Simple but effective precautions include ensuring that no piles of rubbish are left lying around (they can harbour pests and diseases) and that weeds do not become established (these can act as temporary hosts in the life cycle of some pests and diseases of trees).

Carry out pruning such as the removal of dead wood (which can encourage further diseases) and overcrowded wood, when necessary, to ensure good air circulation within the crown of the tree. Still, stagnant air trapped in the crown can actually encourage diseases to establish. Similarly, make sure that all large pruning cuts, and any other wounds, are sealed immediately with a pruning compound to prevent diseases such as wood-rotting fungi from entering the trees.

Traditionally, spraying trees with a systemic pesticide as and when necessary has been the preferred method of controlling pests and diseases. More recently, however, experiments with biological methods of control have given interesting results.

CONTROL BY SPRAYING

Many pests and diseases can be controlled by spraying the trees with suitable pesticides. It is one of the main methods of controlling problems and is therefore frequently recommended in the lists of pests and diseases. It does, of course, presume that the trees are of a realistic size for spraying. There is no way that amateurs, nor indeed professionals, can spray large trees. Having said that, however, professional orchardists can spray quite large standard fruit trees with tractor-mounted spraying equipment.

Young, and naturally small, trees (such as standard apples or other fruit trees) can be sprayed with a pressure sprayer. A knapsack sprayer can be recommended as this gives you a free hand, especially useful if you want to spray trees from platform steps. If you are using steps to spray trees get someone to hold them steady while you work – they have a nasty habit of sinking into the ground and toppling over in gardens.

The alternative to the knapsack sprayer is the pressure type which has to be carried around with one hand. Both types, however, generally have a reasonably long spray lance, enabling you to direct the spray well up into a tree.

Wherever possible choose systemic insecticides and fungicides as these are long lasting. Specific recommendations are given in the lists of pests and diseases.

Systemics are sprayed on to the leaves and are then absorbed by the tree. They are taken into the sap stream where they move around. Therefore, unlike contact pesticides, you do not have to drench every square centimetre for

When spraying trees, it is important to choose a calm and dry day – dull conditions are best. Use a fine spray and pay particular attention to the undersides of leaves.

effective control. This is a great advantage when you are faced with a difficult spraying situation such as you will find with a tree. Furthermore, systemics are not washed off the plants by rain so you do not have to spray as frequently in wet weather as when contact pesticides are used. If the action of a pesticide is systemic, this will be stated on the container. Systemic insecticides are particularly useful for controlling sap-sucking insects such as aphids.

Contact insecticides work by hitting the actual pest, or by coating the pest's food source – the leaves – and are generally recommended for biting and chewing pests such as caterpillars. With these, you have to give a thorough, drenching spray. A number of contact pesticides have been recommended in the pest and disease lists. Most fungicides have a contact action.

It cannot be stated too strongly how essential it is to use pesticides strictly according to the

Malus species, including M. baccata *shown here, may possibly need more spraying than some other trees to control pests and diseases.*

94

manufacturer's instructions. This means thoroughly reading the directions for use on the container and following these recommendations to the letter. *Never* be tempted to mix a stronger solution than recommended as this could severely damage trees. A solution which is too weak, on the other hand, may not control the pest or disease.

It is essential to choose the correct pesticide for the problem in hand. Also do make sure that the product is recommended for the particular plant; some cannot be used on all plants – sensitive plants will be stated on the container. With fruits, ensure the interval between spraying and picking for eating is acceptable.

Make sure you are wearing sufficient protective clothing when mixing and using sprays, as they must not come in contact with the skin. The minimum recommendations are goggles to protect the eyes, and rubber gloves. If any pesticide comes in contact with the skin, wash it off immediately. Never eat, smoke or drink while handling pesticides.

Choose the right time to spray trees. Never spray trees while they are in flower as this can kill essential pollinating insects such as bees. The weather must be completely calm as windy conditions result in spray drift. Do not allow pesticides to drift on to other plants, into neighbours' gardens, or over the highway. The weather must be dry and the leaves of the trees should also be dry, but do not spray during sunny weather as you risk leaf scorch. Dull conditions are best.

A fine spray is generally more penetrating than a very coarse spray pattern.

When using contact pesticides make sure every part of the plant is covered. Pay particular attention to the undersides of the leaves and shoot tips, where pests or diseases are often found. You have applied sufficient when the solution just starts to run off the leaves. With systemic pesticides you should still aim for relatively good/coverage but do not apply so much solution that it runs off the foliage.

After spraying thoroughly wash out equipment with plain clean water. Never store spray solution, instead tip excess on to bare soil. Store containers in a safe place, well away from children and pets.

OTHER METHODS

It is not always necessary to use chemicals to control pests and diseases. Small numbers of caterpillars, for instance, can be picked off by hand, and small populations of bugs such as aphids squashed between a finger and thumb. Other non-chemical methods of control are given as appropriate in the lists; these include trapping codling-moth caterpillars with bands of hessian or burlap tied around the trunk of apple trees, and cutting out diseased shoots.

If you are growing trees under glass for part or all of the year (citrus fruits, for example, or figs), different methods of pest and disease control can be used. The most common is a smoke canister, which distributes the pesticide through the greenhouse in dense smoke.

Alternatively, biological control, that is, using predators and parasites to attack specific pests, can be used. This is still in its infancy but developing constantly. For example, the parasitic wasp, *Encarsia formosa*, is now commonly used to control glasshouse whitefly; and the predatory mite, *Phytoseiulus persimilis*, is used for red spider mite control. To a lesser extent at present, the Australian ladybird predator, *Cryptolaemus*, is used to control mealy bugs and scale insects.

Introduce parasites and predators only when pests are found on the plants and never use chemicals after they have been introduced.

Biological methods of pest control – using one insect to eradicate another – are becoming more popular.

5

PROPAGATING

TREES

*T*he amateur gardener is unlikely to want to propagate trees in any quantity
unless, perhaps, it is to plant a screen or windbreak or start a woodland
garden from scratch.

Many species are easily increased from seeds and some, such as betula,
fraxinus and some acers, even self-sow freely. Buying packets of seeds of
ornamental species certainly represents a cheap way of obtaining trees. You may
end up with far too many seedlings of course, but you could always give
unwanted ones away.

If you want to propagate an existing tree you could try a technique known as
air layering, whereby a shoot is encouraged to form roots while still attached to
the parent plant (see pages 104–5).

Nurserymen propagate many trees – especially cultivars, which do not
come true from seeds – by budding or grafting. These techniques involve
forming a permanent union between portions of two separate plants so that
they develop into a complete new plant. Both grafting and budding are complex
and skilled operations and amateur gardeners who want to know more or try
their hand at it are advised to consult a book on plant propagation. Here, the
easier methods of seed raising and air layering are considered.

Many trees can be grown from seed, including some betula species.

SEEDS

Only species should be raised from seeds, either collected from existing trees or bought from a reputable seedsman.

COLLECTING AND STORING

Seeds could, perhaps, be collected from friends' and neighbours' trees. Never collect from other people's trees without first obtaining their permission, however; this includes trees in public parks and gardens.

Be sure to collect seeds only from species, not from cultivars or hybrids. The time of year to collect depends on the type of tree, but most are ready for harvesting in late summer and autumn.

Ideally collect seeds when they are dry. They should be ripe and, with small seeds, collected before they are shed by the plant. However, large seeds, such as those of quercus, castanea and aesculus, can be allowed to fall to the ground, when they are easily gathered. An indication of ripeness is when seed capsules, pods and cones turn brown, and berries and fruits change to various colours such as red, orange or yellow.

Seeds produced in dry pods, capsules, cones and the like (as opposed to fleshy fruits and berries) will need drying after collecting. Lay them out on sheets of newspaper in a warm, airy place, such as in a greenhouse. When thoroughly dry and the seed containers have opened to release the seeds (if they do not do this, gently crush them), place the seeds in envelopes and store for the winter in a cool, dry, airy place. They are sown in the spring.

If you have collected seeds of acer, fagus and fraxinus a better method of storage is to mix the seeds with damp peat, seal in polythene or plastic bags and place in a refrigerator with a temperature of 1–5°C (35–40°F) until sowing time in spring.

Fleshy fruits and berries such as those of ilex, sorbus, malus and prunus are stored by a

Seeds of acers are best stored by mixing them with damp peat, sealing in plastic bags and placing in a refrigerator until sowing time.

technique known as stratification, which softens their hard seed coats and ensures better germination. To do this, crush the fruits or berries until the seeds are exposed, then mix them with moist horticultural sand – up to three times their own volume of sand. There is no need to separate the seeds from the pulp. Place the mixture in a flower pot and stand it outdoors in the cold.

The stratification period lasts from six to eighteen months, according to species. The seeds of arbutus, juniperus, malus, prunus, sorbus and taxus, for example, need six months, those of crataegus, ilex and magnolia, eighteen.

Protect the seeds from rodents and do not allow the sand to dry out. Seeds and sand are sown together.

The seeds of some trees are best sown in autumn immediately after collecting as they do not store well. These include aesculus, castanea and quercus. If desired, fraxinus can also be sown in autumn.

SOWING

The majority of tree seeds can be sown outdoors in early to mid-spring. Unless the soil is extremely well drained prepare raised beds for sowing, about 90cm (3ft) wide and 10cm (4in) high. This preparation can be done in autumn. In spring, just prior to sowing, apply a balanced fertilizer, firm the soil by treading and rake the surface of the beds to a fine tilth.

TREES TO GROW FROM SEED

Name	Sow
Acer	Outdoors
Arbutus	Indoors
Quercus	Outdoors
Rhododendron	Indoors

SOWING SEEDS INDOORS

*V*ery small or dust-like seeds are best sown in containers and germinated under glass – preferably in a heated greenhouse.

1 *Fill a pot with well-drained seed compost and moderately firm it with a wooden presser. Soil-based compost can be used but peat is more suitable for rhododendrons.*

2 *Sow seeds as thinly and evenly as possible from the palm of your hand. Mix fine seeds such as rhododendrons with some fine dry silver sand to make handling and sowing easier.*

3 *Scatter a layer of compost over all but very small seeds, using a sieve with fine mesh. The depth of compost should equal about twice the diameter of the seeds you have used.*

SOWING SEEDS OUTDOORS

S eeds of most trees can be sown outdoors in early to mid-spring. It is best to prepare a raised bed for sowing, unless the soil is extremely well drained.

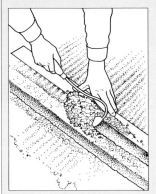  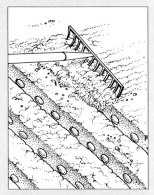

1 *Make shallow furrows across the bed with an onion or draw hoe, spacing them about 10cm (4in) apart. They should be 6–12mm (¼–½in) deep.*

2 *Large seeds, such as those of oak, popularly known as acorns, can be spaced out individually. Always sow seeds thinly to prevent dense colonies of seedlings.*

3 *After sowing, cover the seeds with fine soil by raking it into the furrows. Alternatively seeds can be covered with pea shingle, which helps to keep the soil moist.*

Sow in shallow furrows across the bed, 10cm (4in) apart, and 6–12mm (¼–½in) deep according to the size of the seeds. Sow thinly, then cover the seeds either with fine soil or pea shingle. The latter prevents rapid drying out and protects the seeds from birds. Keep the beds watered and weeded as necessary.

Very small seeds such as those of rhododendron are best sown in containers under glass. Likewise seeds of those trees from mild or warm climates.

Sow thinly in pots or seed trays using a well-drained soil-based compost. However, pure sphagnum peat is suitable for rhododendrons. Very small dust-like seeds are not easy to sow thinly unless mixed with some fine, dry, silver sand. Cover the seeds evenly with a depth of compost that equals about twice their diameter. Do not cover very small seeds.

Water the compost, then place the containers on the bench in a heated greenhouse or in a propagating case. Cover with a sheet of glass and newspaper to prevent the compost from drying out. As soon as germination is apparent remove the coverings and provide maximum light. Seedlings must be shaded from strong sunshine, however.

GROWING ON SEEDLINGS

When seedlings raised outdoors are large enough to handle, which could be in the autumn of the same year or spring of the following year, transplant them to a nursery bed to give them more room to grow. If sufficiently large they can be planted direct into their final positions in the garden. If some seeds do not germinate in the first spring leave them for another year.

Seedlings raised under glass can be planted individually in small pots as soon as they are large enough to handle, using a soil-based or soil-less compost. Once established in their pots transfer them to a garden frame to harden, then plant them in nursery beds or in their final positions. Small, delicate seedlings might be better kept in a garden frame over the first winter and planted out in the spring.

Above: Fraxinus or ash sets large quantities of seeds which germinate freely if sown in the autumn immediately after collecting. Often, ash self-sows freely and becomes a "weed".

Left: Oaks (quercus) are easily raised from seeds and germinate well if they are sown in the autumn immediately after collecting. This is the growth to expect in one year.

103

AIR LAYERING

Layering is a method of encouraging a shoot to form roots while it is still attached to the parent plant. When rooted the shoot is removed and planted. It will then develop into a new plant resembling its parent in every respect.

Generally shoots are encouraged to root in the soil around the parent plants, but with most trees this is not possible because the branches are not sufficiently near to the ground. With trees shoots can be rooted without coming into contact with the ground, a technique known as air layering.

Trees are air layered between mid-spring and late summer. Spring is the best time. Both young and old trees can be propagated by this method, provided young shoots are used. Old wood will not root, or will take an excessively long time to do so.

To encourage a shoot to form roots it must first be wounded. This can be carried out approximately 30cm (1ft) from its tip. Remove some leaves to give a clear area for working. The wound can be made by cutting the shoot half way through its length to form a tongue about 5cm (2in) long. Use a really sharp knife as a clean, smooth cut is important.

The cut surfaces should be dusted with a hormone rooting powder to speed rooting. Choose a type formulated for semi-ripe or hardwood cuttings.

The tongue should be kept open by packing it with a wad of moist sphagnum moss. Then wrap the wounded part of the shoot with more moss. This is the rooting medium.

The moss is held in place by wrapping it with a square of clear polythene or plastic sheeting. Form it into a "bandage" and seal both ends with a few turns of waterproof adhesive tape. Also seal the overlapping edge of the polythene bandage with a strip of tape. The idea of sealing the bandage is to prevent rainwater from entering and soaking the moss. If the moss becomes excessively wet rooting may be inhibited.

You will know when the shoot has rooted as white roots will be visible through the polythene.

One cannot be precise regarding the length of time that a shoot takes to root, as it depends on the subject, but with many trees rooting takes place within a year.

When it is apparent that rooting has occurred, the shoot can be removed. This is best done during an appropriate planting season, in spring or autumn. Carefully remove the polythene but leave the moss in place. If you remove the moss the roots could be damaged. The shoot should be cut away from the parent tree just beyond the rooted area.

Rooted shoots can be planted in pots of suitable size and allowed to establish in a garden frame. Then the young plants can be planted out, either into nursery beds to grow on, or direct into their permanent positions.

TREES SUITABLE FOR AIR LAYERING

Name	Type of tree Deciduous	Evergreen
Amelanchier	•	
Cercidiphyllum	•	
Cornus	•	
Davidia	•	
Eucryphia		•
Halesia	•	
Liquidambar	•	
Magnolia	•	•
Mespilus	•	
Morus	•	
Nyssa	•	
Parrotia	•	
Rhododendron		•
Stewartia	•	

PROPAGATING BY AIR LAYERING

*A*useful vegetative method of propagating trees for the amateur is air layering whereby a shoot is encouraged to form roots while it is still attached to the parent plant. This is both easy and reliable.

1 *Select a young shoot. About 30cm (12in) from the tip of the chosen shoot remove some leaves so that you have a clear area for working. A stripped length of 15cm (6in) should be sufficient.*

2 *To encourage the shoot to form roots it must be wounded. To do this, cut the shoot halfway through its length to form a tongue about 5cm (2in) long. Be sure to use a really sharp knife.*

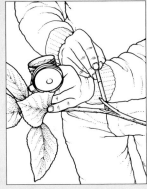

3 *Dust the cut surfaces of the shoot with hormone rooting powder to speed rooting. Choose a type formulated for semi-ripe or hardwood cuttings, and apply it with care with a soft brush.*

4 *To keep the cut tongue open, use a wad of sphagnum moss. This is available from many garden centres or from florists and should be moist, but not soaking wet, before use. Pack it into the cut.*

5 *Wrap the wounded part of the shoot with more moist sphagnum moss. The sphagnum moss acts as the rooting medium so be fairly generous with it and form a substantial wad around the tongue.*

6 *Hold the moss in place by wrapping it with a square of clear plastic sheeting. Form it into a "bandage" and seal both ends plus the overlapping edge with waterproof adhesive tape so that no water penetrates.*

TREE TRAINING

Generally young trees can be allowed to grow naturally without artificial manipulation. Unless you wish to train a tree to a particular shape, the only time you will need to carry out pruning is if a tree produces a double central leader (the continuation of the trunk). Obviously if two leaders are allowed to grow the trunk will end up being forked and the tree will not attain its proper shape or height. Therefore, as soon as noticed remove the weakest of the two leaders.

Much more pruning and training will be required if you want to train a tree into a standard or half-standard – that is, a tree with a trunk devoid of branches but with a head of branches at the top. A standard tree has a clear trunk to a height of at least 1.8m (6ft). This form is necessary for street planting and, of course, if you want to sit or walk under the tree. Half-standards have a clear trunk of about half this height. It is a form often used for fruit trees such as apples and pears. Fruits can also be grown as standards but the trees will be taller, of course, which may present problems when it comes to picking the fruit.

Here is the technique for training a standard (or half-standard) tree. In its second year the stem of a young tree will start to produce side branches or "feathers". These result in an increased stem diameter and stronger trunk and should not be removed too soon or you will end up with a weak tree.

Leave the feathers untouched until late summer, except for the removal of any really thick ones that are competing with the leader. After late summer no regrowth will occur from feathers that have been pruned. Remove the lower third of feathers using a really sharp knife, or secateurs or pruning shears, cutting them off as close as possible to the trunk. The feathers that remain should be cut back to leave three pairs of leaves.

A standard tree is one with a trunk devoid of branches but with a head of branches at the top. This form is necessary for street planting and if the tree is required for sitting under.

TRAINING A STANDARD

*T*raining a tree into a standard (or indeed into a half-standard) is a comparatively simple operation for the amateur gardener.

1 *In the tree's second year, remove the lower third of side branches and reduce others to three leaves.*

2 *In the third year remove the middle third of branches and shorten the remainder to three leaves.*

3 *Finally, in the fourth year, remove the top third of branches but leave at least four to form the head.*

The training of a fan-shaped tree, such as a plum, is a complex operation for the amateur.

TREES SUITABLE FOR TRAINING

Name	Type of tree		Style				
	Deciduous	Evergreen	Standard	Half-standard	Espalier	Cordon	Fan
Acer negundo	•		•				
Acer platanoides	•		•				
Aesculus species	•		•				
Crataegus species	•		•				
Fagus species	•		•				
Fraxinus species	•		•				
Malus (inc apples)	•		•	•	•	•	
Platanus × *acerifolia*	•		•				
Prunus (inc cherry, plum)	•		•	•			•
Pyrus (inc pears)	•		•	•	•	•	•
Quercus species	•		•				
Sorbus species	•		•				
Tilia species	•		•				

At the same time the following year remove the "middle" third of feathers and cut back the remainder to leave three pairs of leaves.

Finally, in the next year, during late summer, remove the top third of feathers. Allow at least four side branches at the top of the stem to form the head of the tree and allow the leader to grow. By now the tree is four years old and formative pruning is complete.

Usually a young tree that is being trained is tied to a bamboo cane to ensure a straight leader. A lot of research has been carried out on the validity of caning. It has been found, among other things, that caned young trees do not thicken as much at the base as un-caned trees. Also, they may grow more in height. A caned tree may have difficulty in supporting itself once the cane is removed and may have a weak point at the top of the trunk.

Experience has shown that some trees grow well without cane support. Examples include species of fraxinus; various prunus including *P. avium* (sweet cherry) and *P. dulcis* (common almond); quercus species; sorbus with a vigorous habit of growth; and *Malus tschonoskii* (large-leaved crabapple).

Trees that need caning include *Crataegus laevigata* (*C. oxyacantha*) (hawthorn/May hawthorn); species of nothofagus; platanus species; *Prunus cerasifera* (cherry plum); *Prunus sargentii* (Sargent cherry); tilia species; and *Ulmus glabra* (wych elm).

If a standard stem is needed, a 2.7m (9ft) bamboo cane should be used. Insert it close to the tree and well down into the soil. Tie the tree to it with raffia or soft string. The number of ties should suit the length and straightness of the stem: three are usually sufficient.

6

ENCYCLOPEDIA

OF

TREES

*T*his comprehensive directory of trees contains over 100 genera and in
excess of 300 species, all commonly grown in the USA and Europe.
It includes trees suitable for small, medium and large gardens, as well as
for parks and estates.
To make selection easy, the trees have been grouped into sections covering
Small Ornamental Deciduous, Small Ornamental Evergreen, Medium to Large
Deciduous, and Medium to Large Evergreen specimens, and, finally,
Trees with Edible Fruits.
The trees are listed alphabetically under generic names. Then follows
the common name or names if applicable, and the family name. The general
introduction to the genus includes suggestions on uses, and may embrace
origins, habits of growth and other useful or interesting details.
Then follow species, including cultivars if applicable. If there is a common
name, this is given, followed by origin, hardiness rating (as zone numbers,
see right), and shape (see key right).
Ultimate height is given, plus descriptions of the leaves, flowers, fruits
and bark as applicable.
Cultivation details embrace suitable aspects and soils
(as symbols, see key right).
Any special requirements, pruning hints and problems (pests, diseases
or disorders) are outlined as applicable.

HARDINESS RATING

The Plant Hardiness Zone System, devised by the United States Department of Agriculture, which embraces the United States of America and southern Canada, has been used to denote the hardiness of each tree (see the map on pages 112–113). Each tree has been given a zone number, for example ⑧, to offer a guide to its suitability for your area.
There are 10 climatic zones, numbered from 1 to 10, with Zone 1 being the coldest and Zone 10 the warmest.

AVERAGE MINIMUM WINTER TEMPERATURES FOR THE CLIMATIC ZONES

①	Below −45°C (−50°F)	⑥	−23 to −18°C (−10 to 0°F)
②	−45 to −39°C (−50 to −40°F)	⑦	−18 to −12°C (0 to 10°F)
③	−39 to −35°C (−40 to −30°F)	⑧	−12 to −6°C (10 to 20°F)
④	−35 to −29°C (−30 to −20°F)	⑨	−6 to −1°C (20 to 30°F)
⑤	−29 to −23°C (−20 to −10°F)	⑩	−1 to 4°C (30 to 40°F)

In this book the system has been applied also to Western Europe, including the UK (see the map on pages 114–115).
Trees should thrive in the zone numbers given and in zones with higher numbers (and therefore higher minimum winter temperatures). It must be remembered, however, that there can be local variations in climate within each zone. No system dealing with plant hardiness can be 100 per cent accurate.

KEY TO SYMBOLS

Shape		**Aspect**		**Soils**	
♤	Conical	☼	Full sun	**A**	Acid
♀	Spreading	☀	Partial shade	**AL**	Alkaline
♉	Broad columnar	●	Shade	**A-N**	Acid to neutral
◊	Fastigiate	☉	Sheltered from cold winds	■	Rich in humus
♔	Weeping			▦	Well drained

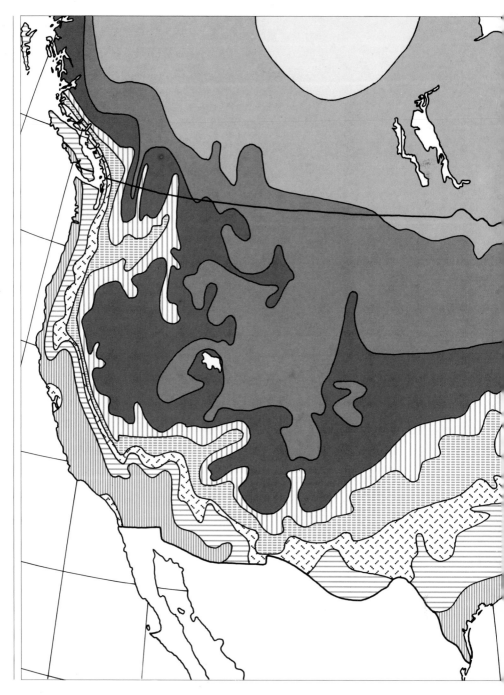

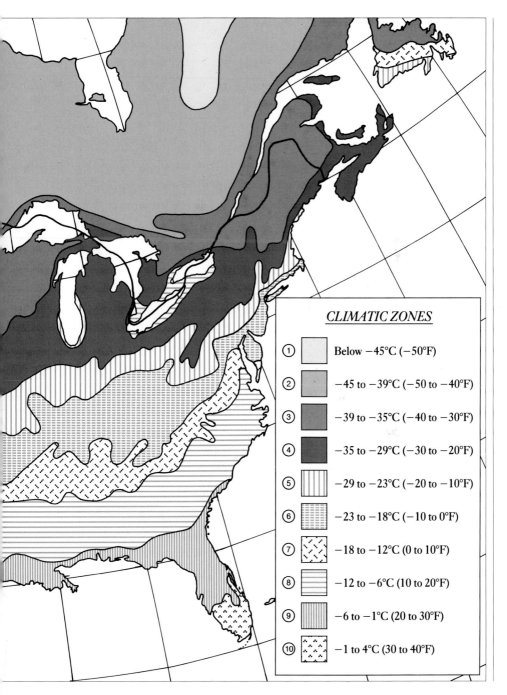

CLIMATIC ZONES

① Below −45°C (−50°F)

② −45 to −39°C (−50 to −40°F)

③ −39 to −35°C (−40 to −30°F)

④ −35 to −29°C (−30 to −20°F)

⑤ −29 to −23°C (−20 to −10°F)

⑥ −23 to −18°C (−10 to 0°F)

⑦ −18 to −12°C (0 to 10°F)

⑧ −12 to −6°C (10 to 20°F)

⑨ −6 to −1°C (20 to 30°F)

⑩ −1 to 4°C (30 to 40°F)

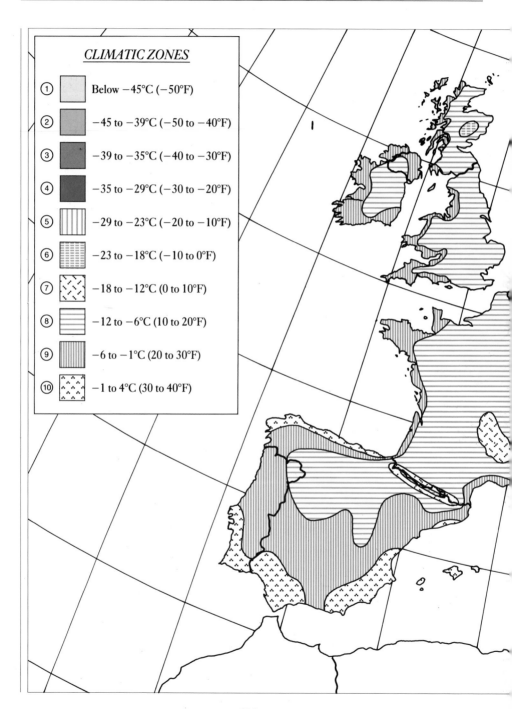

CLIMATIC ZONES

① Below −45°C (−50°F)

② −45 to −39°C (−50 to −40°F)

③ −39 to −35°C (−40 to −30°F)

④ −35 to −29°C (−30 to −20°F)

⑤ −29 to −23°C (−20 to −10°F)

⑥ −23 to −18°C (−10 to 0°F)

⑦ −18 to −12°C (0 to 10°F)

⑧ −12 to −6°C (10 to 20°F)

⑨ −6 to −1°C (20 to 30°F)

⑩ −1 to 4°C (30 to 40°F)

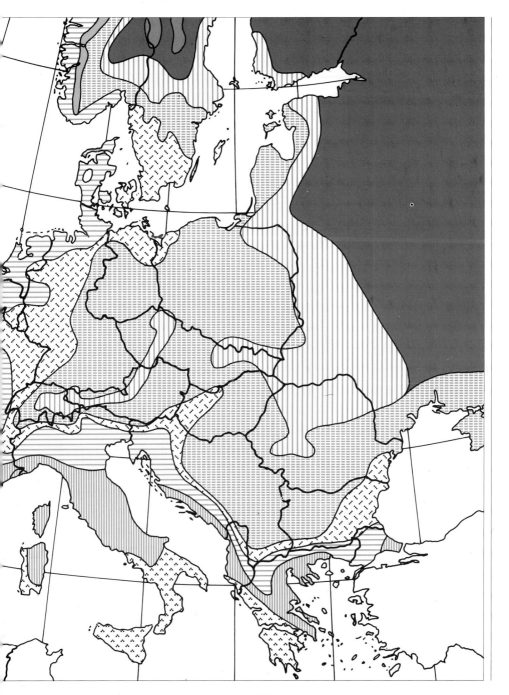

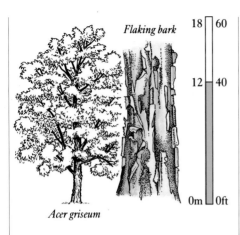

Flaking bark

18 / 60

12 / 40

0m / 0ft

Acer griseum

ACER

Maple

Aceraceae

*T*he acers originated mainly from northern temperate parts of the world and many are noted for attractive (often lobed) foliage and/or bark. Shallow-rooted, they are frequently used as lawn specimens in private gardens, where their distinctive characteristics are shown to advantage. Species with ornamental bark look particularly attractive with winter-flowering shrubs. Those noted for autumn leaf colour need a dark background, such as evergreen conifers, if they are to show up well. They look good near water. In many private gardens, and those open to the public, acers noted for autumn leaf colour are often planted adjacent to lakes, where their foliage is beautifully reflected when the surface of the water is calm. Acers are also highly recommended for inclusion in woodland gardens where their autumn foliage adds a useful splash of colour, and the bark of the snake-bark species provides interest during the winter.

● *A. capillipes* (Snake-bark maple, Hakkoda maple) Japan ⑥ ♀
Height 10.6m (35ft). Leaves three-lobed, flushed with red when they unfurl. Autumn colour is crimson. Flowers green-white, spring.

Young shoots bright red. Bark green, striped with white.
● *A. davidii* (Snake-bark maple, David maple) China ⑥ ♀
Height 10–15m (33–50ft). Leaves ovate, deep green, flushed bronze when young, turning red and gold in autumn. Flowers yellow, spring. Bark grey, striped white; best pattern in partial shade.
● *A. forrestii* (Snake-bark maple) China ⑦ ♀
Height 10–15m (33–50ft). Leaves dark green above, paler below, three-lobed. Flowers yellow-green, spring. Bark striped with white.
● *A. griseum* (Paper-bark maple) China ⑥ ♀
Height 6–12m (20–40ft). Leaves trifoliate, medium green, turning scarlet in autumn. Flowers green, spring. Bark flaking, to reveal orange-brown underbark. Grown mainly for attractive bark.
● *A. grosseri* (Snake-bark maple) China ⑥ ♀
Height 6–10m (20–33ft). Leaves three-lobed, shiny, yellowish-green, red in autumn. Flowers green, spring. Bark striped with white. Variety *hersii* is similar.
● *A. nikoense* (*A. maximowiczianum*) (Nikko maple) Japan, central China ⑥ ♀
Height 15m (50ft) but often much less. Leaves trifoliate, medium green, turning scarlet in autumn. Flowers yellow, spring.
● *A. pensylvanicum* (Striped maple, Pennsylvania maple, Moose wood maple) eastern North America ③ ♀
Height 4.5–6m (15–20ft), sometimes to 10.6m (35ft). Leaves rounded, three-lobed, light or medium green, turning pure yellow in autumn. Flowers yellow, spring. Bark green, strikingly striped with white.

Cultivation

☼ ☀ ☉ A AL ▨

A. forrestii needs acid soil. Shallow chalk soils are best avoided for *A. pensylvanicum*. No pruning required.

Problems
Aphids, coral spot, honey fungus, tar spot.

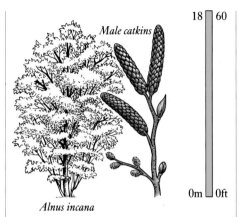

Male catkins

18 | 60

0m | 0ft

Alnus incana

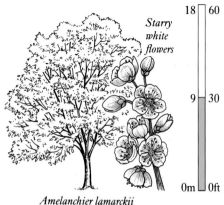

Starry white flowers

18 | 60

9 | 30

0m | 0ft

Amelanchier lamarckii

ALNUS

Alder

Betulaceae

*T*he alders are found in the northern hemisphere and are especially useful for damp or wet soils and exposed situations, often being used for screens and windbreaks. Some have attractive catkin-like flowers in the spring.

● *A. incana* (Grey alder) ④ ♀
Height can be up to 18m (60ft) but often is less; can be reduced by pruning. Fast grower. Leaves usually oval, greyish below. The yellow male catkins produced in early spring are quite showy. Cultivars include 'Aurea', yellow foliage, slow grower; and 'Pendula', weeping habit, foliage grey-green.

Cultivation

☼ ☕ A AL ■

Very adaptable to a variety of soils although shallow chalk is best avoided. Can be pruned hard if necessary, to reduce height of screen for example.

Problems

Fungal leaf spots, but not serious.

AMELANCHIER

June berry, Snowy mespilus, Service-berry

Rosaceae

*T*hese beautiful trees and shrubs from Europe, North America and northern Asia make excellent specimens in a lawn or mixed border where they produce a profusion of white flowers in spring. Superb when underplanted with spring-flowering bulbs. Foliage often colours well in autumn. Also known as Shadbush.

● *A. lamarckii* (*A.* × *grandiflora*)
Origin uncertain ④ ♀
Height 9m (30ft). Leaves copper-coloured when young, turning scarlet in autumn. Starry white flowers in spring. Cultivar 'Rubescens' has pink-tinged flowers.

Cultivation

☼ ☕ A AL ▦

Easily grown in any fertile soil that does not dry out. No pruning needed.

Problems

Fireblight in some areas.

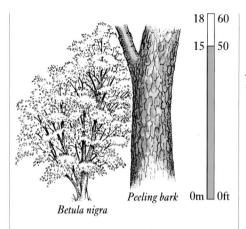

Peeling bark

Betula nigra

18 ⌐ 60
15 ⊢ 50
0m ⌐ 0ft

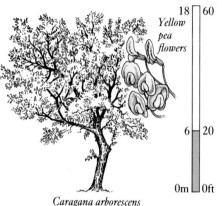

Yellow pea flowers

18 ⌐ 60
6 ⊢ 20
0m ⌐ 0ft

Caragana arborescens

BETULA

Birch

Betulaceae

*W*idely distributed throughout the temperate northern hemisphere, the birches are among the most popular garden trees for use as lawn specimens and focal points or for creating light woodland conditions. They have a graceful habit of growth and often attractive bark. Many produce conspicuous male catkins in spring.

● *B. nigra* (River birch, Black birch)
North America ⑤ ⚐

One of the smaller birches yet can attain a height of 15m (50ft) or more. Leaves have whitish undersides. Bark is the distinctive feature: rugged, peeling, red-brown or greyish.

Cultivation

☼ ◑ **A AL** ■

Although tolerant of poor sandy soils, best results in moisture-retentive, fertile, loamy soils. No pruning needed.

Problems

Aphids, caterpillars, sawflies, honey fungus.

CARAGANA

Pea tree, Pea shrub

Leguminosae

*T*he caraganas come from Asia and are grown for their pea-like flowers and attractive pinnate foliage. Also make good windbreaks. There are up to 60 species but only a few are grown. Many species are quite spiny. Some spines consist of the spine-tipped stalks of the leaves and these eventually become quite hard and woody. Sometimes stipules (leaf-like organs at the base of leaf stalks) are spine tipped.

● *C. arborescens* (Siberian pea tree)
Siberia, Manchuria ② ♀

Height up to 6m (20ft). Leaves are pinnate, the main stalk being spine tipped. Pea flowers yellow in late spring or early summer. The form *lorbergii* has very fine foliage, almost fennel-like. There is also a weeping form called *pendula*.

Cultivation

☼ **A AL** ▨

Best soil is a light sandy type of lowish fertility. No regular pruning needed. To ensure a good tree form, train the leading shoot of the young plant and remove all suckers and lower branches.

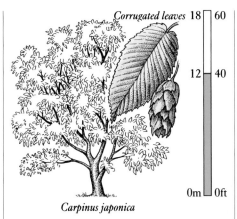

Corrugated leaves 18 / 60
12 / 40
0m / 0ft

Carpinus japonica

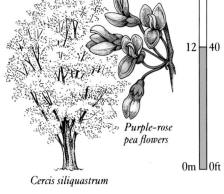

18 / 60
12 / 40
Purple-rose pea flowers
0m / 0ft

Cercis siliquastrum

CARPINUS

Hornbeam

Betulaceae

Very hardy trees originating from the temperate areas of the northern hemisphere. Of good shape, they are generally used as specimen trees to create focal points. Some can also be used for windbreaks and hedges.
- *C. caroliniana* (American hornbeam, Blue beech) eastern North America ④ ♀
Height up to 12m (40ft) but usually less. Leaves oval and shiny, taking on orange and scarlet tints in autumn. Bark grey, fluted; an attractive feature.
- *C. japonica* (Japanese hornbeam) Japan ④ ♀
Height about 12m (40ft). Leaves conspicuously corrugated. Fruiting catkins are also attractive. The bark is scaly.
- *C. turczaninovii* (Tatarian hornbeam) northern China and Korea ④ ♀
Height up to 6m (20ft). Leaves small, oval, bright red when they first unfurl.

Cultivation

☼ ☢ A AL ▦

Best growth in a deep loamy soil. No regular pruning needed.

Problems

Honey fungus.

CERCIS

Judas tree, Redbud

Leguminosae

Coming from North America, southern Europe and Asia, the Judas trees are noted for their pea flowers which appear before the leaves in late spring. Highly recommended for mixed borders and especially attractive with an underplanting of late-spring bulbs.
- *C. canadensis* (Redbud, Eastern redbud) eastern North America ⑤ ♀
Height to 12m (40ft). Attractive almost circular leaves. Clusters of rose-pink pea flowers in late spring.
- *C. siliquastrum* (Judas tree) southern Europe, western Asia ⑦ ♀
Height up to 12m (40ft). Leaves glaucous, virtually circular. Clusters of purple-rose pea flowers in late spring. Red seed pods follow in summer. There is a white-flowered variety, *alba*.

Cultivation

☼ ☉ A AL ▦

Best to plant young pot-grown specimens as cercis resent root disturbance. Fertile soil is best. No regular pruning required.

Problems

Coral spot.

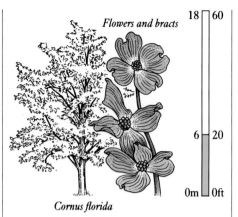

Flowers and bracts

18 / 60

6 / 20

0m / 0ft

Cornus florida

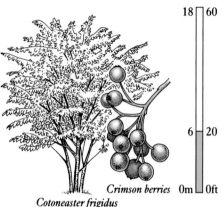

Crimson berries 0m / 0ft

18 / 60

6 / 20

Cotoneaster frigidus

CORNUS

Dogwood, Cornel

Cornaceae

A variable genus from North America, Europe and Asia. The more shapely and distinctive can be used as isolated specimens in lawns as well as in shrub or mixed borders.

● *C. controversa* (Giant dogwood)
Japan, China ⑤ ♀
Height usually 9–15m (30–50ft). Branches held in horizontal layers. Leaves ovate, medium green, purple-red in autumn. White flowers in profusion, early summer. Berries bluish black, autumn. There is a white and green variegated form, 'Variegata'.
● *C. florida* (Flowering dogwood)
eastern North America ⑤ ♀
Height 6m (20ft) or more. Leaves oval, dark green, turning scarlet and orange in autumn. Flowers inconspicuous but surrounded by showy white petal-like bracts, late spring. Red fruits, strawberry-like, late summer/autumn. 'Rubra' has rose or pink bracts.

Cultivation

 ☼ A AL 🏵

Adaptable, growing in any fertile soil but shallow chalky types best avoided for *C. florida*. No regular pruning needed.

COTONEASTER

Cotoneaster

Rosaceae

T he cotoneasters, from temperate areas of the northern hemisphere, especially China and the Himalayas, are mainly deciduous and evergreen shrubs, although the genus does contain a few small trees, including the species described here. This is an excellent berrying subject for shrub and mixed borders, where it associates particularly well with autumn-flowering perennials or bulbs.

● *C. frigidus* (Himalayan cotoneaster)
Himalayas ⑦ ♀
Height 6m (20ft), maybe slightly more. Fast-growing species. Leaves deciduous or semi-evergreen. Small white flowers carried in clusters, early summer. Large clusters of crimson berries in autumn and winter.

Cultivation

☼ ☾ A AL 🏵

Cotoneasters are especially recommended for chalky soils.

Problems
Aphids, scale insects, fireblight, honey fungus, silver leaf.

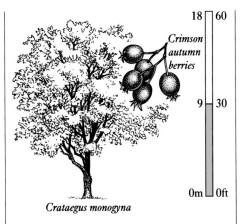

18 ┌ 60

Crimson autumn berries

9 ─ 30

0m └ 0ft

Crataegus monogyna

CRATAEGUS

Thorn, Hawthorn

Rosaceae

Usually thorny trees from temperate areas of the northern hemisphere. Most are noted for their extreme hardiness and are mainly grown as specimen trees. They are admired for their prolific flower display, the colour of which varies from white, to pink, and red, in spring or early summer, often followed by heavy crops of berries. The foliage of some species takes on colourful autumn tints. Especially recommended for coastal areas and town and city gardens.

● *C. crus-galli* (Cockspur thorn)
North America ⑤ ♀
Height up to 9m (30ft). Extremely thorny species with oval, shiny, green leaves that turn scarlet in autumn. White flowers in clusters, early summer. Red berries in autumn.

● *C. laevigata* (*C. oxyacantha*) (Hawthorn, May hawthorn, English hawthorn) Europe ⑤ ♀
Height 6m (20ft). Leaves lobed, medium green. Clusters of white fragrant flowers in late spring. Crimson berries in autumn. Cultivars include 'Coccinea Plena', double scarlet flowers; 'Masekii', double pale pink; 'Plena', double white; 'Punicea', single scarlet; and 'Rosea', single pink.

● *C. × lavallei* (Lavalle hawthorn)
Garden origin ⑤ ♀
Height 6m (20ft). A dense, almost thornless species with oval, shiny, deep green leaves which often do not fall until early winter. Flowers in clusters, white, early summer. Long-lasting orange-red berries in autumn, persisting well into winter.

● *C. monogyna* (English hawthorn, Quick, May)
Europe ⑤ ♀
Height up to 9m (30ft). A very dense and spiny species much used in Britain for hedging and screening. Also a useful specimen tree. Leaves lobed, shiny, deep green. Flowers white, fragrant, carried in clusters during late spring. Berries crimson, autumn. Cultivars include 'Biflora' ('Praecox'), the Glastonbury thorn, which produces a second flush of flowers in winter if the weather is mild; 'Pendula Rosea', pendulous branches carrying pink blossoms; and 'Stricta' ('Fastigiata') with upright branches and white flowers.

● *C. phaenopyrum* (Washington thorn)
North America ⑤ ♀
Height 7.6m (25ft). Long spines. Leaves lobed, shiny green, orange and scarlet in autumn. Flowers white, mid-summer. Scarlet berries in autumn, long-lasting.

● *C. × prunifolia* Garden origin ⑥ ♀
Height 6m (20ft). Very spiny. Leaves oval, shiny, green, downy undersides, turning scarlet and orange in autumn. Flowers white, in clusters, early summer. Berries red, in autumn, lasting well into winter.

Cultivation

☼ ◐ A AL ▦

Tolerant of exposure, atmospheric pollution, drought and wet conditions. No regular pruning required.

Problems
Caterpillars, fireblight, honey fungus, leaf spot, powdery mildew, rust.

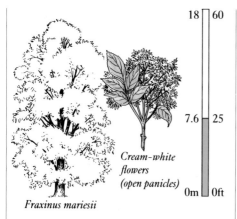

18 | 60

7.6 | 25

Cream-white flowers (open panicles)

0m | 0ft

Fraxinus mariesii

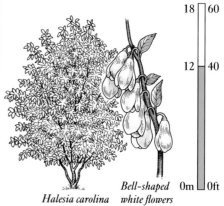

18 | 60

12 | 40

0m | 0ft

Halesia carolina   *Bell-shaped white flowers*

FRAXINUS

Ash

Oleaceae

*F*rom the cool temperate areas of the northern hemisphere, the ashes are mainly large forest-type trees suited only to parks and estates, although some, including the species described below, are small and ideal for use as lawn specimens.

● *F. mariesii* (Flowering ash) China ⑦ ♀
Height up to 7.6m (25ft). A slow-growing tree. Leaves pinnate. Flowers cream-white in open, wide panicles (a notable feature), early summer. Deep purple fruits follow later on in summer.

Cultivation

 ☼ ☙ A AL ▨

Ashes are very wind resistant and therefore can be recommended for exposed situations. Also suitable for town and city gardens and coastal areas. Ideally grown in deep loamy soil. No regular pruning needed.

Problems
Canker, honey fungus.

HALESIA

Snowdrop tree, Silver-bell tree

Styracaceae

A genus of trees and shrubs originating from North America and China. Very attractive in spring when in flower. Invariably planted in light woodland gardens, although they are also suitable for shrub borders and make fine specimen trees.

● *H. carolina* North America ⑤ ♀
Height 12m (40ft). With a wide-spreading habit, this species has oval, pale green leaves that have downy undersides. Flowers white, bell-shaped, pendulous, in clusters, late spring. The conspicuous fruits are four-winged.

Cultivation

☼ ☙ ⊙ A ■

Suitable for moist, well drained soils. Halesias do not need regular pruning but, if necessary, excessively long shoots can be pruned back after flowering so that a well-balanced shape is maintained.

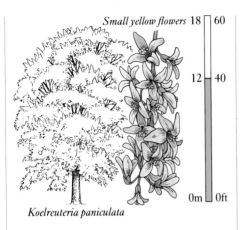

Small yellow flowers

18 — 60

12 — 40

0m — 0ft

Koelreuteria paniculata

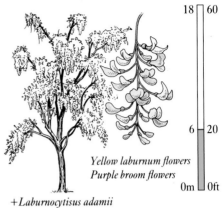

18 — 60

6 — 20

Yellow laburnum flowers
Purple broom flowers

0m — 0ft

+Laburnocytisus adamii

KOELREUTERIA

Koelreuteria

Sapindaceae

A small genus from eastern Asia with attractive pinnate foliage and large terminal panicles of small yellow fragrant flowers that attract bees, in summer. They make handsome trees for specimen planting in lawns or other parts of the garden.

• *K. paniculata* (Pride of India, Varnish tree, Golden-rain tree) China, Korea, Japan ⑤ ♀
Height up to 12m (40ft). Leaves pinnate, to 45cm (18in) in length, turning yellow in autumn. Small yellow flowers in large pyramid-shaped terminal panicles produced in mid-summer. Bladder-like yellow-brown fruits follow. The cultivar 'Fastigiata' forms a narrow columnar tree and is slow growing.

Cultivation

☼ ☉ A AL ▨

No regular pruning needed and no problems from pests or diseases.

+ LABURNOCYTISUS

+ Laburnocytisus

Leguminosae

*T*his is a graft chimera, the result of grafting *Cytisus purpureus* onto *Laburnum anagyroides*. The scion was inadvertently knocked off the rootstock but a little remained. Both grew, however, the cytisus within the laburnum. Propagation is effected by grafting it onto seedling rootstocks of the common laburnum. An unusual and quite attractive tree with a combination of yellow and purple flowers. Essentially a specimen tree for lawns or shrub borders.

• + *L. adamii* Garden origin ⑥ ♀
Height up to 6m (20ft). Rather irregular habit of growth. Leaves similar to those of *Laburnum anagyroides*. The tree bears both pendulous racemes of yellow laburnum flowers and clusters of purple broom flowers. Also, intermediate purplish-pink blooms are carried in racemes.

Cultivation

☼ ◕ A AL ▨

No regular pruning required. Stake young tree well until established.

Problems
Honey fungus.

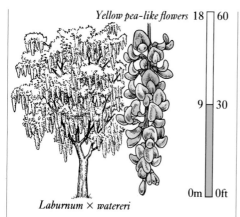

Yellow pea-like flowers 18 / 60
9 / 30
0m / 0ft

Laburnum × watereri

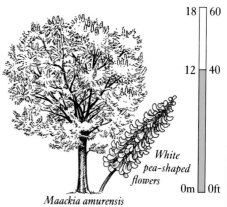

18 / 60
12 / 40
White pea-shaped flowers
0m / 0ft

Maackia amurensis

LABURNUM

Golden rain tree, Bean tree

Leguminosae

A small genus of trees from southern Europe and western Asia with trifoliate leaves and chains of yellow flowers in spring. Very widely planted in urban gardens, often in association with lilac, the equally popular spring-flowering shrub.

● *L. anagyroides* (Common laburnum) central and southern Europe ⑤ ♀
Height up to 9m (30ft). Leaves mid-green, dull. Flowers yellow, pea-shaped, from mid-spring to early summer. The cultivar 'Pendulum' has pendulous branches and is better suited to small gardens.

● *L.* × *watereri* 'Vossii' Garden origin ⑤ ♀
Height up to 9m (30ft). Leaves shiny, medium green. Long racemes of yellow pea-like flowers in late spring. Very few seeds produced.

Cultivation

☼ ☽ A AL 🏵

Very adaptable and easy. Provide a stake for newly planted trees until well established. No pruning needed.

Problems
Honey fungus, silver leaf.

MAACKIA

Maackia

Leguminosae

*F*rom eastern Asia, these somewhat unusual slow-growing trees with pinnate foliage and white pea flowers can be recommended for shrub or mixed borders.

The genus was named for a Russian naturalist, Richard Maack, and contains six species of small trees which, under cultivation, may only attain the proportions of shrubs. The maackias are close relations of *Cladrastis* and at one time were included in that genus. Despite the fact that they are rather unusual, maackias are easy-going and have no special requirements in respect of soil or climate. It is a genus that deserves to be more widely grown.

● *M. amurensis* (Amur maackia) Manchuria, China Hardiness rating uncertain ♀
Height up to 12m (40ft), but often less under cultivation when it may grow as a shrub. Leaves pinnate, up to 30cm (12in) long, young shoots downy. Flowers white, pea-shaped, mid- to late summer.

Cultivation

☼ ☉ A AL 🏵

Easy-going, no special treatment needed.

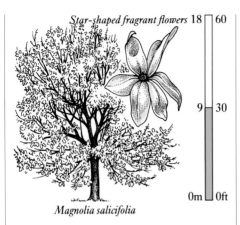

Star-shaped fragrant flowers 18 ⌐ 60

9 ⌐ 30

0m ⌐ 0ft

Magnolia salicifolia

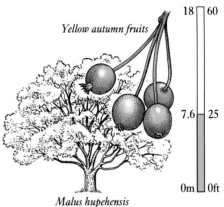

Yellow autumn fruits 18 ⌐ 60

7.6 ⌐ 25

0m ⌐ 0ft

Malus hupehensis

MAGNOLIA

Magnolia

Magnoliaceae

A popular genus of trees and shrubs native to North and Central America, eastern Asia and the Himalayas. Most are shapely enough to be treated as lawn specimens.

● *M. × kewensis* Garden origin ⑤ ⌂
A hybrid of *M. kobus* and *M. salicifolia*. Height up to 9m (30ft). Habit is slender. Leaves ovate-lanceolate, up to 12.5cm (5in) in length. Flowers pure white, 10cm (4in) in diameter, freely produced in mid-spring.

● *M. salicifolia* Japan ⑤ ⌂
Height up to 9m (30ft). Upright habit, fast-growing. Leaves narrow and willow-like, up to 12.5cm (5in) long, aromatic when crushed. Flowers produced on bare branches, star-shaped, 10cm (4in) in diameter, white, fragrant, mid-spring. Not for alkaline soils.

Cultivation

 ☼ ☁ ⊙ A AL A-N ■ ▣

Magnolias dislike transplanting so plant container-grown specimens in early spring. Avoid frost pockets and early morning sun.

Problems
Honey fungus.

MALUS

Crabapple, Flowering crabs

Rosaceae

*V*ery popular small trees from the northern temperate zone noted for attractive flowers and/or fruits. Generally planted as specimen trees in lawns or other parts of the garden where they make good focal points. Suitable also for inclusion in shrub or mixed borders. The apple-like small fruits, although ornamental, are edible and can be used for preserves such as crab-apple jelly.

● *M. baccata* (Siberian crab) eastern Asia ② ♀
Height 4.5m (15ft). Leaves ovate, glossy above. Flowers white, scented, mid- to late spring. Fruits berry-like, red or yellow, autumn. The variety *mandshurica* has slightly larger berries.

● *M. coronaria* (American crab, Wild sweet crabapple) North America ② ⌂
Height not more than 9m (30ft). The young shoots of this species are downy and carry oval leaves which have coarsely toothed edges. The leaves can attain a length of 10cm (4in) and they are up to 8cm (3in) in width. The rose-white flowers, about 3.8cm (1½in) in width, are scented, carried on slender stalks and come in clusters of up to half a dozen. The flowering period is late spring and early summer. The fruits that follow are globose, but are rather

flattened, and about 3.8cm (1½in) in diameter, being yellow-green in colour and very acid. The cultivar 'Charlottae' is an especially attractive tree, with big lobed leaves which take on spectacular autumn tints, and large semi-double flowers which, surprisingly, have the fragrance of violets. They are the same colour as those of the parent.

● *M. floribunda* (Japanese crab, Floribunda crabapple) Japan ⑤ ♀
Height up to 7.6m (25ft). Leaves ovate, medium green, tooth-edged. Flowers pale pink from bright red-pink buds, in profusion, late spring. Fruits yellow, autumn.

● *M. hupehensis* (Tea crabapple)
China, Assam ⑤ ♀
Height up to 7.6m (25ft). Leaves oval, dark green, tooth-edged. Flowers white, flushed pink, scented, late spring and early summer. Fruits yellow, flushed with red, autumn.

● *M.* × *purpurea* (Purple crabapple)
Garden origin ⑤ ♀
Height 7.6m (25ft). Leaves ovate, medium green, tinted with purple. Flowers purple, mid-spring. Small purple fruits in autumn. Cultivars include 'Eleyi' and 'Lemoinei'.

● *M. spectabilis* 'Van Eseltine' (Chinese flowering crabapple) Garden origin ⑤ ◊
Height 7.6m (25ft). Leaves elliptical. Flowers semi-double, pale pink and white from rose-scarlet buds, mid-spring. Fruits yellow, autumn.

● *M. tschonoskii* (Large-leaved crabapple)
Japan ⑤ ◊
Height up to 12m (40ft). Leaves oval, with grey felt on the undersides, turning fiery red in autumn, this tree's main attraction. Flowers white, late spring. Fruits yellow-green, flushed red.

Cultivation

☼ ◑ A AL ▦

Stake young trees well until established and mulch annually with manure or garden compost. No regular pruning needed.

Problems
Aphids, woolly aphids, capsid bugs, caterpillars, fruit-tree red spider mites, apple mildew, apple scab, honey fungus.

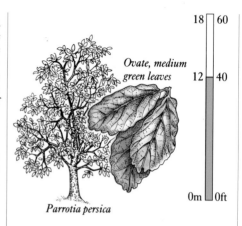

Ovate, medium green leaves

18 / 60
12 / 40
0m / 0ft

Parrotia persica

PARROTIA

Parrotia

Hamamelidaceae

*T*here is only one species in this genus and it is invariably grown as a specimen tree that is at its most spectacular in autumn, when it generally takes on brilliant leaf tints. It can also be recommended for shrub borders provided it is not too hemmed in by other subjects.

● *P. persica* (Iron tree) Iran, Caucasus ⑧ ♀
Height to 12m (40ft) and very wide spreading, but slow-growing. Leaves ovate, medium green, colouring in autumn to gold, crimson and orange. Tints can vary from one year to another; sometimes the leaves simply turn yellow. Flowers inconspicuous, early spring. Flaking bark creates a patchwork effect on the trunks of older trees.

Cultivation

☼ A AL ▦

Best results in a deep fertile loamy soil. No regular pruning needed.

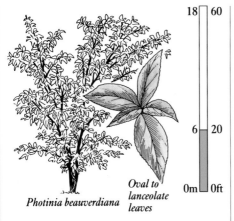

18 | 60

6 | 20

Oval to lanceolate leaves

0m | 0ft

Photinia beauverdiana

White to pink flowers

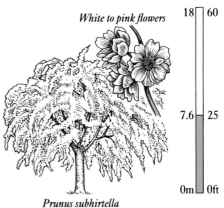

18 | 60

7.6 | 25

0m | 0ft

Prunus subhirtella

PHOTINIA

Photinia

Rosaceae

A genus of mostly shrubs, but containing a few small trees, from southern and eastern Asia. Many notable for their attractive foliage and berries. Flowers not particularly showy. Suitable for inclusion in shrub and mixed borders or woodland gardens.
• *P. beauverdiana* China (8) ♀
Height 6m (20ft). Leaves narrowly oval to lanceolate, pink tinged when they unfurl, and colouring well in autumn. Flowers white. Deep red berries in autumn.
• *P. villosa* China, Korea, Japan (5) ♀
Height 4.5m (15ft). Leaves somewhat lanceolate, turning deep red and yellow in autumn. The small white blossoms are followed by brilliant red berries.

Cultivation

☼ A AL ■ ▩

Moisture-retentive soil gives best results, but generally easily grown. No regular pruning needed.

PRUNUS

Cherry, Plum, Peach, Apricot, Almond

Rosaceae

T his is a very large and diverse genus of trees and shrubs from temperate climates, mainly from the northern hemisphere, and contains some of the most popular small deciduous spring-flowering trees for specimen planting. Ornamental prunus are found in suburban, town and city gardens, often planted in lawns or in pairs to "frame" entrances and other features. They should be chosen with care, for many lack interest once flowering is over.
• *P. cerasifera* (Cherry plum, Myrobalan) central Asia (4) ♀
Height up to 7.6m (25ft). Leaves ovate, the white flowers appearing late winter/early spring before the foliage. Yellow or red edible fruits follow. Cultivars are more attractive and very widely grown, such as 'Nigra', with black-purple stems and foliage and single pink flowers; and 'Pissardii' ('Atropurpurea'), the popular purple-leaved plum with deep red young leaves that change to dark purple, and masses of white blossoms from pink buds.
• *P. davidiana* (Ornamental peach) China (4) ♀
Height 3–9m (10–30ft). The medium green leaves are lanceolate, and the white flowers appear before them from mid-winter to early

spring. Valued on account of its early blossoms, which need a dark background to show them off. The cultivar 'Alba' is similar, and 'Rubra' bears pink blossoms.

● *P. dulcis* (Common almond)
western Asia ⑦ ♀
Height up to 9m (30ft). Leaves medium green, lance-shaped. Flowers pink, on the bare branches in early to mid-spring. Several cultivars, including 'Roseoplena', the double almond, with double light pink blossoms.

P. dulcis 'Roseoplena'

Double blossom

● *P. incisa* (Fuji cherry) Japan ⑥ ♀
Height 4.5m (15ft) or more. Habit shrubby but can be trained to a tree form. Leaves flushed red when they unfurl, tooth-edged. Flowers white, from pink buds, on the bare shoots during early spring.

● *P. maackii* (Manchurian cherry)
eastern Asia ② ♀
Height up to 15m (50ft) but may be shorter under cultivation. Leaves somewhat elliptic. Flowers small, white, mid-spring. A particular attraction is the golden-brown, glossy, flaking bark. Makes an attractive specimen tree.

● *P. mume* (Japanese apricot)
Japan, China ⑦ ♀
Height up to 9m (30ft). Leaves oval. Flowers white to pink with an almond fragrance, late winter and early spring. Many cultivars, including 'Alboplena', white, semi-double; 'Alphandii', pink, semi-double; and 'Ben-shi-don', deep pink, double, strong fragrance.

P. persica 'Klara Meyer'

Double pink flowers

● *P. persica* (Common peach) China ⑤ ♀
Height up to 9m (30ft). Leaves lance-shaped. Flowers pink, mid-spring, before the leaves. Cultivars are normally grown for their flowers, including the double pink 'Klara Meyer', popular in Britain.

● *P. subhirtella* (Spring cherry, Higan)
Japan ⑥ ♀
Height up to 7.6m (25ft). Leaves oval to lance-shaped, serrated. Flowers freely produced, white to pink, before the leaves, early to mid-spring. Popular cultivars include 'Autumnalis' (Autumn cherry), semi-double white blossoms between mid-autumn and early spring; 'Autumnalis Rosea', semi-double palest pink flowers, same period; 'Pendula Rosea' (weeping spring cherry), pale pink blossoms from deep pink buds, weeping habit; and 'Pendula Rubra', similar habit but with dark rose flowers from bright red buds.

Cultivation

☼ ◓ A AL ▣

These shallow-rooting trees dislike deep cultivation around them. Keep soil mulched with organic matter. Avoid soils that are very dry or prone to waterlogging.

Problems
Aphids, caterpillars, birds (damage buds), bacterial canker, honey fungus, peach leaf curl, silver leaf.

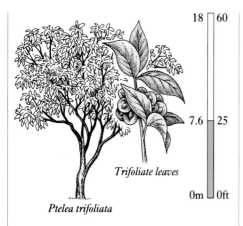

18 ┌ 60

7.6 ┤ 25

0m └ 0ft

Trifoliate leaves

Ptelea trifoliata

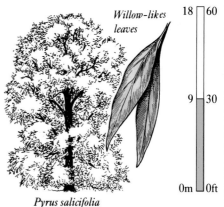

Willow-likes leaves

18 ┌ 60

9 ┤ 30

0m └ 0ft

Pyrus salicifolia

PTELEA

Hop tree

Rutaceae

*A*small genus of trees and shrubs native to North America. The generic name is the old Greek name for the elm. Pteleas do not seem to be commonly grown and deserve to be more widely planted for they require no special soil or conditions, apart from adequate drainage. They generally have trifoliate leaves and greenish-white flowers, followed by conspicuous bunches of green fruits. They make unusual specimen trees.

● *P. trifoliata* (Hop tree, Common hop tree, Stinking ash) eastern North America ⑤ ♀
Height up to 7.6m (25ft). Leaves trifoliate, turning yellow in autumn. Flowers dull green-white, early summer. Fruits winged, green, in clusters. Bark reddish brown. The cultivar 'Aurea' has bright yellow foliage.

Cultivation

Easily grown, only requiring good drainage. No pruning, no particular problems.

PYRUS

Pear

Rosaceae

*A*genus of small trees from Eurasia and North Africa. Some species of shapely habit make good specimen trees. Certain pyrus are most attractive when in flower while others are admired for their foliage.

● *P. betulifolia* (Birchleaf pear) northern China ⑤ ♀
Height at least 6m (20ft). Leaves oval, opening grey-green, then turning shiny green. Clusters of white, red-anthered flowers in mid-spring followed by pea-sized brown fruits. Pleasing habit; makes a good specimen tree.

● *P. calleryana* China ⑤ ♀
Height up to 9m (30ft). Leaves oval, becoming red in autumn. White flowers in spring. A pleasing ornamental tree, resistant to the disease fire blight. The cultivar 'Chanticleer' is particularly recommended for temperate climates. It has a narrow conical habit of growth, white flowers and shiny foliage which turns deep purple and red in autumn.

● *P. nivalis* Asia Minor ⑤ ♀
Height not more than 9m (30ft). The young shoots are thickly covered with white wool and carry oval leaves up to 8cm (3in) in length which are similarly covered when young. The pure

white flowers, at least 2.5cm (1in) in diameter, are freely produced in mid-spring, when they create quite a spectacular display. Following these are long-stalked globose fruits up to 3.8cm (1½in) in diameter and of a yellow-green colour. This is indeed a most attractive small tree, especially as the white flowers are produced with the white young leaves.

P. salicifolia

White flower clusters

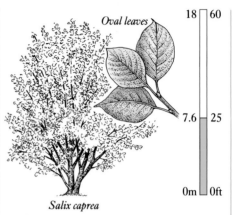

Oval leaves

18 | 60
7.6 | 25
0m | 0ft

Salix caprea

SALIX

Willow, Osier

Salicaceae

● *P. salicifolia* (Willow-leaved pear) south-eastern Europe, Caucasus, Armenia ⑤ ♀ Height up to 9m (30ft). Leaves are narrowly lance-shaped or willow-like. Woolly when they first open; an attractive feature. Flowers white, in clusters, mid-spring, followed by small yellowish pear-like fruits. Shoots are thickly covered with white down. The cultivar 'Pendula' is one of the finest small weeping trees with silvery-grey foliage, cream-white flowers and brown fruits. Excellent specimen tree for lawn or poolside; a much better choice for small gardens than weeping willows.

Cultivation

☼ A AL 🔲

Best results in deep fertile moisture-retentive loamy soils without too much lime. No regular pruning needed.

Problems

Aphids, birds (damage flower buds), canker, fireblight, honey fungus, pear scab.

A large genus of trees and shrubs mainly from the temperate areas of the northern hemisphere. Very diverse in habit but invariably with narrow lanceolate leaves. Flowers are in the form of catkins and are sometimes very decorative; in other species the bark is an appealing feature. The tree willows are invariably used as specimens in lawns and by lakes and pools. Indeed willows are very tolerant of wet and waterlogged soils and can be especially recommended for gardens where drainage may be a problem. They are often seen planted alongside river banks, where they not only enjoy the moist conditions but also help to stabilize the soil with their roots. Many willows are extremely hardy and therefore make good windbreaks or shelter for other plants. Although they do not require regular pruning, willows can be cut back if desired, although this, of course, spoils their natural shape.

● *S. aegyptiaca* eastern Turkey, Iran, USSR ⑥ ♀ Height 3.6m (12ft). This is on the borderline between a large shrub and a small tree, but as it can assume a tree-like habit it is included here. By any criteria it is a very desirable species. The thick grey-felted shoots carry elliptic leaves 15cm (6in) long and in late winter or early spring large eye-catching yellow male catkins.

• *S. caprea* (Goat willow, Great sallow, Pussy willow) Europe ⑤ ♀
Height up to 7.6m (25ft). Leaves are broadly oval and woolly grey below. Male plants produce large, conspicuous yellow catkins in spring. Female plants have silvery catkins. Better for gardens is the male cultivar 'Pendula' ('Kilmarnock'), the Kilmarnock willow, with stiff weeping branches. This is an excellent specimen beside a pool or lake.

• *S. daphnoides* (Violet willow) Europe, Asia ⑤ ♀
Height up to 9m (30ft). Leaves narrowly lanceshaped, shiny deep green above, glaucous below. Catkins appear in early spring before the leaves. Conspicuous in winter when its dark purple young shoots are covered with waxy white 'bloom'.

• *S. purpurea* 'Pendula' (Pendulous purple osier) Garden origin ⑤ ♠
Height 3m (10ft) or more. Leaves narrow, bluish-green. The catkins are slender, appearing before the leaves. It produces long, slender, pendulous branches and is one of the best small weeping trees for limited space.

• *S. viminalis* (Common osier, Basket willow) central Europe, Asia ④ ♀
Height up to 9m (30ft). Leaves long and lanceshaped, silky silver-white below. Catkins produced on bare shoots in spring. Young shoots grey woolly. Grown as an ornamental and also to produce material for basket making.

Cultivation

 A AL

Best grown in moist soil; avoid soils prone to drying out. No regular pruning needed.

Problems
Aphids, caterpillars, willow anthracnose, canker, honey fungus.

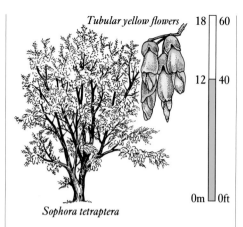

Tubular yellow flowers

Sophora tetraptera

SOPHORA

Sophora

Leguminosae

Widely distributed trees and shrubs with pinnate leaves and pea flowers. Ideal for very sunny places in shrub or mixed borders. Distinctive enough to be used as specimen trees, although for this purpose they should be grown in a very warm sheltered position that is open enough to receive plenty of sun.

• *S. tetraptera* (Kowhai) New Zealand, Chile ⑧ ♀
Height up to 12m (40ft). Leaves large and pinnate, semi-deciduous. Flowers deep yellow, somewhat tubular, in pendulous clusters, late spring, followed by four-winged seed capsules. The form 'Grandiflora' has larger leaflets and flowers.

Cultivation

☼ ☉ A AL ▩

Ideally grown against a sheltered sunny wall. No pruning needed.

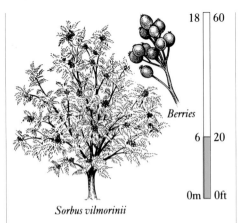

18 | 60

Berries

6 | 20

0m | 0ft

Sorbus vilmorinii

SORBUS

Mountain ash, Rowan, Whitebeam, Service tree

Rosaceae

A genus of deciduous trees and shrubs from Europe, North America and northern Asia. Some have simple oval leaves, as in the Aria group, while species in the Aucuparia group have pinnate foliage. The white flowers are quite showy but even more striking in some species (particularly those in the Aucuparia group) are the clusters of colourful autumn berries. The foliage of some species takes on attractive tints in autumn. The sorbus are very hardy and adaptable and make fine specimens in lawns or other parts of the garden such as shrub borders. Also recommended for planting in woodland gardens, or for helping to form this type of garden.

● *S. americana* (American mountain ash) eastern North America ② ♀
Height up to 9m (30ft). Leaves pinnate, colouring well in autumn. Flowers cream-white in late spring and early summer. Fruits globular, bright red. Winter buds conspicuous, red and sticky.
● *S. commixta* eastern Asia, Japan ⑥ ⚥
Height at least 6m (20ft). The winter buds are sticky. The shiny green leaves are more than 15cm (6in) in length and consist of 11 to 15 leaflets, each one somewhat lance-shaped,

pointed at the tip and with toothed margins. The foliage colours well in the autumn. The white flowers are carried in clusters during late spring and followed by bunches of globular bright red berries. As a young tree it is broadly columnar and is often used for street planting.
● *S. hupehensis* China ⑥ ♀
Height approximately 9m (30ft). The leaves are up to 25cm (10in) in length and consist of 11 to 17 leaflets, each one oblong in shape and 3.8–8cm (1½–3in) long. The foliage is an unusual bluish-green colour. Long-stalked clusters of white flowers are produced in early summer. These are followed by pendulous clusters of white or pink-flushed berries that last on the tree until well into winter. This is one of the popular and widely planted species of sorbus.
● *S. sargentiana* western China ⑦ ♀
Height 6–9m (20–30ft). Leaves pinnate, with red petioles, colouring well in autumn. Flowers white in late spring. Fruits globular, scarlet. Red winter buds somewhat downy.
● *S. scalaris* western China ⑥ ♀
Height up to 6m (20ft). Leaves pinnate, grey downy below, colouring deep red in autumn. Flowers dull white in late spring and early summer. Globular bright red fruits.
● *S. × thuringiaca* Garden origin ⑥ ♀
Height up to 9m (30ft). Leaves a combination of deeply divided and shallowly lobed. Flowers white followed by large clusters of deep red fruits.
● *S. vilmorinii* China ⑥ ♀
Height up to 6m (20ft). Leaves pinnate, grey undersides, turning red and purple in autumn. Flowers white, in early summer. Globular rose-pink berries.

Cultivation

☼ ☽ **A AL** 🌸

Very tolerant of both atmospheric pollution and coastal or exposed areas. No regular pruning required.

Problems

Apple canker, fireblight, honey fungus, silver leaf.

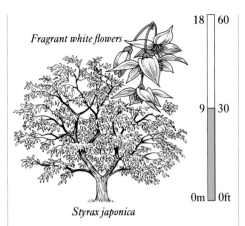

Fragrant white flowers

18 — 60

9 — 30

0m — 0ft

Styrax japonica

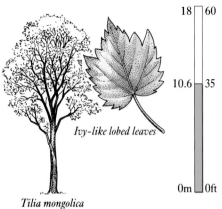

18 — 60

10.6 — 35

Ivy-like lobed leaves

0m — 0ft

Tilia mongolica

STYRAX

Snowbell, Storax

Styracaceae

Styrax are native to tropical and temperate parts of Asia, south-west Europe and the USA. They are noted for pendulous white flowers produced in late spring or early summer. Suitable for planting in woodland or shrub gardens. They are extremely beautiful trees and not particularly difficult given the right growing conditions. They deserve to be more widely grown. Some are on the tender side but one of the hardiest species is described here.

● *S. japonica* (Japanese snowbell)
Japan, China ⑤ ♀
Height up to 9m (30ft). Wide-spreading species. Leaves elliptic. Fragrant, white, bell-shaped, pendulous flowers produced along the shoots in early summer.

Cultivation

They succeed in moisture-retentive, light loamy soil. Add plenty of peat before planting. No regular pruning needed.

TILIA

Lime, Linden, Basswood

Tiliaceae

Tilias are mainly medium-size or large trees from temperate parts of the northern hemisphere and make fine specimen trees or avenues in large gardens, parks and estates. There are smaller-growing species suitable for more limited space.

● *T. mongolica* (Mongolian lime)
China, Mongolia ⑤ ♀
Height up to 10.6m (35ft). Of compact rounded habit, a shapely tree making a good lawn specimen. The lobed shiny green leaves are rather ivy-like and in autumn become bright yellow before they fall. Flowers yellowish, nectar-rich and fragrant, in summer.

Cultivation

☼ ☽ A AL ▨

Easy-going but thrive in moisture-retentive soil. No regular pruning needed, except to remove suckers if necessary.

Problems
Aphids, caterpillars, gall mites, cankers, honey fungus, leaf spot.

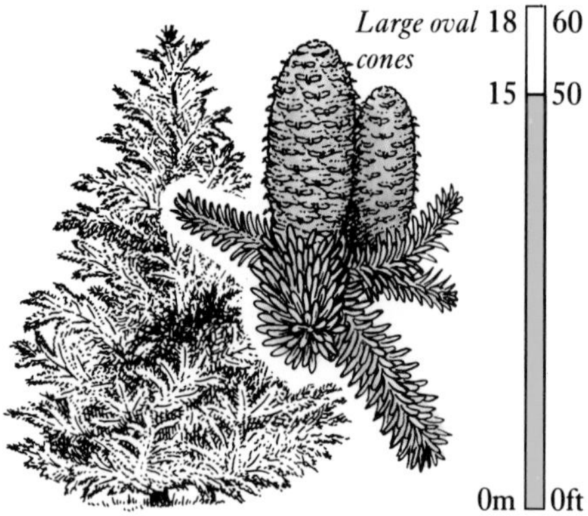
Large oval cones
18
60
15
50
0m
0ft

Abies koreana

ABIES

Silver fir

Pinaceae

Coniferous trees from temperate areas of the northern hemisphere and found mainly in mountainous regions. Generally very hardy. Habit mainly conical, foliage needle-like, somewhat oval cones formed on the upper branches. Used as specimen trees in lawns and as backgrounds for planting schemes. Smaller forms are suitable for shrub or mixed borders and as specimens on large rock gardens.

● *A. koreana* (Korean fir) Korea ⑤ ♤
Height up to 15m (50ft) but may be less under cultivation. Leaves dark green, brilliant silver below, thinly produced. Female flowers conspicuous, erect, deep red, pink or green, late spring. Male flowers globe-shaped, reddish brown, becoming yellow. Cones oval, 8cm (3in) long, glaucous with brown bracts.

Cultivation

☼ ◒ ⊙ **A-N** ⛉

It is best to plant small trees, approximately 30cm (12in) high, with a strong leading shoot, as it can be difficult to establish older ones. New growth may be damaged by frosts late in spring. The ideal site is shaded from early morning sun to avoid frost damage. Mulch young trees with organic matter. Train a strong leading shoot to a stake, removing competing side shoots or forking shoots if necessary in early or mid-spring.

Problems

Adelgids, die-back (fungal disease).

KEY TO SYMBOLS

Shape		**Aspect**		**Soils**	
♤	Conical	☼	Full sun	**A**	Acid
♀	Spreading	◒	Partial shade	**AL**	Alkaline
⍑	Broad columnar	●	Shade	**A-N**	Acid to neutral
◊	Fastigiate	⊙	Sheltered from cold winds	■	Rich in humus
☂	Weeping			⛉	Well drained

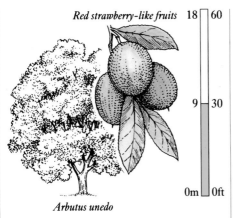

Red strawberry-like fruits

18 | 60

9 | 30

0m | 0ft

Arbutus unedo

ARBUTUS

Strawberry tree, Madrone

Ericaceae

Coming from the Mediterranean region, the Canary Islands and western North America, the arbutus are broad-leaved trees and shrubs with attractive foliage, flowers and red strawberry-like fruits. The bark is also distinctive. Some species are hardy, others half-hardy. They are mainly used as specimen trees in lawns and in mixed or shrub borders.

In mixed plantings it is a good idea to select companion plants that associate pleasingly with arbutus. Heaths and heathers are a good choice for creating ground cover around the trees, including cultivars of *Calluna vulgaris* which flower in the autumn, and cultivars of the winter-flowering *Erica herbacea* (*E. carnea*) and *E. × darleyensis*. Shrubs noted for autumn leaf colour also associate well with arbutus, including *Acer palmatum* and cultivars (Japanese maples). Arbutus are also effectively underplanted with autumn-flowering bulbs such as colchicum and crocus species.

● *A. andrachne* (Grecian strawberry tree)
south-east Europe, Asia Minor ⑧ ♀
Height up to 12m (40ft) in the wild, often shorter under cultivation. Young plants tender, becoming hardier as they age. Leaves oval, with entire or serrated edges, deep green and leathery. Flowers urn-shaped, in pendulous clusters, white, early to mid-spring. Fruits globular, orange-red. Bark peeling, smooth, orange-red; an attractive feature.

● *A. × andrachnoides* (*A. × hybrida*)
Natural hybrid (*A. andrachne × A. unedo*)
south-east Europe, Asia Minor ⑧ ♀
Height up to 9m (30ft). Foliage, flowers, fruits and bark as *A. andrachne*, but flowers produced in late autumn and winter. Fruits not often produced.

A. × andrachnoides

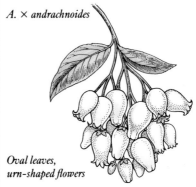

Oval leaves,
urn-shaped flowers

● *A. unedo* (Killarney strawberry tree)
southern Europe, south-west Ireland, Asia ⑧ ♀
Height up to 9m (30ft). Leaves oval or elliptic with serrated edges, deep green, shiny. Flowers urn-shaped, in pendulous clusters, white or pink, mid-autumn to early winter, appearing with fruits that formed previous year. Fruits as *A. andrachne*. Bark rough, shredding, brown.

Cultivation

☼ ☉ A ▦

Young plants are tender, needing protection in winter, but becoming hardier as they age. *A. unedo* is lime-tolerant and best grown only in milder areas.

Problems
Leaf spot.

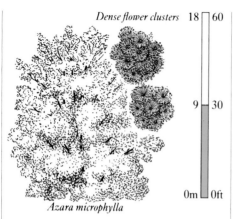

Dense flower clusters 18 60

9 30

0m 0ft

Azara microphylla

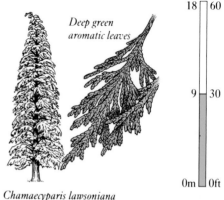

Deep green aromatic leaves

18 60

9 30

0m 0ft

Chamaecyparis lawsoniana

AZARA

Azara

Flacourtiaceae

Chilean shrubs and small trees best grown against a warm sheltered wall. Attractive foliage and, in early spring, fragrant flowers. The species described below is the hardiest, but it should be borne in mind that a particularly severe winter can damage or even kill this tree. Even so it is well worth growing and deserves to be more widely planted.

● *A. microphylla* Chile ⑨ ♀
Height 3.6–9m (12–30ft). Leaves obovate, toothed, deep green, shiny. Stems densely covered with dark hairs. Flowers very small, in dense clusters, yellow, vanilla scented, late winter to mid-spring. Small globular red fruits.

Cultivation

☼ ☽ ☉ A AL ■ ▨

Could be grown in more open situation in mild areas that are also sheltered. No regular pruning is required.

CHAMAECYPARIS

False cypress, White cedar

Cupressaceae

The false cypresses are coniferous trees from North America and Asia. The species are large, but there are more diminutive cultivars suited to smaller gardens. They are extremely popular conifers of neat, cone-shaped habit and make excellent specimen trees in lawns or other parts of the garden. They also look very impressive when planted in groups. In addition, some varieties can also be used for creating hedges and screens.

Chamaecyparis are very tolerant of clipping, but this should only be undertaken when they are grown as formal hedges. If specimen trees are clipped their natural shape will be ruined and they will tend to look rather artificial. Some of the smaller-growing species and cultivars are happy to be grown in large tubs, making handsome features on a patio or terrace, for example. Alternatively, a pair could be positioned either side of a gateway or the front door of the house. This idea is particularly recommended for more formal locations as chamaecyparis have a regular outline.

The foliage is scale-like and formed into flat sprays. It comes in all shades of green, grey and gold, depending on species and cultivars.

● *C. lawsoniana* (Lawson cypress,
Lawson false cypress, Port Orford cedar)
North America ⑥ ◬
Height up to 30m (100ft) but many cultivars
much shorter. It is not often grown in gardens.
Leaves deep green, greyish beneath, aromatic.
Peeling bark. Together with its cultivars, this
species is suitable for hedges and screens. Cultivars that form small trees include 'Columnaris',
narrow habit, upright branches, very dense glaucous foliage; and 'Elegantissima', of broader
habit, pendulous shoots, foliage silver-grey.
Height of these should not exceed 9m (30ft).

● *C. obtusa* (Hinoki white cedar,
Hinoki cypress) Japan ⑤ ◬
Height up to 36m (120ft) but many cultivars,
which are normally grown, are much shorter.
Leaves bright green, aromatic. Bark reddish
brown. Cultivars that form small trees, up to 9m
(30ft) in height, include 'Crippsii', with sprays of
deep yellow foliage, an excellent small golden
conifer; and 'Tetragona Aurea', deep golden-
yellow foliage in irregular mossy sprays.

● *C. pisifera* (Sawara cypress) Japan ⑤ ◬
Height up to 36m (120ft), but many cultivars
much shorter. Ferny sprays of bright green
aromatic foliage. Attractive brown bark. This
species is not often grown. Cultivars that form
small trees up to 9m (30ft) in height include
'Plumosa', with soft plume-like sprays of bright
green foliage; 'Plumosa Aurea', similar, but with
yellow young foliage; 'Squarrosa', dense, soft,
feathery sprays of grey-green foliage; and
'Squarrosa Sulphurea', similar, light yellow
foliage.

Cultivation

Prefer moderate climate with adequate moisture; not suitable in areas with drying winds.
Golden cultivars best in full sun. Prune only to
maintain single leading shoot.

Problems
Honey fungus.

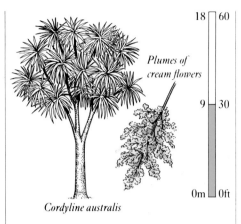

*Plumes of
cream flowers*

18 — 60

9 — 30

0m — 0ft

Cordyline australis

CORDYLINE

Cabbage palm

Agavaceae

*T*his genus, from India, Australia and tropical America, contains both tender and half-
hardy shrubs and trees which are grown for their
attractive foliage and somewhat palm-like habit.
Useful for patio planting and tubs to provide a
sub-tropical touch. Suitable also for beds and
borders.

● *C. australis* (Cabbage palm)
New Zealand, Australia ⑧ ⵁ
Height 9m (30ft). Leaves narrow, lance-shaped,
arching, grey-green, carried in tufts at tips of
branches. The stem develops branches when the
plant reaches flowering age, approximately 10
years. Large plumes of fragrant cream flowers
produced in early summer, followed by globular
white fruits.

Cultivation

Excellent for mild maritime gardens where it
will tolerate winds. No pruning needed.

Problems
Leaf spot.

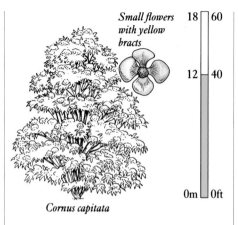

Small flowers with yellow bracts

18 | 60
12 | 40
0m | 0ft

Cornus capitata

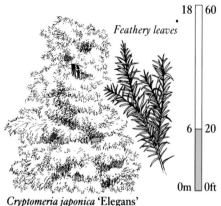

Feathery leaves

18 | 60
6 | 20
0m | 0ft

Cryptomeria japonica 'Elegans'

CORNUS

Dogwood, Cornel

Cornaceae

A variable genus from North America, Europe and Asia. The more shapely and distinctive species can be used as isolated specimens in lawns as well as in shrub or mixed borders. The species described here is very popular and a highly desirable garden tree. It is very adaptable and easily grown in any reasonably good soil. It is noted for conspicuous bracts and unusual fruits.

● *C. capitata* Himalayas ⑨ ♀
Height up to 12m (40ft). Leaves oval to lance-shaped, leathery, greyish green. Flowers very small, encircled by showy, light yellow, 5cm (2in) long bracts, early to mid-summer. Red strawberry-like fruits follow.

Cultivation

☼ A AL ▣

Adaptable, growing in any fertile soil. No regular pruning needed.

CRYPTOMERIA

Japanese cedar

Taxodiaceae

T here is only one species in this genus, a Japanese coniferous tree that makes an imposing specimen in lawns and is good as a focal point in the garden.

● *C. japonica* (Japanese Cedar) Japan ⑦ ♀
Height 45m (150ft). A massive fast-growing forest tree with scale-like dark green leaves. Bark soft and shredding, orange-brown; a distinctive feature. Its cultivar 'Elegans' is much more popular and suited to smallish gardens. Of similar shape, it attains a height of at least 6m (20ft). The soft, feathery, juvenile foliage is glaucous in summer and deep reddish bronze in winter: a tree for all seasons.

Cultivation

☼ ☉ A-N ▣

Plant small specimens, as they establish better than larger ones: maximum height 60cm (2ft). Young plants benefit from feeding with a general-purpose fertilizer in late spring. Do not let the soil dry out as this can be fatal for young plants. Moisture-retentive soil is desirable. No regular pruning required.

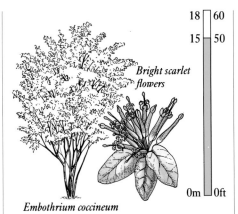

18 60
15 50

Bright scarlet flowers

0m 0ft

Embothrium coccineum

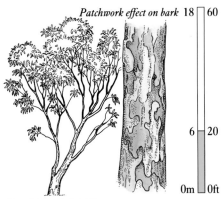

Patchwork effect on bark 18 60

6 20

0m 0ft

Eucalyptus niphophila

EMBOTHRIUM

Chilean fire bush

Proteaceae

A South American genus of evergreen trees and shrubs. The species generally grown, *E. coccineum*, provides an exotic touch to gardens with its racemes of bright scarlet flowers. It is often grown in light woodland conditions but is also at home in a sheltered shrub border.

• *E. coccineum* (Chilean fire bush)
Chile, Argentina ⑧ ♀
Height 12–15m (40–50ft). Leaves oval to lance-shaped, medium green, glossy. Flowers in long racemes, bright scarlet, late spring and early summer. Suckering habit. Hardier than the species and with longer leaves is *E. c. lanceolatum*.

Cultivation

☼ ☉ A-N ■ ▥

They relish deep moist soils free from lime. In cold areas young plants need to be protected from frost in winter by surrounding them with straw. No regular pruning needed, but shorten any over-long or untidy shoots as soon as flowering is over.

EUCALYPTUS

Gum tree

Myrtaceae

A very large genus of more than 500 species from Australia, including Tasmania. Useful as lawn specimens and as focal points on account of their distinctive habit. Suitable for helping to form woodland gardens as they provide dappled shade, which is relished by woodland plants and shrubs. Many eucalyptus eventually make large trees but some species do not grow excessively tall.

Often the bark is an extremely attractive feature and species are worth growing for this alone. The leaves of young trees are often completely different from those of mature specimens. In Australia the genus is extremely important for forestry, eucalyptus being classed as a hard wood. Various species produce essential oils and tannins.

In countries other than Australia, species have to be carefully chosen to suit the climate. If too cold (ie, a winter temperature below −12° to −6°C/10–20°F), they may not survive.
• *E. niphophila* (Alpine snow gum)
New South Wales, Victoria ⑧ ♀
Height 6m (20ft). Growth slow at first but then speeds up. Adult leaves are lance-shaped, thick, glaucous or green, shiny and aromatic. Shoots

red in winter and covered with bluish-white "bloom" in spring. Flowers white, in clusters, early summer, but the most interesting feature of this species is its extremely attractive bark, on young trees it is bluish-white; later the bark shreds each year in autumn. New bark is cream but it changes to grey and reddish brown, creating a patchwork effect of several colours. This is one of the hardiest species.

• *E. pauciflora* (Cabbage gum)
Australia, including Tasmania ⑧ 🝔
In height it is generally considered to be a small tree, up to 12m (40ft) within 20 years; but it can grow into a large tree up to 30m (100ft) tall. Somewhat like *E. niphophila* (considered by some to be a variant of *E. pauciflora*), but twigs not covered with "bloom". Has a flaking bark that is mottled dark grey and white.

Cultivation

☼ ☉ A-N ▦

The best planting time is early to mid-summer in well-drained soil. Plants should be small, up to 30cm (12in) high, as they establish better than larger ones. Keep young plants moist. Stake plants for first year. Base of stem should be protected with straw or sacking during first winter. Young plants should be protected from cold winds by erecting a screen of windbreak netting.

Pruning hints: after the first year the young tree should be able to support itself without the aid of a stake. If not, prune back the stem to within 2.5cm (1in) of ground level in early spring. Thin out the resulting shoots (produced from the swollen base or ligno-tuber) in summer to leave one which will form the main stem. This drastic treatment encourages the formation of a strong root system so that the tree is fully capable of supporting itself.

Problems
Few encountered normally, perhaps silver leaf occasionally.

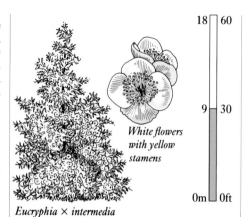

White flowers with yellow stamens

Eucryphia × intermedia

EUCRYPHIA

Eucryphia

Eucryphiaceae

*E*ucryphias are handsome trees and shrubs from Chile and Australia. Recommended only for mild areas, they make fine specimens or groups in light woodland or well-protected shrub borders.

• *E. × intermedia* (*E. glutinosa* × *E. lucida*)
Garden origin (Northern Ireland) ⑧ 🝔
Height about 9m (30ft). Rate of growth is fast. Leaves vary from simple to trifoliate and are deep green with grey undersides. Flowers up to 5cm (2in) in diameter, white, each with a conspicuous boss of yellow stamens, late summer and early autumn. The cultivar 'Rostrevor' is very free-flowering.

Cultivation

☼ ☁ ☉ A-N ▦

The ideal soil is light and cool. Young plants are best protected from severe frosts over winter with a surround of straw. No regular pruning required.

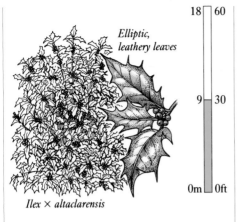

Elliptic, leathery leaves

18 — 60

9 — 30

0m — 0ft

Ilex × altaclarensis

ILEX

Holly

Aquifoliaceae

*T*he hollies are native mainly to temperate and tropical areas of North and South America and Asia. The evergreen tree species and cultivars are often very shapely and attractive, being grown for their pleasing foliage, which is often prickly, and/or winter berries. They make superb focal points in gardens and are often grown as specimens in lawns. Sometimes hollies are used in pairs to "frame" gates or front entrances. In large gardens and estates hollies may be planted as avenues and, in addition, the English or European holly, *I. aquifolium* (see Medium to Large Evergreen trees), is commonly used as hedging.

Hollies are also amenable to tub cultivation, at least when comparatively small, when they make distinctive features on patios or perhaps as a pair placed each side of the front door of a house. They are easily grown, very adaptable and especially suitable for cultivation in towns, cities and industrial areas.

The white or greenish flowers are hardly noticeable, males and females generally being produced on different trees, so trees of both sexes are obviously needed in order for berries to be produced.

● *I.* × *altaclarensis* (*I. aquifolium* × *I. perado*) Garden origin ⑥ ♀
Height variable but usually 7.6–9m (25–30ft). Leaves elliptic, leathery, with a few spines, dark green. Cultivars are grown, including 'Camelliifolia', virtually spineless deep green leaves, flushed with purple when they unfold, purple stems, large red berries; 'Hodginsii', oval dark green leaves, spines many or few, purple stems, male; 'Lawsoniana', leaves usually spineless, splashed yellow in centre, female; and 'Wilsonii', large spiny leaves, female.

● *I. latifolia* (Luster-leaf holly, Tara holly) China, Japan ⑦ ♀
Height up to 15m (50ft) in the wild but may be shorter under cultivation. The large, oblong, dark green, shiny leaves have a thick leathery texture and serrated edges. Berries red, freely produced in clusters.

● *I. pernyi* (Perny holly) China ⑥ ◬
Height 7.6m (25ft). The small, leathery, olive-green, spiny leaves are of triangular shape. Clusters of tiny brilliant red berries.

Cultivation

☼ ☗ ● A AL ▩

Very adaptable, tolerating industrial atmospheric pollution, exposure, maritime conditions and any soil but they relish moisture-retentive loam. Try to site variegated cultivars in full sun to ensure optimum foliage colour. Best to plant small young specimens, which establish better, and to protect them from cold winds in winter by erecting windbreak screens around them. Do not let the soil dry out. Hollies do not need regular pruning, but specimen trees can be trimmed annually to ensure a neat shape. This is best carried out in mid- to late summer. If any green-leaved shoots are produced by variegated hollies cut them out completely.

Problems

Holly leaf miner, birds (which eat the berries), honey fungus.

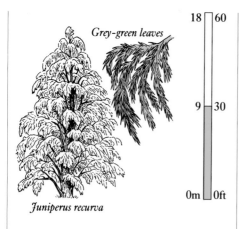

Grey-green leaves

18 | 60

9 | 30

0m | 0ft

Juniperus recurva

JUNIPERUS

Juniper

Cupressaceae

*A*n extremely variable genus of coniferous trees and shrubs scattered over the northern hemisphere. They have scale-like or needle-like leaves in all shades of green and also bluish or greyish shades. Some cultivars have yellow or golden foliage.

The tree species are invariably used as specimen plants, for example in lawns, or they may be included in groups of conifers for contrast in shape, colour and texture.

● *J. chinensis* (Chinese juniper)
China, Mongolia, Japan ④ △ and ♀
Height up to 18m (60ft) but the cultivars that are grown are shorter, maybe half this height. Leaves deep green, often a combination of juvenile and adult. Cultivars include 'Aurea', golden-yellow foliage; 'Kaizuka', leaves dense, bright green; and 'Keteleeri', dense, bright green, scale-like foliage.

● *J. recurva* (Drooping juniper,
Himalayan juniper) Himalayas ⑧ △
Height up to 9m (30ft). Drooping shoots. Leaves grey-green. The variety *coxii* (the coffin juniper) has a very graceful drooping habit and orange-brown bark. Train the leading shoot vertically from an early stage.

● *J. rigida* (Needle juniper)
eastern Asia ⑥ ♀
Height up to 9m (30ft). This species has attractive pendulous branchlets. The leaves are quite rigid, hence the specific name, and are very sharply pointed or needle-like. This is why it is called the needle juniper. The green foliage turns a pleasing bronze-green shade in the winter. The tiny female cones are brown-black or glaucous. This is not one of the hardiest junipers and needs to be well protected from cold drying winds during the winter. At its best it is a handsome, broadly columnar small tree, but it can also grow as a large shrub. There are various sub-species, the typical one being *J. rigida rigida*. This is the plant that is normally grown. It originates from Japan, Korea and northern China.

J. rigida

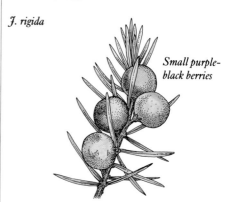

Small purple-black berries

● *J. scopulorum* (Rocky mountain juniper,
Colorado red cedar) North America ④ △
Height at least 9m (30ft). Leaves scale-like, green or grey-green. Bark red-brown, peeling.
Cultivation

☼ ☻ A AL ▦

An excellent choice for alkaline and/or dry soils. No regular pruning needed.
Problems
Juniper webber moth caterpillars, scale insects.

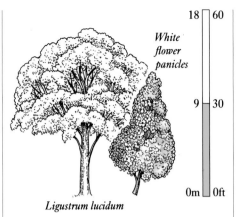

White flower panicles

18 | 60

9 | 30

0m | 0ft

Ligustrum lucidum

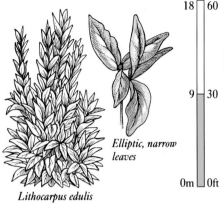

Elliptic, narrow leaves

18 | 60

9 | 30

0m | 0ft

Lithocarpus edulis

LIGUSTRUM

Privet

Oleaceae

A genus of mostly shrubs, but including a few small tree species, native mainly to Asia and Australia. The one species described here is often used as a street tree in the USA, but is equally suitable for planting in private gardens, such as in shrub borders and lawns.

• *L. lucidum* (Glossy privet, Chinese privet) China, Korea ⑧ ♀
Height 9m (30ft). The long, pointed, oval leaves are deep green and shiny. Large showy panicles of white flowers in autumn. Cultivars include 'Excelsum Superbum', leaves variegated cream, yellow and green; and 'Tricolor', leaves margined white, flushed pink when they unfurl.

Cultivation

No regular pruning needed. This species is often grown on a 60–90cm (2–3ft) high trunk and allowed to branch low down.

Problems
Leaf miner, thrips, honey fungus.

LITHOCARPUS

Lithocarpus

Fagaceae

A lthough a large genus, few lithocarpus are grown in gardens as most come from tropical and sub-tropical regions of Asia. They are rather oak-like, and indeed are related to *Quercus*, with leathery foliage and seeds in the form of acorns. Grown as specimen trees.

Lithocarpus are not very commonly grown, possibly due to the fact that they are not very hardy. The hardiest species are recommended only for very mild areas and in the USA are occasionally grown in the South and in California. However, they are handsome trees and well worth growing where conditions are suitable.

• *L. edulis* (*Quercus edulis*) Japan ⑧ ♀
Height 9m (30ft). Leaves elliptic, narrow, yellow-green, leathery. Acorns up to 2.5cm (1in) long.

Cultivation

☼ ☉ A 🛡

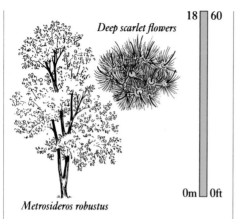

18 | 60

Deep scarlet flowers

0m | 0ft

Metrosideros robustus

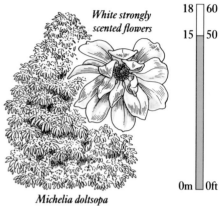

18 | 60

15 | 50

White strongly scented flowers

0m | 0ft

Michelia doltsopa

METROSIDEROS

Iron tree, Bottlebrush

Myrtaceae

A genus of evergreen trees, shrubs and climbers, mainly from New Zealand and Polynesia, generally with highly colourful bottle-brush flowers containing numerous stamens. Metrosideros can be grown outdoors in temperate climates only in very mild areas, and they should be sited in a warm sheltered part of the garden. With the increasing interest in New Zealand plants, metrosideros are becoming better known outside their native country and seem likely to become popular. At least five species are grown in California, and the species described here is the one most commonly cultivated in Britain.

● *M. robustus* (New Zealand Christmas tree, Rata) New Zealand ⑨ ♀

Height up to 18m (60ft) but generally much less under cultivation. Leaves elliptic, thick-textured, deep green. Flowers numerous, in terminal clusters, deep scarlet, summer.

Cultivation

MICHELIA

Michelia

Magnoliaceae

E vergreen trees and shrubs from tropical and temperate areas of Asia, like magnolias, to which they are related, but with smaller flowers. They are recommended only for mild areas in temperate regions of the world, and even then, they should be given warm sheltered conditions.

● *M. doltsopa* eastern Himalayas, Tibet, western Yunnan ⑨ ♀

Height up to 27m (90ft) in the wild but much less under cultivation, usually in the region of 9–15m (30–50ft). In less favourable conditions it may lose its leading shoot and grow as a shrub. Leaves elliptic, leathery texture. Flowers white, strongly scented, up to 8cm (3in) long, occurring in spring. This species is used for timber in the Himalayas.

Cultivation

☼ ☉ A 🛡

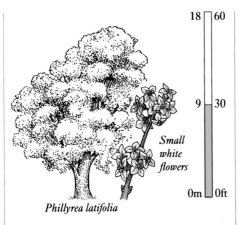

Small
white
flowers

18 ⎡ 60

9 ⎼ 30

0m ⎣ 0ft

Phillyrea latifolia

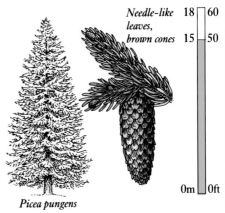

Needle-like 18 ⎡ 60
leaves,
brown cones 15 ⎼ 50

0m ⎣ 0ft

Picea pungens

PHILLYREA

Phillyrea

Oleaceae

*E*vergreen shrubs and small trees from the Mediterranean. Attractive plants with handsome foliage and white flowers, they are well suited to inclusion in mixed plantings of shrubs and trees. There are several attractive species grown in gardens but the majority are classed as medium to large shrubs. The species described below, however, is generally considered to be a small tree.

● *P. latifolia* (Tree phillyrea)
southern Europe, Asia Minor ⑦ ♀
Height up to 9m (30ft). Leaves oval, toothedged, shiny and deep green above. Racemes of small white flowers in late spring.

Cultivation

No regular pruning needed, but note that new shoots are readily produced from old wood if pruned hard.

PICEA

Spruce, Fir

Pinaceae

A genus of cone-shaped conifers widely distributed in the northern hemisphere. They have short needle-like leaves and in some species the branches droop attractively. Many species develop into large, tall trees but there are shorter ones available, especially among cultivars. They make fine specimen trees or can be included in groups; some are suitable for forming screens and windbreaks.

● *P. pungens* (Colorado spruce, Blue spruce, Colorado blue spruce) North America ③ ◬
Height up to 30m (100ft) but the cultivars recommended make small trees, growing up to about 15m (50ft). Leaves stiff and needle-like, bluish-green. Cones up to 10cm (4in) long, light brown. Cultivars include 'Hoopsii', silvery-blue leaves; 'Koster', brilliant silvery-blue foliage; 'Moerheimii', intense grey-blue leaves; and 'Spekii', grey-blue foliage. These cultivars are among the best piceas for specimen planting. They also create contrast in groups of conifers.

Cultivation

They like a deep soil that is able to retain moisture without becoming waterlogged. Avoid planting in frost pockets; young growth can be damaged by spring frosts. In winter protect young plants with a screen of windbreak netting until well established. Plant only small specimens up to 90cm (3ft) high as they establish better than larger ones. No regular pruning needed but make sure young trees carry only one leading shoot; reduce double leaders to one.

Problems

Adelgids (spruce gall), aphids (spruce), honey fungus.

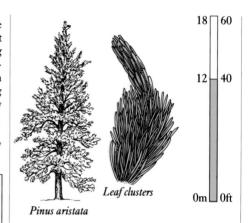

Leaf clusters

Pinus aristata

18 | 60
12 | 40
0m | 0ft

CLIMATIC ZONES

①   Below −45°C (−50°F)

②   −45 to −39°C (−50 to −40°F)

③   −39 to −35°C (−40 to −30°F)

④   −35 to −29°C (−30 to −20°F)

⑤   −29 to −23°C (−20 to −10°F)

⑥   −23 to −18°C (−10 to 0°F)

⑦   −18 to −12°C (0 to 10°F)

⑧   −12 to −6°C (10 to 20°F)

⑨   −6 to −1°C (20 to 30°F)

⑩   −1 to 4°C (30 to 40°F)

PINUS

Pine

Pinaceae

D istributed over the northern hemisphere, the pines are coniferous trees, often extremely tall, although there are some shorter species for gardens. They have various uses including the provision of windbreaks and woodland, and some of the more attractive ornamental species are used as lawn specimens. There are even dwarf pines that can be grown on rock gardens. The pines have long needle-shaped leaves (in clusters of two, three or five, depending on species) and produce woody cones which are quite conspicuous in some species.

● *P. albicaulis* (White-bark pine)
North America ④ ⚘
Height up to 9m (30ft). Although classed as a small tree, this species can also grow as a shrub. The red-brown new shoots are quite an attractive feature and eventually change to white. The stiff deep green or grey-green leaves are carried in fives and attain a length of 6cm (2½in). The purple-brown oval cones are about 8cm (3in) long.

● *P. aristata* (Bristle-cone pine, Hickory pine)
North America ⑥ ⚘
Height 4.5–12m (15–40ft). A slow grower.

Dense head of branches. Young shoots red-brown. Leaves in clusters of five, green above, glaucous below. Cones cylindrical, at least 8cm (3in) long.
• *P. cembroides* (Mexican stone pine, Mexican pinyon) Arizona and Mexico ⑦ ♀
Height at least 7.6m (25ft). Deep orange branchlets. The leaves are usually carried in clusters of three but sometimes in twos, fours or fives. They are deep green, rigid, usually curved, with sharply pointed tips and almost 8cm (3in) in length. The cones are somewhat globose and almost 8cm (3in) in diameter.
• *P. mugo* (Mountain pine)
central and south-east Europe ③ ♀
Height at least 4.5m (15ft). Leaves in groups of two, bright deep green. Oval brown cones about 5cm (2in) long.
• *P. patula* (Mexican yellow pine)
Mexico ⑧ ♀
Height about 15m (50ft). The leaves are usually carried in clusters of three and attain a length of between 15 and 30cm (6 and 12in). They are pendulous and fresh bright green in colour. The conical cones are more than 10cm (4in) in length. Attractive reddish bark. This species will not tolerate alkaline soils.

Cultivation

☼ A AL A-N 🏱

Most species described above will tolerate alkaline soils and, when established, moderate drought conditions. Two-needled pines are the hardiest and will take exposed conditions. Do not plant large specimens: plants up to 60cm (2ft) high establish much better. No regular pruning needed. If leading shoot is damaged or killed, which results in several apical shoots, reduce these to the strongest one so that a new leader is formed.

Problems
Adelgids, caterpillars (pine-shoot moth), sawfly larvae, honey fungus.

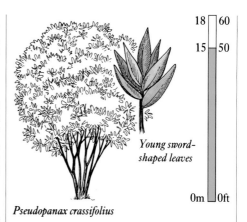

Young sword-shaped leaves

Pseudopanax crassifolius

PSEUDOPANAX

Pseudopanax

Araliaceae

A small genus of shrubs and small trees, mainly from New Zealand. They are of distinctive habit and make unusual focal points or specimen plants in gardens with a mild climate.
• *P. crassifolius* (Lancewood)
New Zealand ⑨ ♀
Height 6–15m (20–50ft). Leaves are variable in shape: seedlings have simple oval to lance-shaped leaves about 5cm (2in) long; those of young plants are sword-shaped, stiff, tooth-edged, up to 90cm (3ft) in length; and mature plants have trifoliate or simple leaves. Greenish flowers are borne in umbels. Young plants are unbranched but branching occurs in the third growth stage when leaves become trifoliate or simple.

Cultivation

☼ ❀ ☉ A AL ■ 🏱

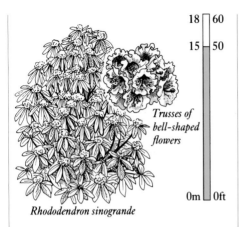

18 — 60
15 — 50

Trusses of bell-shaped flowers

0m — 0ft

Rhododendron sinogrande

RHODODENDRON

Rhododendron

Ericaceae

A very large genus of evergreen and decid-uous shrubs and small trees found mainly in temperate parts of the northern hemisphere. There is a great concentration of species in the Himalayas and south-east Asia. The simple leaves are often quite large and can be an attractive feature, but rhododendrons are grown mainly for their sumptuous bell-shaped or tubu-lar flowers, of various colours, which are often carried in large heads or trusses. Rhododen-drons are frequently grown in woodland gardens or in mixed plantings of shrubs and trees. They can be grown only in acid soils.

There are also numerous hybrid rhododen-drons, which fall outside the scope of this book.

● *R. arboreum* Himalayas ⑧ ♀
Height up to 12m (40ft). Wide-spreading habit. Leaves lanceolate, up to 20cm (8in) long, deep green with silvery undersides. Dense trusses of bell-shaped blood-red flowers in early to mid-spring. Moderately hardy.

● *R. barbatum* Himalayas ⑧ ♀
Height up to 12m (40ft). Leaves oblong, up to 20cm (8in) in length. Flowers in globular trusses, bell-shaped, blood red, mid-spring. Bark grey, smooth and peeling.

● *R. falconeri* Himalayas ⑨ ♀
Height up to 12m (40ft). Leaves oval, up to 30cm (1ft) in length, with deeply set veins, rust-coloured and woolly below. Large round trusses of bell-shaped cream-white to light yel-low flowers, each with a purple basal blotch, mid-spring.

● *R. fictolacteum* China ⑦ ♀
Height up to 14m (45ft). Leaves elliptic, to 30cm (1ft) in length, with brown felted under-sides. Trusses of bell-shaped white, cream or pink-tinted flowers, blotched with crimson, mid- to late spring.

● *R. rex* China ⑦ ♀
Height 6m (20ft). Leaves lanceolate, up to 30cm (1ft) long, deep green with buff or grey felt below. Flowers bell-shaped, in large trusses, pink or white, with crimson basal blotches, mid- to late spring.

● *R. sinogrande* China, Burma, Tibet ⑧ ♀
Height 9–15m (30–50ft). Leaves oval or oblong, 50cm (20in) or more in length and half as wide, deep green, shiny, with silver-grey undersides. Trusses of bell-shaped cream-white to light yellow flowers, generally with crimson basal blotches, mid-spring.

Cultivation

☀ ⊙ A ■ ▥

They thrive in moisture-retentive soil sheltered from cold winds. Add plenty of peat or leaf-mould before planting. Keep plants mulched with peat, leafmould or pulverized bark. Never allow the soil around rhododendrons to dry out; they are shallow-rooting and therefore unable to search deeply for moisture. Make sure plants are protected from early morning sun as frozen buds and young shoots can be killed if they thaw out too rapidly. In addition, dead blooms should be removed to prevent seed formation; this process also results in more prolific flowering. No regu-lar pruning required.

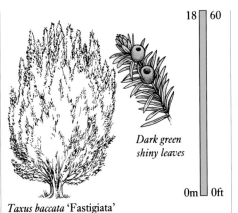

18 | 60

0m | 0ft

Dark green shiny leaves

Taxus baccata 'Fastigiata'

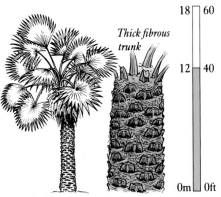

Thick fibrous trunk

18 | 60

12 | 40

0m | 0ft

Trachycarpus fortunei

TAXUS

Yew

Taxaceae

A small genus of coniferous trees and shrubs native to Europe, Asia Minor, eastern Asia and North America. Of bushy habit, they make excellent focal points in a garden and also look good when planted in groups.

● *T. baccata* (English yew)
Europe, north Africa, western Asia ⑦ ♀
Height 12–18m (40–60ft). Very wide spreading with age. Leaves linear, dark green, shiny, paler below. Cultivars include 'Adpressa', spreading, very dense habit; 'Dovastoniana', wide spreading, pendulous branchlets, black-green leaves; and 'Fastigiata' (Irish yew) – really classed as a shrub but included here because of its suitability for small gardens – which has a columnar habit of growth.

Cultivation

 ☼ ☺ ● A AL ▨

They are extremely adaptable and grow particularly well on chalk. Tolerant of exposure and atmospheric pollution. No regular pruning needed.

Problems
Scale insects, honey fungus.

TRACHYCARPUS

Chusan palm, Fan palm

Palmae

A small genus of palms from eastern Asia with big fan-shaped leaves supported by a tall thick trunk. Most commonly used as lawn specimens in gardens.

● *T. fortunei* (Chusan palm) China ⑧ ♀
Height variable, according to climate: 3.6m (12ft) in cool conditions to 12m (40ft) in warmer areas. Leaves produced at top of trunk, medium green, fan-shaped, 76cm (30in) long and at least 90cm (3ft) wide, carried on spiny stalks up to 90cm (3ft) long. Panicles of yellow flowers in late spring or early summer. Fruits globular, blue-black. Thick cylindrical trunk clothed with fibres.

Cultivation

☼ ☺ ⊙ A AL ▨

No pruning needed. Any leaves badly damaged by wind should be removed. To help prevent this, grow in a really sheltered position.

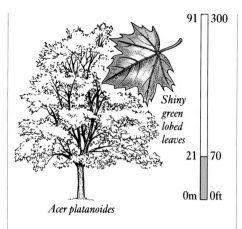

Acer platanoides

Shiny
green
lobed
leaves

91 300

21 70

0m 0ft

ACER

Maple

Aceraceae

*T*he acers originate mainly from northern temperate parts of the world and many are noted for their attractive (often lobed) foliage. Shallow-rooted, the large acers described here are frequently used as lawn specimens in very large gardens and estates where their grandeur can be appreciated. (They are not so suitable for smaller gardens.) Some of those recommended below are among the finest coloured-foliage trees and others rank among the best choices where brilliant autumn leaf colour is desired. These species would also make fine avenues where space is available.

● *A. negundo* (Box elder) North America ⑤ ♀
Height 15–21m (50–70ft). Growth is fast. Leaves pinnate, three to five leaflets, fresh green. Flowers yellow-green but not very conspicuous. Cultivars (not so tall as species) include 'Auratum', golden foliage; 'Elegans', leaves edged yellow; and 'Variegatum', leaves edged white. The variety *violaceum* is noted for its pendulous trusses of red-pink flowers in spring.

● *A. platanoides* (Norway maple)
Europe, Caucasus ④ ♀
Height 18–21m (60–70ft). Shiny green lobed leaves, turning yellow in autumn. Flowers conspicuous, green-yellow, on bare twigs, mid-spring. Cultivars include 'Columnare', fastigiate; 'Crimson King', dark crimson-purple foliage; 'Drummondii', white-edged leaves; and 'Schwedleri', new shoots and young leaves deep crimson-purple, leaves turning red in autumn. Fast growing, Norway maple also makes a good street tree.

● *A. rubrum* (Red maple, Scarlet maple)
North America ③ ♀
Height up to 36m (120ft). Three- to five-lobed leaves, glaucous below, turning scarlet in autumn. Best colour on acid soil. The cultivar 'Scanlon' is not so tall as species, of broad columnar habit and leaves turn red and orange in autumn. Cultivar 'Schlesingeri' is also less tall, of broad columnar habit and with brilliant red foliage in early autumn.

● *A. saccharinum* (Silver maple)
North America ③ ♀
Height 27–39m (90–130ft). Fast growing. Five-lobed bright green leaves with silvery undersides, turning red and yellow in autumn. Cultivars include 'Laciniatum', with pendulous branches and deeply cut leaves; and 'Pyramidale', of fastigiate habit.

● *A. saccharum* (Sugar maple)
North America ③ ♀
Height up to 39m (130ft). Leaves three- to five-lobed, turning to brilliant shades of scarlet, crimson, orange and gold in autumn. Although very hardy, it does not perform so well in Europe. Maple syrup obtained from sap. Cultivars include 'Temple's Upright' ('Monumentale'), of broad columnar habit, foliage turning orange in autumn.

Cultivation

☼ ☽ ⬤ A AL 🏵

No regular pruning needed.

Problems

Aphids, coral spot, honey fungus, tar spot.

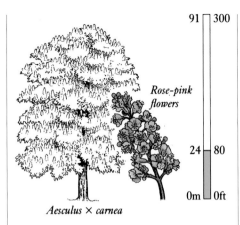

Rose-pink flowers

91 | 300

24 | 80

0m | 0ft

Aesculus × carnea

AESCULUS

Horse chestnut

Hippocastanaceae

*T*rees and shrubs native to North America, south-east Europe and eastern Asia, noted for their palmate compound leaves and pink or white flowers, carried in upright panicles during spring. They make fine specimen trees in large lawns and other grassed areas.

● *A. × carnea* (*A. hippocastanum × A. pavia*) (Red horse chestnut) Origin unrecorded ④ ♀ Height at least 15m (50ft), sometimes up to 18 or 24m (60 or 80ft). Leaves medium green, unfurling from sticky buds. Flowers rose-pink,

late spring and early summer. The cultivar 'Briotii' has darker flowers.

● *A. hippocastanum* (Common or European horse chestnut) northern Greece, Albania ⑤ ♀ Height up to 30m (100ft). Leaves medium or deep green from sticky buds. Flowers white, marked with red, late spring. Seed pods prickly, each containing a single glossy brown seed – the familiar "conker" of childhood. The cultivar 'Baumannii' has double white flowers and does not set seeds.

● *A. indica* (Indian horse chestnut) northern India ⑥ ♀ Height up to 30m (100ft). Leaves medium to deep green, shiny, from sticky winter buds. Flowers white, flushed with pale pink and blotched red and yellow, early to mid-summer.

● *A. turbinata* (*A. sinensis*) (Japanese horse chestnut) Japan ⑤ ♀ Height up to 30m (100ft). A rapid grower. The leaves are composed of five to seven leaflets which attain a length of 38cm (15in). They colour well in the autumn. The panicles of flowers are about 25cm (10in) in length, the blooms yellow-white, each with a red mark. The fruits are rather warty.

Cultivation

☼ ☀ A AL ▨

Although adaptable, they grow best in well-drained deep loam. No regular pruning needed.

Problems

Leaf spot.

KEY TO SYMBOLS

Shape	**Aspect**	**Soils**
� Conical	☼ Full sun	A Acid
♀ Spreading	☀ Partial shade	AL Alkaline
♬ Broad columnar	● Shade	A-N Acid to neutral
◊ Fastigiate	☉ Sheltered from cold winds	■ Rich in humus
♔ Weeping		▨ Well drained

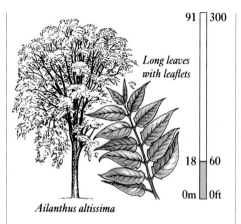

91 ⌐ 300

*Long leaves
with leaflets*

18 ⊢ 60

0m ⌐ 0ft

Ailanthus altissima

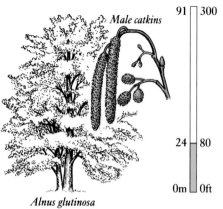

91 ⌐ 300

Male catkins

24 ⊢ 80

0m ⌐ 0ft

Alnus glutinosa

AILANTHUS

Ailanthus

Simaroubaceae

A small genus found in southern and eastern Asia and northern Australia, with pinnate foliage and panicles of green-white flowers. The species described here makes a good specimen tree for lawns and is also used as a street tree in some areas.

● *A. altissima* (Tree of heaven) China ④ ♀

Height 18m (60ft) or more. Young trees grow vigorously. Leaves up to 60cm (2ft) long, with 13 to 25 leaflets. Flowers green-white, late summer, followed by bunches of reddish fruits on female trees.

Cultivation

Prefer a light yet moisture-retentive soil, but are adaptable. They tolerate atmospheric pollution and thrive in towns and cities, hence their use as street trees. No regular pruning needed and no particular problems.

ALNUS

Alder

Betulaceae

*F*or additional details, see entry under Small Ornamental Deciduous.

● *A. cordata* (Italian alder)
Corsica, southern Italy ⑧ ◬
Height up to 24m (80ft). Leaves rounded, deep green and shiny above. Male catkins up to 8cm (3in) long in early spring. Considered to be one of the most attractive alders.

● *A. glutinosa* (Common, black, or European alder) Europe, North Africa, Asia ④ ♀
Height up to 24m (80ft). Leaves roundish, deep green and glossy. Male catkins 10cm (4in) long, early to mid-spring. The cultivar 'Imperialis' has deeply cut leaves, giving a feathery appearance.

Cultivation

☼ ☕ A AL ■

Very adaptable regarding soils, but shallow chalk soil is generally best avoided, although *A. cordata* will grow well on chalk. The trees can be pruned hard if necessary, to reduce the height of a screen, for example.

Problems
Fungal leaf spots, but not serious.

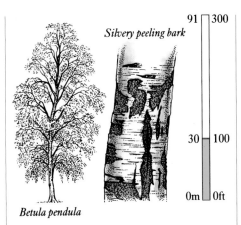

Silvery peeling bark

91 ⎡ 300

30 ⎯ 100

0m ⎣ 0ft

Betula pendula

BETULA

Birch

Betulaceae

*T*he birches are widely distributed throughout the temperate northern hemisphere and are among the most popular garden trees for use as lawn specimens and focal points, or for creating light woodland conditions. They have a graceful habit of growth and often attractive bark. Many produce conspicuous male catkins in the spring.

They associate well with many other ornamental trees, contrasting beautifully in shape and texture. The bark, which is often white, creates another pleasing contrast. It shows up best against a dark background such as a group of deep green conifers or evergreen broad-leaved shrubs. Some particularly lovely effects can be achieved by planting rhododendrons with birches.

● *B. albo-sinensis septentrionalis*
(Chinese paper birch) China ⑤ ⌇
Height up to 27m (90ft). Leaves ovate, toothed, silky hairy. This species is noted for its orange-brown bark.
● *B. ermanii* China, Korea, Japan ⑤ ♀
Height 18–24m (60–80ft). Leaves ovate, medium green, toothed. Bark orange-brown, then cream-white, peeling; a notable feature.

● *B. jacquemontii* Himalayas ⑤ ♀
Height 18–21m (60–70ft). Leaves ovate, serrated. Bark white, peeling; highly attractive.
● *B. maximowicziana* (Monarch birch)
Japan ⑤ ♀
Height 24–30m (80–100ft). Leaves heart-shaped, the largest of any birch, turning clear yellow in autumn. Bark is the attractive feature, being light orange or grey.
● *B. papyrifera* (Paper birch, Canoe birch)
North America ③ ♀
Height 21–30m (70–100ft). Leaves oval, turning yellow in autumn. Bark white, papery, peeling.
● *B. pendula* (Silver, white, common, or European birch)
Europe, Asia Minor ② ⌒
Height 18m (60ft), sometimes up to 30m (100ft). Leaves somewhat diamond-shaped, medium green. Graceful pendulous branchlets. Bark silvery, peeling. Cultivars include 'Dalecarlica' (Swedish birch), graceful drooping habit and deeply cut leaves; 'Fastigiata', narrow erect habit; 'Purpurea', purple foliage; and 'Tristis', of rather broad columnar habit.
● *B. platyphylla* China and Korea ⑤ ♀
Height 18m (60ft). Leaves somewhat triangular. Bark white. The variety *szechuanica* has even whiter bark and is more vigorous.
● *B. pubescens* (White birch, European white birch) Europe to Siberia ② ♀
Height 18m (60ft). Leaves broadly ovate. Bark white, peeling, eventually rugged. Grows in moist soils in the wild.
● *B. utilis* (Himalayan birch) Himalayas ⑤ ⌇
Height up to 21m (70ft). Leaves oval, with coarsely toothed edges. Bark cream-white, peeling.
Cultivation

☼ ◐ A AL ■

Although tolerant of poor sandy soils, best results in moisture-retentive, fertile, loamy soils. No pruning needed.
Problems
Aphids, caterpillars, sawflies, honey fungus.

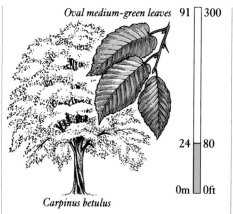

Oval medium-green leaves 91 ☐ 300

24 ┤ 80

0m └ 0ft

Carpinus betulus

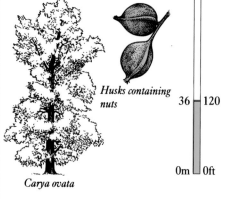

91 ☐ 300

Husks containing nuts 36 ┤ 120

0m └ 0ft

Carya ovata

CARPINUS

Hornbeam

Betulaceae

The hornbeams are very hardy trees originating from the temperate areas of the northern hemisphere. Of good shape, they are generally used as specimen trees to create focal points. The large species recommended here needs plenty of space to develop and is one of the best known in the genus.

• *C. betulus* (European hornbeam) Europe, Asia Minor ④ ♀

Height up to 24m (80ft). Leaves oval, medium green, turning gold in autumn. Bark grey. This species is often used for hedging. Cultivars include 'Fastigiata', of conical habit, especially when young.

Cultivation

☼ ☾ A AL ▥

Best growth in a deep loamy soil. No regular pruning needed when grown as a tree.

Problems

Honey fungus.

CARYA

Hickory

Juglandaceae

The hickories come mainly from North and Central America and eastern Asia. They have pinnate leaves which generally turn yellow in autumn, and are used as specimens in large gardens, estates and parks. They are of rather slow growth but make fine specimens eventually.

• *C. cordiformis* (Bitternut, Pignut, Swamp hickory) North America ⑤ ♀

Height up to 27m (90ft). Leaves usually composed of seven leaflets, from bright yellow winter buds. Bark brown and scaly.

• *C. ovata* (Shagbark hickory, Shellbark hickory) North America ⑤ ♀

Height up to 36m (120ft). Leaves composed of five leaflets, turning deep yellow in autumn. Bark shaggy, flaking.

Cultivation

☼ ☾ A AL ▥

Best soil is a deep loam. Hickories resent root disturbances so plant only small specimens.

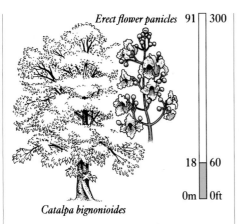

Erect flower panicles 91 | 300

18 | 60

0m | 0ft

Catalpa bignonioides

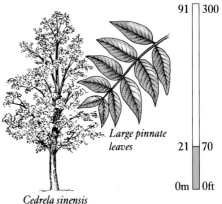

91 | 300

Large pinnate leaves 21 | 70

0m | 0ft

Cedrela sinensis

CATALPA

Catalpa

Bignoniaceae

*F*rom North America and eastern Asia, the catalpas make imposing specimen trees in large gardens and estates, in town or country, with their very large heart-shaped leaves and conspicuous panicles of foxglove-like flowers in summer.

● *C. bignonioides* (Indian bean tree, Southern catalpa) North America ⑤ ♀
Height up to 18m (60ft). Leaves heart-shaped, bright green, aromatic when bruised. Flowers in erect panicles, white, marked yellow and purple, mid-summer. Bean-like seed pods follow. The cultivar 'Aurea' has yellow foliage.

● *C. speciosa* (Western catalpa, Northern catalpa) North America ⑤ ♀
Height up to 30m (100ft). Leaves ovate. Flowers white with brown spots, mid-summer.

Cultivation

☼ ☉ A AL ▣

They thrive in any fertile moisture-retentive soil. To produce a good trunk in young trees ensure a single leading shoot to a height of about 3m (10ft) and then allow to branch.

CEDRELA

Cedrela

Meliaceae

*S*mall genus of trees from tropical America, south-east Asia and Australia, with pinnate leaves and large panicles of white, green or pink flowers. The genus is noted for its soft timber which is light in colour. This timber has many uses in the countries of origin. In South America and the West Indies the aromatic wood of *C. odorata* is used in the manufacture of cigar boxes. The hardiest species is described below, a handsome and fast-growing tree, making a fine lawn specimen.

● *C. sinensis* (Toon, Chinese cedrela) China ⑥ ♀
Height up to 21m (70ft). Leaves up to 60cm (2ft) in length, pinnate, turning yellow in autumn. Flowers white, scented, in drooping panicles, early summer. Shaggy peeling bark.

Cultivation

☼ ☻ A AL ▣

Grows best in a deep, fertile, loamy soil. Otherwise no special requirements or problems.

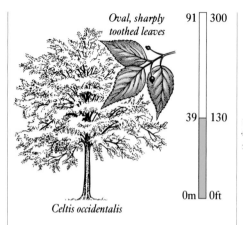

Oval, sharply toothed leaves

91 | 300

39 | 130

0m | 0ft

Celtis occidentalis

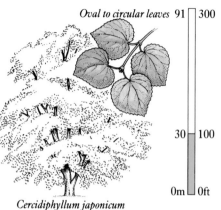

Oval to circular leaves 91 | 300

30 | 100

0m | 0ft

Cercidiphyllum japonicum

CELTIS

Hackberry, Nettle tree, Sugarberry

Ulmaceae

The hackberries in general are native to temperate parts of the northern hemisphere, although a few are native to the tropics. Although some species make shapely specimen trees and are worth growing for this reason, they do not have particularly distinctive flowers, foliage or fruits. The foliage turns yellow in the autumn. Some species are used as street trees in southern Europe and North America as they are excellent for providing shade.

● *C. occidentalis* (Sugarberry, Common hackberry) North America ④ ♀
Height up to 39m (130ft). Fast growing. Leaves oval, glossy above, with sharply toothed edges, turning yellow in autumn. Orange-red to deep purple berries freely produced by mature trees. Bark corky.

Cultivation

CERCIDIPHYLLUM

Cercidiphyllum

Cercidiphyllaceae

There are only two species in this genus and they hail from eastern Asia. They are attractive trees of shapely appearance. Their foliage colours well in autumn and this is one of the main reasons for planting them in shrub borders or woodland gardens, or as lawn specimens, particularly near water.

● *C. japonicum* (Chinese katsura tree, Katsura tree) China, Japan ⑤ ♀
Height 30m (100ft). Leaves oval to circular, opening red, becoming deep green above and glaucous below, turning yellow or red in autumn. The petal-less flowers are insignificant.

Cultivation

They thrive in any fertile soil that retains moisture. Although they will grow in alkaline soils, autumn foliage colour is generally better when the soil is acid. *C. japonicum* is best protected from spring frosts, accomplished perhaps in woodland conditions. No pruning needed.

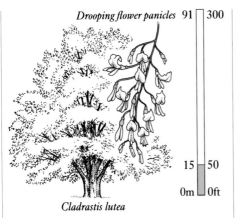

Drooping flower panicles 91 300

15 50

0m 0ft

Cladrastis lutea

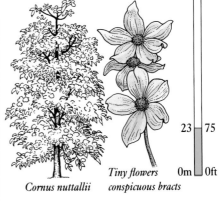

91 300

23 75

0m 0ft

Tiny flowers
conspicuous bracts

Cornus nuttallii

CLADRASTIS

Yellow wood

Leguminosae

A small genus of trees native to North America and eastern Asia, with pinnate leaves and white pea-like flowers in abundance. Useful and handsome lawn specimens.

● *C. lutea* (Yellow wood) North America ⑧ ♀
Height 15m (50ft). Leaves are up to 30cm (1ft) in length, consisting of seven or nine leaflets, colouring deep yellow in autumn. White scented flowers are carried in drooping panicles, up to 35cm (14in) in length, during early summer. These are followed by 10cm (4in) long flat seed pods. It is interesting to note that a yellow dye is obtained from the heartwood of this species, hence the common name.

Cultivation

☼ A AL 🏵

Best growth in a fertile loamy soil. Easy going, needing no regular pruning and having no particular problems.

CORNUS

Dogwood, Cornel

Cornaceae

*S*ee entry under Small Ornamental Deciduous. The species described here makes a fine and shapely lawn specimen.

● *C. nuttallii* (Mountain dogwood, Pacific dogwood) North America ⑨ 🏵
Height 23m (75ft) but usually less under cultivation. Leaves oval, with glaucous undersides, turning yellow or sometimes red in the autumn. Heads of tiny flowers surrounded by six to eight conspicuous cream-white bracts which eventually become flushed with pink, are produced in late spring. Sometimes more flowers appear in autumn. Fruits are red or orange and strawberry-like in appearance. This cornus is considered to be one of the most attractive and desirable of the tree species and is very widely planted in gardens.

Cultivation

☼ A AL 🏵

Adaptable, growing in any fertile soil but thin chalky types best avoided for this species. No regular pruning needed.

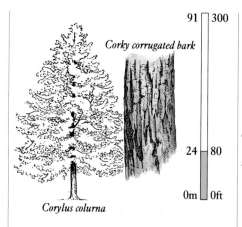

Corky corrugated bark

91 300

24 80

0m 0ft

Corylus colurna

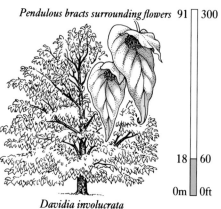

Pendulous bracts surrounding flowers 91 300

18 60

0m 0ft

Davidia involucrata

CORYLUS

Filbert, Hazel

Betulaceae

A genus of mainly shrubs, but including a few trees, native to temperate parts of the northern hemisphere. The leaves are generally oval and the male flowers (the flowers are unisexual) are in the form of catkins and appear before the leaves. The flowers are followed by edible nuts. Corylus are not particularly outstanding as specimen plants.

● *C. colurna* (Turkish hazel)
south-east Europe, western Asia ⑧
Height 24m (80ft). Leaves oval, deep green. Male catkins yellow, up to 8cm (3in) in length, early to mid-spring. Clusters of oval nuts, each one enclosed in a sheath of bracts, follow the flowers. Bark grey, corky, corrugated; a notable feature.

Cultivation

☼ ☉ A AL ▨

To form the above species into a tree, a leading shoot should be selected and trained early in the life of the plant. Remove any suckers produced.

Problems

Caterpillars, squirrels (which feed on the nuts), weevils, honey fungus, powdery mildew.

DAVIDIA

Handkerchief tree, Dove tree

Nyssaceae

There is only one species in this genus and it makes a most unusual and handsome specimen tree with its white handkerchief-like bracts. It is invariably grown in woodland conditions but also makes a fine specimen in more open parts of the garden, such as the lawn.

● *D. involucrata* (Handkerchief tree, Dove tree) western China ⑥ ♀
Height 18m (60ft). Leaves large, oval, light to medium green, with downy undersides. Flowers green-yellow, surrounded by two oval, cream-white, pendulous bracts of unequal length, the longest being about 15cm (6in), late spring. The variety *vilmoriniana* is frequently grown and is very similar to the species, except that the leaves have smooth undersides.

Cultivation

☼ ☻ A AL ▨

Try to provide a moisture-retentive soil that does not dry out in summer. No regular pruning needed and no particular problems.

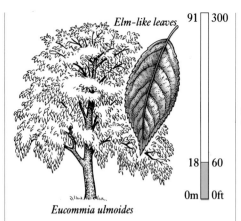

Elm-like leaves

91 300

18 60

0m 0ft

Eucommia ulmoides

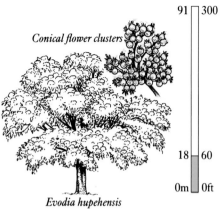

Conical flower clusters

91 300

18 60

0m 0ft

Evodia hupehensis

EUCOMMIA

Hardy rubber tree, Tu-chung

Eucommiaceae

There is only one species in this genus, a native of China, with elm-like leaves, making a fine and rather unusual specimen tree. It produces rubber, although the tree is not used commercially for this purpose. If a leaf is gently torn in half, threads of rubber will be revealed. In China the bark is used medicinally. It appears that male plants are the most common to be found in cultivation.

● *E. ulmoides* China ⑤ ♀
Height up to 18m (60ft). Leaves oval, with long pointed tips, up to 20cm (8in) in length, and somewhat elm-like in appearance. The flowers are insignificant.

Cultivation

☼ A AL 🏠

A rapid grower in any ordinary garden soil. No regular pruning needed and no particular problems.

EVODIA

Evodia

Rutaceae

Trees and shrubs from Asia and Australia with pinnate or simple leaves and white flowers. They are easily grown and generally recommended as lawn specimens.

● *E. hupehensis* (Hupeh evodia)
China Considered hardy ♀
Height up to 18m (60ft). Wide spreading habit. Leaves pinnate, consisting of five to nine leaflets. Flowers white, in wide conical clusters, late summer. Fruits red-brown, with a hooked "beak".

Cultivation

☼ ☽ A AL 🏠

Easily grown in any reasonably fertile soil. *E. hupehensis* grows particularly well in chalky soils. No regular pruning needed and no particular problems. Branching is not extensive and young plants should have a strong leading shoot trained vertically from an early age. Aim for a 1.8m (6ft) clear trunk. The trees need plenty of light around them.

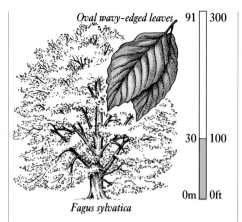

Oval wavy-edged leaves

91 | 300

30 | 100

0m | 0ft

Fagus sylvatica

FAGUS

Beech

Fagaceae

*L*arge trees from temperate regions of the northern hemisphere, noted for their very smooth grey bark. They make magnificent specimen trees in large gardens, parks and estates and have also been planted to form woodland and avenues. The European beech, *F. sylvatica*, is extensively used for formal hedging. When used in this way the plants hold onto their dead leaves over the winter, when they are a rich golden-brown colour.

● *F. crenata* (*F. sieboldii*) (Japanese beech)
Japan ⑥ ♀
Height up to 27m (90ft). Leaves oval, with wavy margins, similar to those of *F. sylvatica*. It is an important forest tree in Japan.

● *F. englerana* China ⑥ ♀
Height up to 21m (70ft), often multi-stemmed. The grey-green elliptic leaves attain a length of about 10cm (4in). This is a fine species but is quite rare in cultivation, although it is supplied by some specialist tree and shrub nurserymen and worth searching out.

● *F. grandifolia* (*F. americana*) (American beech)
eastern North America ④ ♀
Height 24m (80ft) or more. Produces suckers. Leaves up to 12.5cm (5in) in length, somewhat oval, with long-pointed tips, the margins having coarse teeth, taking on yellow tints in the autumn before they fall. The seed capsules are downy and prickly. The timber is used for a wide variety of purposes. Not a good species for Britain, where it does not grow well. Good for North America.

● *F. orientalis* (Oriental beech)
Europe ⑥ ♀
Height 30m (100ft) or more. Leaves up to 15cm (6in) long, the largest of all species; obovate, with wavy edges, turning yellow in autumn. The bark is very light grey. Altogether a distinctive tree.

● *F. sylvatica* (European beech)
Europe ⑤ ♀
Height at least 30m (100ft), although sometimes much more. Leaves oval with wavy edges, colouring well in autumn. Makes a massive trunk, covered in grey bark. An important timber tree. Extensively planted as woodland. Cultivars include 'Cuprea', with copper leaves; 'Dawyck' (Dawyck beech), fastigiate; 'Dawyck Gold', fastigiate, golden foliage; 'Dawyck Purple', fastigiate, purple foliage; *F. s. heterophylla* (Fern-leaved beech, Cut-leaved beech), attractively cut and lobed leaves; 'Latifolia', large leaves, to 15cm (6in) in length; 'Pendula' (Weeping beech), arching and pendulous branches; *F. s. purpurea* (Purple beech), purplish leaves; 'Riversii' (Purple beech), large deep purple leaves; 'Rohanii', cut and lobed purple leaves; 'Roseomarginata', leaves purple, edged pink; and 'Zlatia', leaves yellow, eventually turning green, a slow grower.

Cultivation

☼ A AL ▣

Avoid soils that are heavy and wet. Beeches grow particularly well on chalk soils. No regular pruning required for trees.

Problems

Beech aphids, scale insects (beech scale), honey fungus.

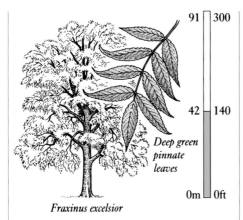

91 | 300

42 | 140

Deep green pinnate leaves

0m | 0ft

Fraxinus excelsior

FRAXINUS

Ash

Oleaceae

*F*rom the cool temperate areas of the northern hemisphere, the ashes are mainly large forest-type trees suited only to parks and estates, although there are some small species and these are included under Small Ornamental Deciduous. The species described here are planted as specimen trees or avenues in large gardens, parks and estates. The timber is valuable and has many uses.

The opposite leaves are mainly pinnate and the small flowers are carried in panicles during early spring, but are not particularly decorative or conspicuous. Some species produce their flowers before the leaves. The flowers are followed by clusters of winged seeds. Some species self-sow themselves very freely, especially *F. excelsior* which can become almost a weed in some gardens. The seedlings should be pulled out as soon as they are noticed, if not required.

● *F. americana* (White ash)
North America ④ ♀
Height to 36m (120ft). Leaves pinnate, with five to nine leaflets, medium green with very pale undersides, colouring well in autumn. It is a fast-growing species and makes a fine lawn specimen where space permits.

● *F. excelsior* (European ash)
Europe, Asia Minor ④ ♀
Height up to 42m (140ft). Leaves pinnate, with seven to eleven leaflets, deep green, from black winter buds. This is a very fast-growing tree with far-reaching roots just below the soil surface and therefore should on no account be planted near buildings or underground pipes and cables. Cultivars include 'Diversifolia', of broad columnar habit, with simple, tooth-edged leaves; 'Jaspidea' ('Aurea') (Golden ash), young shoots and branches yellow, foliage turns clear yellow in autumn; and 'Pendula' (Weeping ash), pendulous branches, forming a mound-like shape.

● *F. latifolia* (Oregon ash)
North America ⑦ ♀
Height 23m (75ft). Leaves pinnate, with five to nine leaflets, downy undersides. A vigorous grower.

● *F. ornus* (Flowering ash, Manna ash)
southern Europe, western Asia ⑥ ♀
Height 18m (60ft). Leaves pinnate, generally with seven leaflets. Cream-white fragrant flowers carried in panicles during late spring followed by clusters of green fruits which eventually turn brown.

● *F. pennsylvanica* (Red ash, Green ash)
North America ③ ♀
Height 18m (60ft). Leaves pinnate, with five to nine leaflets, downy undersides, from conspicuous brown winter buds. A fast grower and a very hardy species.

Cultivation

☼ ☾ A AL 🌣

Are very wind resistant and therefore can be recommended for exposed situations. Also suitable for town and city gardens and coastal areas. Ideally grown in deep loamy soil. No regular pruning needed.

Problems
Canker, honey fungus.

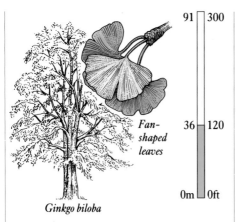

91 | 300

Fan-shaped leaves

36 | 120

0m | 0ft

Ginkgo biloba

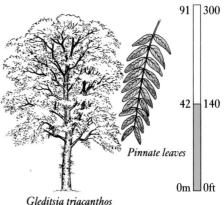

91 | 300

42 | 140

Pinnate leaves

0m | 0ft

Gleditsia triacanthos

GINKGO

Maidenhair tree

Ginkgoaceae

*T*his genus contains only one species, a highly distinctive conical tree from China which makes a superb lawn specimen. It is also used as a street tree. Ginkgo has unusually shaped leaves which colour well in autumn.
● *G. biloba* (Maidenhair tree)
China ⑤ ♈
Height up to 36m (120ft). Leaves two-lobed, fan-shaped, light green, turning clear yellow in autumn. Bark deep grey. Female trees produce plum-shaped green fruits which ripen to yellow and give off an unpleasant odour. Cultivars include 'Fastigiata', of columnar habit; and 'Variegata', leaves variegated cream and green.
Cultivation

☼ A AL ■ ▧

Tolerates atmospheric pollution and is ideal for towns and cities. Trees should not be pruned as this results in die-back. No problems from pests or diseases.

GLEDITSIA

Honey locust

Leguminosae

A genus of spiny pinnate-leaved trees native to North America and Asia. They make handsome lawn specimens, being grown for their attractive foliage. Flowers insignificant.
● *G. triacanthos* (Honey locust)
North America ③ ♀
Height up to 42m (140ft). Leaves pinnate, with 10–15 pairs of leaflets. Spines flattish, simple or branched, on branches and trunk. In Britain the cultivar 'Sunburst' is one of the most popular ornamental trees. It is of medium size with spineless stems and brilliant yellow young foliage.
Cultivation

☼ A AL ▧

These trees tolerate atmospheric pollution and are highly recommended for planting in towns and cities. No pruning needed and no particular problems.

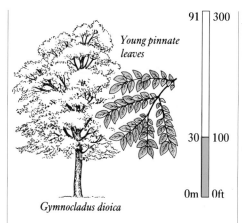

Young pinnate leaves

91 | 300

30 | 100

0m | 0ft

Gymnocladus dioica

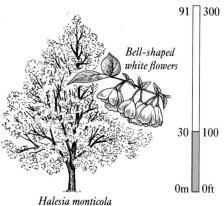

Bell-shaped white flowers

91 | 300

30 | 100

0m | 0ft

Halesia monticola

GYMNOCLADUS

Gymnocladus

Leguminosae

A small genus native to North America and China, grown mainly for the pinnate foliage. The species described here makes a very handsome but rather unusual lawn specimen as it is not too widely grown. The seeds were used as a substitute for coffee by the early settlers in North America, hence the common name of coffee tree.

● *G. dioica* (Kentucky coffee tree)
North America ③ ♀
Height up to 30m (100ft). Pinnate leaves grow up to 90cm (3ft) in length and 60cm (2ft) wide, pink when young, turning clear yellow in autumn. The young shoots are downy and greyish.

Cultivation

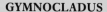 ☼ ◑ A AL ▦

Quite a slow-growing tree that prefers a deep, fertile, loamy soil. No regular pruning needed. No particular problems.

HALESIA

Snowdrop tree, Silver-bell tree

Styracaceae

*T*he halesias are trees and shrubs from China and North America and are very attractive in the spring when in flower. They are invariably planted in woodland gardens with light or dappled shade, although they are also suitable for including in shrub borders.

● *H. monticola* (Mountain silver bell)
North America ⑤ ♀
Height up to 30m (100ft) in the wild but generally less under cultivation. Leaves elliptic, light green. Flowers bell-shaped, white, carried in clusters during late spring. These are followed by winged fruits. The cultivar 'Rosea' has palest pink flowers. The variety *vestita* has larger flowers, sometimes flushed with pink. Both of these form much smaller trees than the species.

Cultivation

☼ ◑ ☉ A ■

Suitable for moist soils. Do not need regular pruning but excessively long shoots can be pruned back after flowering to maintain a balanced shape.

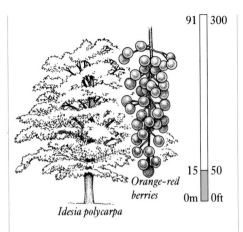

91 | 300

15 | 50

0m | 0ft

Orange-red berries

Idesia polycarpa

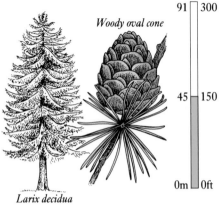

Woody oval cone

91 | 300

45 | 150

0m | 0ft

Larix decidua

IDESIA

Idesia

Flacourtiaceae

There is only one species in this genus, a native of China and Japan, with handsome foliage, sometimes used as a shade tree in parks, streets and in lawns of large gardens. Rather unusual, not widely planted but deserving to be grown where space permits.

● *I. polycarpa* China, Japan ⑦ ♀
Height 15m (50ft). The tree has a tier system of branching. Leaves oval, up to 25cm (10in) in length, deep green with glaucous undersides. Large terminal panicles of tiny yellow-green flowers in early to mid-summer. Female trees produce clusters of orange-red berries in autumn, at which season trees are particularly attractive.

Cultivation

☼ A–N ⊞

No regular pruning needed and no particular problems.

LARIX

Larch

Pinaceae

A genus of tall coniferous trees from temperate areas of the northern hemisphere. They have short needle-like leaves which open bright green and turn yellow in autumn, and produce oval woody cones. Larches are used in forestry, make excellent woodland and when planted alone they form distinctive conical specimens.

● *L. decidua* (European larch, Common larch) Europe ③ ♧
Height up to 45m (150ft). Trees become more spreading as they mature. Leaves light green. Important timber tree; source of turpentine.

● *L. kaempferi* (*L. leptolepis*) (Japanese larch) Japan ⑤ ♧
Height 30m (100ft). Leaves glaucous. Widely used in forestry. The cultivar 'Pendula' has a weeping habit.

Cultivation

☼ A AL ⊞

Best to plant seedlings, no more than 60cm (2ft) high. Avoid very wet soils. No pruning needed, but ensure trees do not develop twin leaders.

Problems
Adelgids, sawfly larvae, honey fungus.

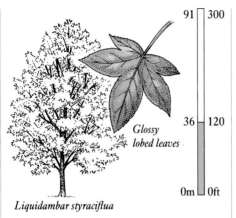

91 | 300

Glossy lobed leaves

36 | 120

0m | 0ft

Liquidambar styraciflua

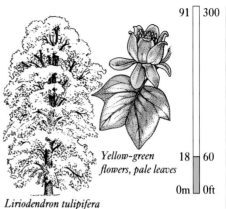

91 | 300

Yellow-green flowers, pale leaves

18 | 60

0m | 0ft

Liriodendron tulipifera

LIQUIDAMBAR

Sweet gum

Hamamelidaceae

*F*rom North America and Asia, the liquid-ambars have palmate or maple-like leaves that colour brilliantly in autumn. Indeed, they are among the best for autumn colour. Generally grown as lawn specimens, they look particularly good near water. Also used as street trees.

● *L. styraciflua* (Sweet gum)
North America ④ 🜊
Height up to 36m (120ft). Leaves five- or seven-lobed, glossy, deep green, becoming scarlet and orange in autumn. With older trees corky wings develop on branches. Various cultivars are available with especially good autumn leaf colour.

Cultivation

☼ ☼ ☉ A AL ▩

Moisture-retentive loam is the best soil. These trees will not thrive on shallow chalky soils. No regular pruning needed and no particular problems.

LIRIODENDRON

Tulip tree

Magnoliaceae

*T*his genus contains two species, native to China and North America. They produce large lobed leaves that are squared-off at the tips, turning clear yellow in autumn, and large flowers shaped like tulips, hence the common name. Superb specimen trees where space permits.

● *L. tulipifera* (Tulip tree, Yellow poplar)
North America ⑤ ♀
Height up to 61m (200ft) but generally about half this under cultivation. Leaves pale to medium green. Flowers yellow-green, marked with orange inside, early to mid-summer. Cultivars include 'Aureomarginatum', leaves edged with yellow; and 'Fastigiatum', of narrow columnar habit.

Cultivation

☼ A AL ▩

Best results in deep, fertile, loamy soil that is moisture-retentive. No regular pruning needed. Not troubled by pests or diseases.

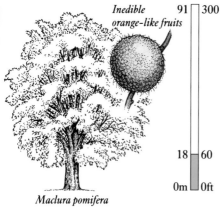

Inedible orange-like fruits 91 300

18 60

0m 0ft

Maclura pomifera

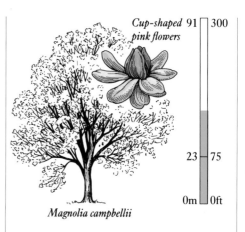

Cup-shaped pink flowers 91 300

23 75

0m 0ft

Magnolia campbellii

MACLURA

Maclura

Moraceae

A genus of a single species native to North America and related to the mulberry. In Europe and the USA it is often used as a hedging plant, creating a dense spiny barrier. It can also be used as a specimen tree or grown with a collection of ornamental shrubs.

• *M. pomifera* (Osage orange, Bow wood)
North America ⑤ ♀
Height up to 18m (60ft). Leaves ovate or oblong-lanceolate, deep green and shiny above with downy undersides. Flowers inconspicuous. Fruits look like oranges but cannot be eaten; they mature in early autumn. To obtain fruits a male and female tree must be planted.

Cultivation

☼ ☀ A AL ▨

The osage orange thrives in poor soils. No pruning needed when grown as a tree and no particular problems.

MAGNOLIA

Magnolia

Magnoliaceae

A popular genus of trees and shrubs native to North and Central America, eastern Asia and the Himalayas. They are grown mainly for their magnificent flowers. Most are shapely enough to be treated as lawn specimens but magnolias can also be grown in shrub or mixed borders.

The following trees make magnificent specimens in sheltered parts of the garden, especially in woodland conditions. These magnolias are considered to be among the finest woodland plants and they associate superbly well with other choice plants such as rhododendrons, especially the tree types with large leaves. Magnolias also make excellent companion plants together with other shrubs such as kalmias, pieris and enkianthus. This is a theme that is justifiably repeated in many large private gardens open to the public.

The alternate leaves of magnolias are entire and often have a somewhat leathery texture. The flowers are large and carried singly at the tips of stems. The number of petals varies from six to more than 20. Flower colour is white, cream, pink or purple. Some species have conspicuous red cone-like fruits.

- *M. acuminata* (Cucumber tree)
eastern North America ③ ♀
Height 30m (100ft). Leaves elliptic, medium green, with downy undersides, turning yellow in autumn. Flowers erect, green-yellow, late spring to mid-summer, not as showy as many other species. Deep red cucumber-shaped fruits. Will tolerate lime.

- *M. campbellii* (Pink tulip tree)
Himalayas ⑧ ♀
Height 45m (150ft) in the wild but about half this under cultivation. Will not grow in alkaline soils. Leaves ovate, up to 30cm (1ft) in length. Flowers cup-shaped, at least 15cm (6in) in diameter, light pink on the outside, deep pink within, scented, early spring, before the leaves. Flower buds liable to frost damage in cold areas. Young trees (under 20 years old) do not flower. Cultivars and varieties include *alba*, white flowers; 'Charles Raffill', deep pink-purple flowers flushed white, vigorous habit; 'Darjeeling', deep rose flowers; 'Lanarth', bright pink-purple waterlily-shaped flowers; *mollicomata*, large pink or pink-purple flowers shaped like waterlilies, produced at an earlier age than species; and 'Wakehurst', deep pink-purple flowers.

- *M. heptapeta* (*M. denudata*) (Yulan)
China ⑤ ♀
Height 15m (50ft) but could be less under cultivation. Unsuitable for alkaline soils. Leaves oval or obovate, up to 15cm (6in) long, with downy undersides. Flowers bell-shaped, 15cm (6in) in diameter, white, fragrant, appearing before the leaves from early to late spring.

- *M. hypoleuca* (*M. obovata*)
(Silverleaf magnolia) Japan ⑤ ♀
Height 30m (100ft) in the wild but may be less under cultivation. Unsuitable for alkaline soils. Leaves obovate, leathery, up to 45cm (18in) in length, glaucous-green above with blue-white undersides. Flowers cup-shaped, 20cm (8in) in diameter, white, fragrant, early summer. Fruits scarlet, 20cm (8in) in length.

- *M. macrophylla* (Large-leaved cucumber tree, Great-leaved magnolia, Bigleaf magnolia)
North America ⑦ ♀
Height 15m (50ft). Not suitable for alkaline soils. Leaves oblong-obovate, 60cm (2ft) or more in length and up to 30cm (1ft) wide (the largest in the genus and inclined to hide the flowers), upper surface bright green, lower surface silver-grey. Flowers cup-shaped, 20cm (8in) or more in diameter, cream-white with purple base, fragrant, late spring and early summer. Flower buds can be damaged by spring frosts.

- *M. sargentiana* China ⑤ ♀
Height 18m (60ft). Not suitable for alkaline soils. Leaves obovate, 20cm (8in) in length, rather dull above, with grey downy undersides. Flowers rose-pink on the outside but a lighter shade within, 20cm (8in) in diameter, appearing before the leaves in mid- to late spring. Trees do not flower until nearing maturity.

- *M. sprengeri* China ⑤ ♀
Height 18m (60ft). Not suitable for alkaline soils. Leaves obovate, about 15cm (6in) in length, deep green. Flowers erect, up to 20cm (8in) in diameter, rose-pink on the outside but a lighter shade within, and appearing before the leaves in mid-spring. The red fruits are 20cm (8in) long.

- *M. × veitchii* (*M. campbellii* × *M. denudata*)
Britain ⑤ ♀
Height uncertain, but at least 26m (85ft). Unsuitable for alkaline soils. Leaves obovate, up to 30cm (1ft) in length, purplish when young. Flowers 15cm (6in) in length, palest pink, produced at an early age, before the leaves in mid-spring.

Cultivation

☼ ☗ ☉ A AL A-N ▓ ▣

Stake young plants well until established and provide an annual mulch of leafmould or peat. Magnolias dislike transplanting so plant container-grown specimens in early spring. Avoid frost pockets and sites exposed to early morning sun. No pruning required.

Problems
Honey fungus.

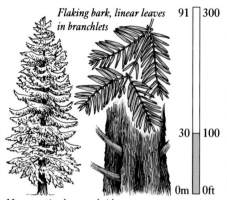

Flaking bark, linear leaves in branchlets

91 | 300

30 | 100

0m | 0ft

Metasequoia glyptostroboides

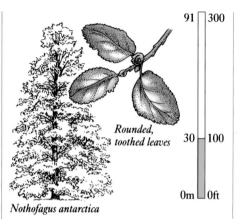

Rounded, toothed leaves

91 | 300

30 | 100

0m | 0ft

Nothofagus antarctica

METASEQUOIA

Meţasequoia

Taxodiaceae

There is only one species in this genus, a most desirable conifer of conical habit with attractive foliage, particularly in the spring and autumn. It makes a superb lawn specimen and looks especially good near water. Also creates an attractive screen. Can be grown as a hedge.

● *M. glyptostroboides* (Dawn redwood) China ⑤ ♌

Height at least 30m (100ft). Leaves linear, carried in two rows on short branchlets (appearing like pinnate leaves), pale fresh green in spring, turning gold or brown in autumn. Bark flaking, reddish brown.

Cultivation

 ☼ ☻ ☉ A AL

Is best grown in fertile, moisture-retentive soil. No regular pruning needed but make sure a strong leading shoot is maintained and retain all lower branches.

Problems
Honey fungus.

NOTHOFAGUS

Nothofagus

Fagaceae

Nothofagus are native to Australia, New Zealand, Tasmania and South America and are related to the true beeches or fagus, although they have smaller leaves. These trees make fine specimens on large estates and in parks, although they are not suitable for very cold regions. The hardiest are the South American species. In the southern hemisphere nothofagus are important timber trees.

● *N. antarctica* (Antarctic beech) Chile, Argentina ⑧ ♌

Height 30m (100ft). Leaves deep green, shiny, rounded, toothed, becoming yellow in autumn.

● *N. obliqua* (Roble beech) Chile, Argentina ⑧ ♀

Height 30m (100ft). The ovate-toothed leaves are larger than most other species, up to 8cm (3in) in length. One of the hardiest species.

● *N. procera* Chile, Argentina ⑧ ♀

Height at least 24m (80ft). Oblong leaves up to 10cm (4in) long, far larger than most, with very conspicuous veins. The leaves generally colour well in autumn.

Cultivation

☼ ☻ ☉ A AL ▥

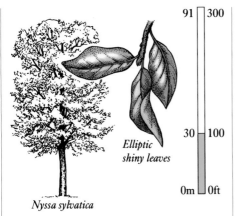

91 | 300

30 | 100

0m | 0ft

*Elliptic
shiny leaves*

Nyssa sylvatica

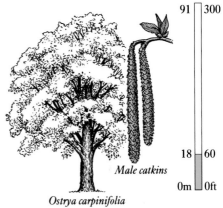

91 | 300

18 | 60

0m | 0ft

Male catkins

Ostrya carpinifolia

NYSSA

Tupelo

Nyssaceae

From North America and south-east Asia, these trees are among the best for autumn leaf colour. They are superb as lawn specimens, particularly near water, or with a background of dark conifers. They are also valued for their quality timber.

● *N. sylvatica* (Tupelo, Black tupelo)
North America ⑥ 🛇
Height up to 30m (100ft). Leaves elliptic, deep green, shiny, turning red, scarlet or orange in autumn. Flowers insignificant.

Cultivation

☼ ☕ A ▦

Soil should be moisture-retentive and reasonably fertile. A deep loamy type will ensure strong growth with a good leading shoot. Intolerant of root disturbance so plant small container-grown specimens. No regular pruning needed and no particular problems. As the tree ages the branches become semi-pendulous and this habit can be aided by removing a few lower branches.

OSTRYA

Ostrya

Betulaceae

A small genus from the northern hemisphere, in the same family as hornbeams (carpinus) and resembling them in foliage. They produce clusters of hop-like fruits. Easily grown in any good soil, they make pleasing lawn specimens.

● *O. carpinifolia* (Hop hornbeam)
southern Europe, Asia Minor ⑧ 🛇
Height up to 18m (60ft). A very shapely tree, lightly and evenly branched. Leaves oval, up to 10cm (4in) in length, with toothed edges, turning yellow in autumn. Male flowers, in the form of catkins, are produced in the spring. The bark is grey.

Cultivation

☼ A AL ▦

No regular pruning needed and no particular problems. Make sure there is plenty of light and air around the tree as branches will be lost if any part is shaded by other trees.

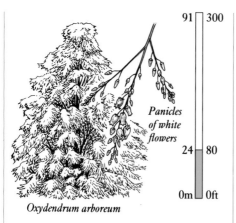

91 | 300

Panicles of white flowers

24 | 80

0m | 0ft

Oxydendrum arboreum

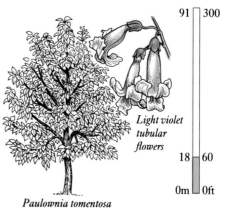

91 | 300

Light violet tubular flowers

18 | 60

0m | 0ft

Paulownia tomentosa

OXYDENDRUM

Oxydendrum

Ericaceae

*T*here is only one species in this genus, a native of the eastern USA, which is grown for magnificent autumn foliage colour. It is quite a slow grower, although very hardy, and eventually makes a fine specimen tree. The flowers are attractive to bees and in the USA the tree is classed as a honey plant.

● *O. arboreum* (*Andromeda arborea*) (Sourwood, Sorrel tree) eastern North America ⑤ ♀
Height up to 24m (80ft), although it can be less under cultivation. Leaves simple, oblong-lanceolate, turning scarlet in autumn. Flowers white, in pendulous panicles, late summer and autumn.

Cultivation

No particular pruning requirements or problems. When young plants are being trained, aim for branching to ground level.

PAULOWNIA

Paulownia, Foxglove tree

Bignoniaceae (*Scrophulariaceae*)

*N*atives of China, these trees make magnificent lawn specimens with their wide-spreading habit, large leaves and upright panicles of tubular flowers in the spring.

● *P. tomentosa* (Royal paulownia)
China ⑦ ♀
Height up to 18m (60ft). Leaves are broadly oval, 30cm (1ft) or more in length, three-lobed, with downy undersides. Flower panicles about 30cm (1ft) long, consisting of fragrant, light violet tubular flowers, spotted within, late spring. Only produced by plants that are very well established. An important timber tree in China.

Cultivation

☼ ⊙ A AL ✍

Relish deep fertile soils. No regular pruning required.

Problems
Honey fungus. In some areas flower buds may be killed by spring frosts.

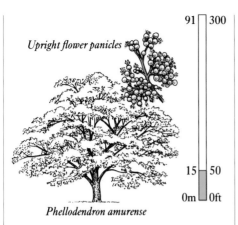

91 ⌐ 300

15 ⊢ 50

0m ⌐ 0ft

Upright flower panicles

Phellodendron amurense

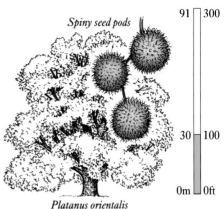

91 ⌐ 300

Spiny seed pods

30 ⊢ 100

0m ⌐ 0ft

Platanus orientalis

PHELLODENDRON

Cork tree

Rutaceae

*F*ast-growing trees with attractive pinnate foliage, native to eastern Asia. Making handsome specimens in lawns or other parts of the garden, they are extremely hardy and easily grown. Cork trees deserve to be more widely planted in gardens.

● *P. amurense* (Amur cork tree)
China, Japan ④ ♀
Height 15m (50ft), with a stiff, sparsely branched habit of growth. Leaves pinnate, consisting of 5–13 bright green shiny leaflets, which turn to yellow in the autumn. The flowers are yellowish green, carried in upright panicles during summer. The bark of older trees becomes corky and is attractive.

Cultivation

☼ ⊙ A AL 🔲

Best growth is obtained in a deep, fertile, loamy soil. In poor soils trees are unlikely to gain their ultimate height.

Problems
In some areas young growths may be damaged by late spring frosts, so if necessary choose a location where the tree is protected from frosts.

PLATANUS

Plane, Buttonwood, Sycamore

Platanaceae

*P*latanus are large trees, natives of the Far East, North America and Mexico. They are widely used as specimen trees in parks and large estates, as avenues and as street trees in towns and cities. The planes are magnificent trees with flaking bark and often lobed, maple-like leaves.

● *P.* × *acerifolia* (*P. orientalis* × *P. occidentalis*)
(London plane) Britain ⑤ ♀
Height up to 36m (120ft). Leaves three to five lobed. The rather inconspicuous pale green flowers are followed by spherical, prickly, pen-

P. × *acerifolia*

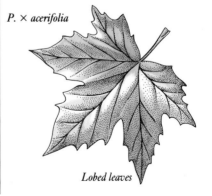

Lobed leaves

171

dulous seed pods. Flaking bark creates a patch-work effect and is a notable feature of this hybrid. Widely planted in London and tolerant of atmospheric pollution.

• *P. occidentalis* (Buttonwood, American sycamore) North America ④ ♀
Height 45m (150ft). Leaves are shallowly three to five lobed. Spherical seed pods are carried singly or in pairs. Not widely grown in Europe. A timber tree in the USA.

P. orientalis

Lobed leaves with toothed edges

• *P. orientalis* (Oriental plane) south-east Europe, Asia Minor ⑥ ♀
Height 30m (100ft). Branches carried in a massive rounded head. Leaves have five or seven lobes with toothed edges, and are deep green and shiny. Spherical spiny seed pods are carried in clusters.

Cultivation

☼ A AL ▣

No regular pruning needed, but they are tolerant of lopping to reduce height and spread, although this spoils their natural habit. It is often carried out on town and city trees. No particular problems.

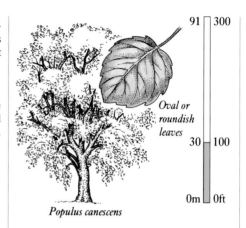

Oval or roundish leaves

Populus canescens

POPULUS
Poplar, Aspen
Salicaceae

*T*his genus contains mainly large trees which are widely scattered throughout the northern hemisphere. Fast growing and of easy culture, most are attractive enough to be planted as specimen trees in parks and other expansive areas. They also make superb and stately avenues, where space permits. As they are extremely hardy and wind-resistant, poplars make excellent windbreaks and are useful for creating screens. They tolerate a polluted atmosphere, wet soils and harsh coastal conditions. They must, however, be planted with caution, for their far-spreading roots can damage drains and other underground services, foundations of buildings, and roads and footpaths. So plant them well away from services and buildings, at least 30m (100ft).

Poplars have catkin-like flowers and the sexes are on separate trees.

• *P. alba* (White poplar, Silver-leaved poplar) Europe, Asia ④ ♀
Height 27m (90ft). Leaves oval, lobed, with white or grey woolly undersides, turning yellow in autumn. Tolerates extreme exposure (drought, salt spray, and so on). Cultivars include the columnar 'Pyramidalis', and

'Richardii', a medium-sized tree whose leaves are yellow on the upper surface.

● *P. balsamifera* (Balsam poplar) North America ②♀
Height up to 30m (100ft). Leaves oval, with a balsam fragrance when young, from conspicuous sticky winter buds. An important timber tree.

● *P.* × *berolinensis* (*P. laurifolia* × *P. nigra* 'Italica') (Berlin poplar) ②♀
Height 18–24m (60–80ft). Leaves oval, bright green, from sticky buds. Shoots downy. A useful specimen tree on account of its broad columnar habit.

● *P.* × *canadensis* (*P. deltoides* × *P. nigra*) (Carolina poplar) ④♀
Height variable but can exceed 18m (60ft). The tree is of vigorous habit. Leaves somewhat triangular. Generally cultivars are grown and these include 'Eugenei', which has a very narrow habit, the leaves being flushed with copper when they unfurl in spring; and 'Serotina', which is a large vigorous spreading tree, whose foliage is reddish copper when it first appears. The catkins are quite conspicuous with their red anthers. 'Serotina Aurea' is the golden poplar, with deep yellow foliage that turns green-yellow as summer progresses and finally deep yellow again in the autumn. This makes a striking specimen tree.

● *P. canescens* (Grey poplar) Europe, western Asia ④♀
Height up to 30m (100ft). Leaves oval or roundish, with woolly grey undersides. Similar to *P. alba* but has smaller leaves. The bark is yellowish grey. The cultivar 'Macrophylla' has larger leaves, up to 15cm (6in) in length, and is very vigorous.

● *P. lasiocarpa* China ⑥♀
Height up to 18m (60ft). A most attractive species which bears fat shoots and extra-large leaves which are oval, pale green with downy undersides and can be up to 30cm (12in) in length. The central vein of each leaf is red. This is one of the largest-leaved of the poplars. Although generally hardy it is best when grown in a sheltered position.

● *P. nigra* (Black poplar) Europe, Asia ②♀
Height up to 27m (90ft). Leaves triangular in shape, with pale green undersides. The cultivar 'Italica' (Lombardy poplar) is one of the most widely planted poplars for ornamental purposes because of its fastigiate habit. It makes an imposing specimen in a large garden but is also sometimes planted as a windbreak. The variety *betulifolia* (Manchester poplar) has a spreading habit and is especially recommended for planting in areas where atmospheric pollution is a problem.

● *P. tremula* (Aspen) Europe, north Africa, Asia ②♀
Height up to 27m (90ft). Leaves circular to elliptic with conspicuously toothed edges, trembling in the slightest breeze and turning yellow in autumn. The grey catkins are conspicuous in the spring.

● *P. trichocarpa* (Black cottonwood, Western balsam poplar) North America ⑤♀
Height 55m (180ft) or more. This is the tallest species of poplar and is very fast-growing. Leaves are broadly oval, deep green above and white or rust-coloured below, from sticky winter buds, with a pleasant balsamic fragrance in spring, turning pure yellow in autumn. Peeling bark.

Cultivation

☼ A AL

Especially suitable for wet and heavy soils but will grow anywhere and tolerate almost any climatic conditions. Newly planted trees should be well staked until they are established, especially if planting in a position exposed to winds. No regular pruning required. If pruning is carried out it should be completed by late winter to prevent the risk of "bleeding". Pruning can result in the excessive production of shoots on the main branches and trunk and these have to be pruned out on an annual basis.

Problems

Aphids, caterpillars, bacterial canker, honey fungus, leaf spot, rust, silver leaf.

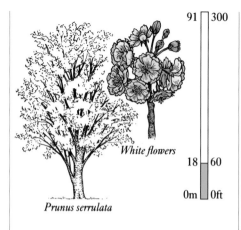

White flowers

91 | 300

18 | 60

0m | 0ft

Prunus serrulata

PRUNUS

Cherry, Plum, Peach, Apricot, Almond

Rosaceae

*F*or additional details, see entry under Small Ornamental Deciduous.

● *P. avium* (Gean, Mazzard, Wild cherry) Europe, western Asia ④ ♀
Height 18m (60ft) or more. Leaves oval. Flowers white, carried in umbels during mid to late spring. Round black-red sweet fruits. Bark reddish brown, peeling. A hardy species. The cultivar 'Plena' has double white flowers in profusion. It is not well known in America but is popular in Europe.

● *P. padus* (Bird cherry) Europe, northern Asia to Japan ④ ♀
Height 15m (50ft). Leaves oval, dull deep green. Flowers fragrant, white, carried in drooping racemes up to 15cm (6in) in length during late spring. Bitter black fruits. A popular cultivar is 'Watereri' with racemes up to 20cm (8in) in length.

● *P. sargentii* (Sargent cherry, North Japanese hill cherry) northern Japan, Korea, Sakhalin ⑤ ♀
Height 15m (50ft). Leaves elliptic, reddish bronze when they first unfurl, turning to flame shades in autumn. One of the best prunus for autumn leaf colour. The single rose-pink

flowers appear in early to mid-spring. Oval crimson fruits follow in autumn.

● *P. serrulata* (Japanese flowering cherry, Oriental cherry) China, Japan ⑥ ♀
Height up to 18m (60ft). Leaves oval and shiny green. Flowers white, produced before or with the leaves, followed by small black fruits. The variety *spontanea* is one of the parents of the Japanese ornamental cherries, such as 'Kanzan', with double purple-pink flowers, and 'Tai Haku' (great white cherry), with large brilliant white blossoms. They should be planted with care, since although these cherries are spectacular for a few weeks when in flower, they do little to enhance the garden for the rest of the year. Nevertheless, they are extremely popular with amateur gardeners and are widely planted, especially as lawn specimens.

● *P. yedoensis* (Yoshino cherry) Japan ⑥ ♀
Height up to 18m (60ft). A fast grower. Leaves broadly oval, deep green. The many racemes of slightly scented flowers open pink and turn white, being produced in mid-spring, generally before the leaves appear. They are followed by small, round, black, bitter fruits. A very desirable early-flowering cherry that is highly recommended.

Cultivation

☼ ◗ A AL ▦

These shallow-rooting trees dislike deep cultivation around them. Keep the soil mulched with organic matter. Avoid soils that are very dry or prone to waterlogging. No regular pruning required. If pruning is carried out it should be done in the summer, but before mid-summer, to prevent silver leaf from infecting the pruning cuts.

Problems

Aphids, caterpillars, birds (damage buds), bacterial canker, honey fungus, peach leaf curl, silver leaf.

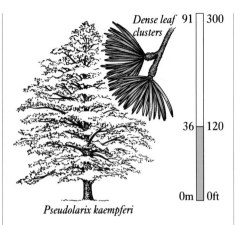

Dense leaf clusters 91 | 300

36 | 120

0m | 0ft

Pseudolarix kaempferi

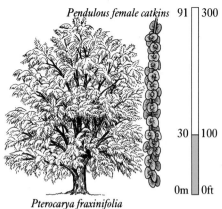

Pendulous female catkins 91 | 300

30 | 100

0m | 0ft

Pterocarya fraxinifolia

PSEUDOLARIX

Golden larch

Pinaceae

There is only one species in this genus, which is related to *Larix* or larch. It is a beautiful tree from spring to autumn and is recommended as a specimen in lawns provided the soil is acid. It is slow-growing and very hardy. When well grown the lower branches sweep down to the ground, carrying an abundance of attractive cones.

● *P. kaempferi* (*P. amabilis*) (Golden larch)
China ⑥ ↧
Height 36m (120ft). Carries horizontal, flattened branches. Leaves arranged in spirals, in dense clusters on short shoots, up to 5cm (2in) long, bright green above, grey-banded below, turning deep golden-yellow in the autumn before they fall. The egg-shaped cones up to 8cm (3in) long are light green and turn red-brown when ripe.

Cultivation

 ☼ A ▩

Needs an open position – not hemmed in by other plants – to develop to its full potential. Provide good growing conditions, especially a fertile soil and adequate moisture. No particular problems.

PTEROCARYA

Wingnut

Juglandaceae

The wingnuts, from Asia, mainly China, are large, handsome trees with pinnate foliage and catkin-like flowers followed by conspicuous winged seed pods. These trees are essentially for specimen planting in large gardens, parks and estates and they look particularly attractive near lakes.

● *P. fraxinifolia* (Caucasian wingnut)
Caucasus, Iran ⑥ ♀
Height up to 30m (100ft). Very wide-spreading and with branches low down the trunk. Leaves pinnate, up to 45cm (18in) in length, with 11–27 leaflets. Female catkins green, pendulous and up to 50cm (20in) long.

Cultivation

☼ ☉ A AL ■ ▩

Although the wingnuts are hardy, young trees (especially the shoots) can be damaged during severe winters and should be well protected. Growing the trees in full sun will ensure well-ripened, harder shoots which should overwinter better. Grow them in fertile, moisture-retentive loam. No regular pruning needed and no particular problems.

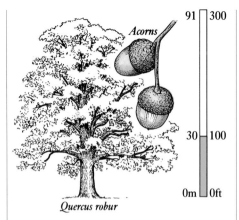

Acorns

91 300

30 100

0m 0ft

Quercus robur

QUERCUS

Oak

Fagaceae

This is a large genus of deciduous and evergreen trees native to the northern hemisphere, being found in cool and warm temperate areas and also in high-altitude, sub-tropical and tropical areas of Asia and South America. The leaves are often lobed and in some deciduous species they take on brilliant tints in the autumn before they fall. The oval nuts are contained in a "cup" and are popularly known as acorns. The oaks have various uses. Many species make magnificent specimen trees. They are also grown as woodland and as avenues. Some species are used in forestry to produce high-quality timber.

• *Q. alba* (White oak) North America ④ ♀
Height up to 30m (100ft). Leaves have five or nine lobes and turn purplish-red in the autumn. An important timber tree in the USA but also a very handsome species for ornamental planting. Not widely planted in Britain. Resembles the English oak in general outline. Grow in acid soil.

• *Q. cerris* (Turkey oak) southern Europe, western Asia ⑦ ♀
Height up to 30m (100ft). A vigorous, fast-growing tree. Leaves with three to eight pairs of lobes, deep green with greyish undersides.

Especially recommended for alkaline soils and coastal planting. Grown for ornamental purposes, its timber is of little value. The cultivar 'Laciniata' has deeply cut leaves and 'Pendula' has weeping branches.

• *Q. coccinea* (Scarlet oak)
North America ④ ♀
Height up to 24m (80ft). Leaves very deeply lobed, bright green and shiny, turning bright red in the autumn. One of the best oaks for autumn leaf colour and widely planted for this purpose. Grow in acid soil. There are several cultivars with especially good autumn leaf colour.

• *Q. frainetto* (Hungarian oak, Italian oak)
southern Europe ⑥ ♀
Height up to 36m (120ft). Growth rapid. Leaves deeply lobed, dark green on the upper surface, with paler and woolly undersides. Suitable for acid or alkaline soils. Makes an excellent specimen tree.

• *Q. palustris* (Pin oak, Spanish oak)
North America ⑤ ♀
Height at least 24m (80ft). The branches have pendulous tips. Leaves with five to seven lobes, vivid shiny green, invariably turning deep red in autumn before they fall. Not considered one of the best oaks for autumn leaf colour. In the USA it is planted as a street tree. This species is grown commercially for timber.

• *Q. petraea* (Durmast oak, Sessile oak)
Europe, western Asia ⑤ ♀
Height 18–30m (60–100ft). Very like *Q. robur* (see below) except that its leaves have longer stalks and the acorns are stalkless. Thrives in moist soils.

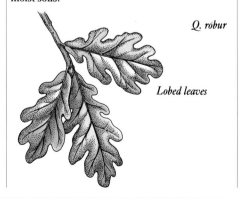

Q. robur

Lobed leaves

● *Q. robur* (*Q. pedunculata*) (English oak)
Europe, North America, Asia Minor ⑤ ♀
Height 18–30m (60–100ft). Slow growing.
Leaves short-stalked, with three to seven pairs
of lobes. Acorns carried on thin stalks. Cultivars
include 'Fastigiata' (Cypress oak), which has a
columnar habit of growth and is an excellent
specimen tree; and 'Variegata', whose leaves are
edged with white.

● *Q. rubra* (*Q. borealis*) (Northern red oak,
Red oak) eastern North America ⑤ ♀
Height up to 24m (80ft). Leaves with 7–11 deep
lobes, dull green, turning reddish brown in the
autumn before they fall. An important timber
tree in the USA. Grow in acid soil.

Cultivation

☼ ◐ **A AL** ▦

Best growth is achieved in full sun with a fertile,
deep, loamy soil. Young trees appreciate a
mulch of organic matter. No regular pruning
needed.

Problems
Caterpillars, honey fungus, powdery mildew.

CLIMATIC ZONES

① Below −45°C (−50°F)

② −45 to −39°C (−50 to −40°F)

③ −39 to −35°C (−40 to −30°F)

④ −35 to −29°C (−30 to −20°F)

⑤ −29 to −23°C (−20 to −10°F)

⑥ −23 to −18°C (−10 to 0°F)

⑦ −18 to −12°C (0 to 10°F)

⑧ −12 to −6°C (10 to 20°F)

⑨ −6 to −1°C (20 to 30°F)

⑩ −1 to 4°C (30 to 40°F)

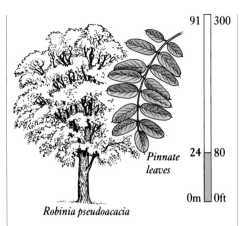

91 ⎸ 300

Pinnate leaves 24 ⎸ 80

0m ⎿ 0ft

Robinia pseudoacacia

ROBINIA

False acacia, Locust

Leguminosae

Natives of North America, the fast-growing
robinias have attractive pinnate leaves and
pendulous racemes of pea-type flowers in white,
pink or purple, followed by flat pods. The stems
are brittle, prone to damage in high winds, and
may be spiny. Very attractive when planted as
lawn specimens.

● *R. pseudoacacia* (False acacia, Black locust,
Yellow locust) eastern and central
North America ③ ♀
Height up to 24m (80ft). Spiny branches.
Leaves pinnate, with nine pairs of pale green
leaflets. Flowers white, scented, early summer,
attractive to bees. The tree has a suckering habit
and furrowed bark. The cultivar 'Pyramidalis' is
spineless and of columnar habit.

Cultivation

☼ ☉ **A AL** ▦

Particularly suitable for poor dry soils. This
species tolerates a polluted atmosphere.

Problems
Scale insects.

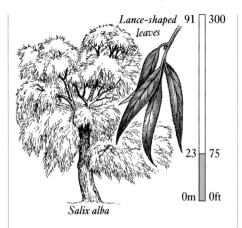

Lance-shaped leaves 91 300

23 75

0m 0ft

Salix alba

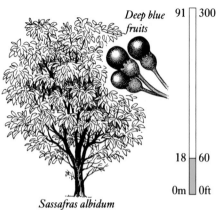

Deep blue fruits 91 300

18 60

0m 0ft

Sassafras albidum

SALIX

Willow, Osier

Salicaceae

*F*or additional details, see entry under Small Ornamental Deciduous.

• *S. alba* (White willow)
Europe, North Africa, Asia ② ♀
Height up to 23m (75ft). Leaves lance-shaped, up to 10cm (4in) in length, covered with silky white hairs on the undersides. Catkins produced at the same time as the leaves. The white willow is versatile and can be used as a specimen or windbreak in wet soils and in exposed coastal areas. Several handsome cultivars.

• *S. matsudana* (Pekin willow)
China, Korea ⑤ ♀
Height up to 18m (60ft). Leaves up to 10cm (4in) in length, lance-shaped, grey-green. Young shoots are yellow. Grows particularly well in dry soils. The cultivar 'Tortuosa' has branches and shoots twisted like corkscrews.

Cultivation

 A AL

Best grown in moist soil (but see above, *S. matsudana*). No regular pruning needed.

Problems
Aphids, caterpillars, willow anthracnose, canker, honey fungus.

SASSAFRAS

Sassafras

Lauraceae

A small genus of ornamental trees from Asia and North America, pleasantly aromatic in all their parts. The species described here is grown for its autumn leaf colour. As it needs sheltered conditions it is best planted in a woodland garden.

• *S. albidum* North America ⑥ ♀
Height 18m (60ft) or more. Leaves oval, sometimes lobed, turning red and orange in autumn. Clusters of green-yellow flowers produced in spring with the leaves, but not showy. Deep blue fruits. Attractive furrowed bark. Oil of sassafras (used for flavouring) obtained from the bark.

Cultivation

☼ ⊙ A ▨

Grow in a fertile loamy soil if possible. No regular pruning needed and no particular problems. The tree is inclined to produce suckers in lawns and beds. These can be removed for propagation, though some gardeners leave them in beds to form colonies.

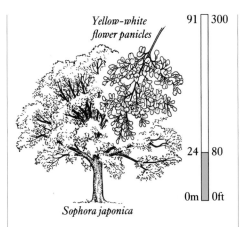

Yellow-white
flower panicles

91 300

24 80

0m 0ft

Sophora japonica

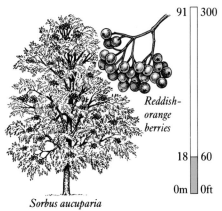

91 300

Reddish-
orange
berries

18 60

0m 0ft

Sorbus aucuparia

SOPHORA

Sophora

Leguminosae

For additional details, see entry under Small Ornamental Deciduous.

● *S. japonica* (Japanese pagoda tree, Chinese scholar tree) China, Korea ⑤ ♀
Height up to 24m (80ft). Leaves pinnate, 30cm (1ft) in length, with up to eight pairs of leaflets, grey-green undersides. Flowers like those of peas, yellow-white, carried in panicles up to 38cm (15in) in length during late summer and autumn, but only on mature trees. These are followed by bean-like seed pods up to 8cm (3in) in length. Plenty of sun is required for trees to set seeds. The bark is corrugated.

Cultivation

No regular pruning required and no particular problems. In time the tree can develop very large heavy lower branches which may eventually break off in high winds. If pruning is needed carry this out in late summer to reduce bleeding.

SORBUS

Mountain ash, Rowan, Whitebeam, Service tree

Rosaceae

For additional details, see entry under Small Ornamental Deciduous.

● *S. aria* (Whitebeam) Europe ⑥ ♀
Height 15m (50ft). Leaves elliptic, about 12.5cm (5in) in length, with toothed edges, grey above but eventually turning green, with white woolly undersides, becoming gold and brown in autumn before they fall. Cream flowers, in flat panicles, occur in late spring and early summer. Large clusters of dark red berries are produced in autumn. Very tolerant of exposed coastal conditions and atmospheric pollution. An extremely ornamental tree, making an attractive specimen, *S. aria* is also good for forming both tall screens and windbreaks. Cultivars include 'Decaisneana' ('Majestica'), which has larger leaves and berries.

● *S. aucuparia* (Mountain ash, Rowan, European mountain ash) Europe, Asia Minor ② ♀
Height up to 18m (60ft). Leaves pinnate, up to 25cm (10in) in length, with 13–15 leaflets, grey undersides, turning to shades of gold and orange in autumn. Flowers white, in flat panicles, produced during late spring and early summer. Large bunches of reddish-orange ber-

ries produced in late summer and autumn, these often being quickly devoured by birds in some areas. Not recommended for shallow chalky soils as the tree is then short-lived, but ideal for very acid conditions. There are several cultivars, most of which are small trees, but 'Edulis' is of medium size and has larger leaves and large bunches of edible berries which can be used for preserves.

• *S. cuspidata* (Himalayan whitebeam) Himalayas ⑦ ♀
Height up to 18m (60ft). The shoots are purplish-brown and carry simple, elliptic, grey-green leaves up to 15cm (6in) in length, with toothed edges, white-felted undersides and of leathery texture. White flowers in 10cm (4in) wide clusters, late spring, followed by comparatively large orange-red berries.

• *S. domestica* (Service tree) Europe ⑥ ♀
Height up to 24m (80ft). Leaves pinnate, up to 22cm (9in) in length, with 13–21 leaflets, from shiny and sticky winter buds. Flowers white, in panicles, late spring and early summer. These are followed by green, red-flushed, pear-shaped or apple-shaped, edible fruits about 2.5cm (1in) long but not particularly palatable.

• *S. torminalis* (Wild service tree) Europe ⑥ ♀
Height up to 24m (80ft). Leaves up to 12.5cm (5in) in length, oval, deeply lobed, deep green and shiny, turning brown-yellow in autumn. Clusters of white flowers in early summer. Brown-speckled berries appear in autumn. Bark scaly. A very attractive tree in the lawn or on the edge of a woodland garden.

Cultivation

Very tolerant of atmospheric pollution and coastal or exposed areas. No regular pruning required.

Problems
Apple canker, fireblight, honey fungus, silver leaf.

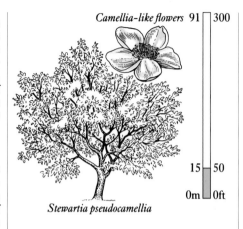

Camellia-like flowers

Stewartia pseudocamellia

STEWARTIA

Stewartia

Theaceae

Natives of eastern Asia and eastern North America, the stewartias are highly ornamental trees with attractive flowers, good leaf colour in the autumn and handsome flaking bark. Although they are rather slow-growing, they are excellent for including in an ornamental woodland garden.

• *S. pseudocamellia* Japan ⑧ ♀
Height 15m (50ft). Leaves elliptic, with pointed tips, becoming red or purple in the autumn before they fall. The white flowers, about 6cm (2½in) across, have wide-spreading petals and look like single camellias; each has a central cluster of conspicuous orange-yellow anthers; mid- to late summer.

Cultivation

Best results in a moisture-retentive soil well enriched with peat or leafmould.

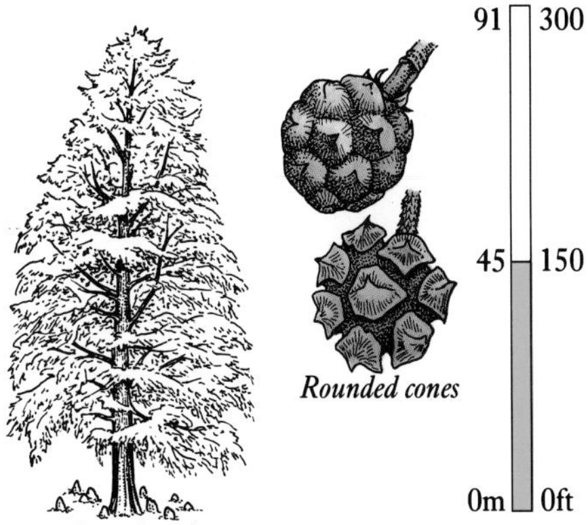
91
300
45
150
Rounded cones
0m
0ft
Taxodium dictichum

TAXODIUM

Taxodium

Taxodiaceae

Coniferous trees inhabiting the edges of rivers and lakes in North America and Mexico. They make excellent specimens near water in gardens and have distinctive ferny foliage and attractive bark.

• *T. dictichum* (Swamp cypress, Bald cypress) North America ⑤ △
Height up to 45m (150ft) in the wild but may be less under cultivation. Leaves linear, two-ranked, bright green, turning red-brown in autumn before they fall. Bark red-brown, fibrous. Trunk buttressed. In wet places growths popularly known as "knees" rise from the roots above water level for breathing purposes. The cultivar 'Pendens' has pendulous branchlets.

Cultivation

☼ ◒ ⊙ A AL

Grow in permanently moist or wet soil. No regular pruning required, but reduce double leading shoots to one. No particular problems.

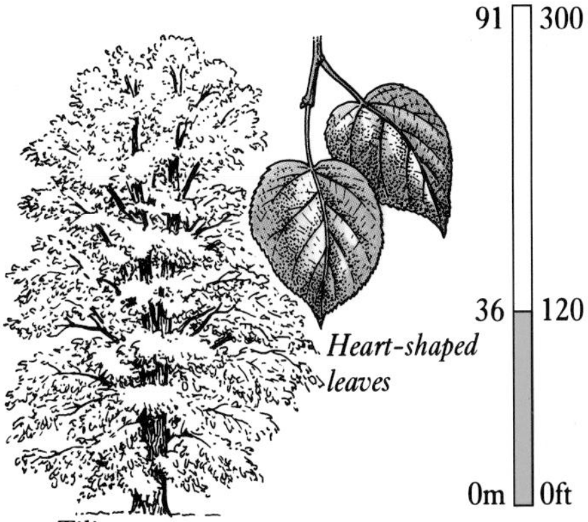
91
300
36
120
Heart-shaped leaves
0m
0ft
Tilia × europaea

TILIA

Lime, Linden, Basswood

Tiliaceae

Tilias are mainly medium-size to large trees from temperate parts of the northern hemisphere and make fine specimens or avenues in large gardens, parks and estates. Some species can also be used as windbreaks and they tolerate atmospheric pollution. The leaves are somewhat heart-shaped. Green-yellow or white fragrant flowers, rich in nectar and much loved by bees, are produced in mid-summer.

• *T. americana* (American lime, American basswood) North America ③ ♀
Height up to 39m (130ft). Leaves large, up to 30cm (1ft) in length, with coarsely toothed edges, deep green with paler undersides. The flowers attract bees. The bark is deeply grooved.

• *T. cordata* (Small-leaved lime) Europe ④ ♀
Height 30m (100ft). Leaves almost circular, thick textured, deep green above with paler undersides. The cream flowers are highly fragrant. This species is often planted as a street tree. Good as a windbreak.

• *T.* × *euchlora* Uncertain origin ⑥ ♀
Height 20m (65ft). Leaves are broadly oval, deep green and glossy. Widely used for street planting, having mainly replaced *T.* × *europaea*

for the purpose as it is less prone to attacks by aphids, which secrete an unpleasant sticky honeydew.

• *T. × europaea* (*T. × vulgaris*) (*T. cordata × T. platyphyllos*) (Common lime) Origin uncertain ④ ♀
Height up to 36m (120ft). A vigorous grower. Leaves heart-shaped with pointed tips, medium green. This species is very prone to attacks from aphids, which secrete an unpleasant sticky honeydew, and so is not as widely planted as in the past. Also produces suckers. The cultivar 'Pallida' has more upright branches which give the tree a conical shape; particularly suitable for exposed windy positions.

• *T. petiolaris* (Pendent silver lime) Origin doubtful, probably south-east Europe ⑥ ♧
Height 23m (75ft). Leaves medium green, downy on the upper surface, white downy below. The leaf stalks (petioles) are more than half as long as the leaf blade. The branches weep, creating a very wide dome-shaped tree, superb as a specimen in large lawns. The white flowers are highly fragrant and much loved by bees.

• *T. platyphyllos* (Broad-leaved or Large-leaved lime, Linden) Europe ④ ♀
Height up to 39m (130ft). Of vigorous habit. Leaves rounded, heart-shaped, about 12.5cm (5in) in length, light to medium green, rather downy. Unlike some other species it produces few suckers. Cultivars include 'Aurea', twigs yellow; 'Fastigiata', conical habit; and 'Rubra' (Red-twigged lime), of broad columnar habit, twigs red.

Cultivation

☼ ☽ A AL ▣

Easy-going, but thrive in moisture-retentive soil. No regular pruning needed, except to remove suckers if necessary.

Problems

Aphids, caterpillars, gall mites, cankers, honey fungus, leaf spots.

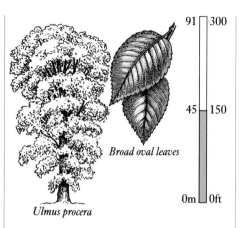

91 ⌐ 300

45 ⌐ 150

Broad oval leaves

0m ⌐ 0ft

Ulmus procera

ULMUS

Elm

Ulmaceae

*T*he elms are native to Europe, Asia and North America. They are shapely, stately trees used for specimen planting or as avenues in parks, estates and large gardens. They have simple toothed leaves and the flowers are inconspicuous. The green fruits are winged and are more conspicuous. Dutch elm disease has devastated elms in parts of Europe and America. The English elm, once a feature of the English landscape, has been wiped out in Britain. *U. americana* is also very prone to the disease. It is therefore not advisable to plant elms where the disease is a problem.

• *U. americana* (American, White or Water elm) North America ② ♀
Height up to 36m (120ft). Forms a wide, rather open crown. Leaves up to 15cm (6in) in length, oval, with double-toothed edges, rough texture in the upper surface. One of the finest elms for planting in the USA but generally does not perform well in Europe.

• *U. carpinifolia* (Smooth-leaved elm) Europe, western Asia ⑤ ♦
Height 30m (100ft). The outermost branches are somewhat drooping. Leaves oval, medium green, shiny, smooth, turning yellow in autumn.

Cultivars include 'Cornubiensis' (*U. stricta*) (Cornish elm), of conical habit with shiny, smooth, deep green leaves. The variety *sarniensis* (*U. sarniensis, U. wheatleyi*) (Wheatley elm, Jersey elm) has very upright branches, and the elliptic leaves are deep green, smooth and shiny.

• *U. glabra* (Wych elm, Scotch elm)
northern Europe ⑤ ♀
Height up to 38m (125ft). The branches form a distinctive egg-shaped head. Makes a good specimen tree. Leaves oval, with toothed edges, medium green, becoming yellow in the autumn before they fall. A non-suckering species. Cultivars include 'Camperdownii' (Camperdown elm), with a dome-shaped crown; 'Exoniensis', with a columnar habit of growth; and 'Pendula', of weeping habit. All these cultivars make superb lawn specimens.

• *U.* × *hollandica* (*U. carpinifolia* × *U.glabra* × *U. plotii*) (Dutch elm) western Europe ⑤ ♀
Height up to 36m (120ft). Large spreading crown, the branches having drooping tips. Suckering habit. Leaves obovate, deep green, glossy, smooth. The cultivar 'Vegeta' (Huntington elm) is similar to the species.

• *U. procera* (*U. campestris*) (English elm)
western and southern Europe ⑥ ♀
Height up to 45m (150ft). Produces suckers. Broad oval leaves, medium or dark green, with a rough upper surface, turning gold in autumn. Once very widely planted in Britain, especially as avenues but also as specimen and street trees. Cultivars include 'Louis van Houttei', with yellow foliage, and the white-variegated 'Variegata'.

Cultivation

☀ **A AL** 🖼

No regular pruning required, but remove suckers as necessary; these could be used for propagation.

Problems
Aphids, caterpillars, elm-bark beetle (which spreads Dutch elm disease), Dutch elm disease, honey fungus.

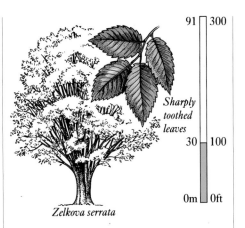

Sharply toothed leaves

91 — 300

30 — 100

0m — 0ft

Zelkova serrata

ZELKOVA

Zelkova

Ulmaceae

Natives of western and eastern Asia, the zelkovas comprise a small genus of elm-like trees which have similar uses to elms in the garden. The elliptical leaves with toothed edges are similar to those of ulmus.

• *Z. carpinifolia* Caucasus ⑤ ♀
Height up to 24m (80ft) but growth is slow. Leaves elliptic, about 5cm (2in) in length, with wavy toothed edges. Bark grey, smooth, but eventually flaking.

• *Z. serrata* (Japanese zelkova) Japan ⑤ ♀
Height up to 30m (100ft). Leaves oval and very sharply toothed, giving it the popular name of saw-leaf zelkova. The foliage turns reddish brown in autumn. Bark grey, smooth, but eventually flaking.

Cultivation

☀ **A AL** 🖼

They thrive in a deep, fertile, loamy soil, but are adaptable to other types.

Problems
Honey fungus.

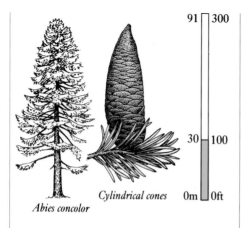

91 | 300

30 | 100

Cylindrical cones 0m | 0ft

Abies concolor

ABIES

Silver fir

Pinaceae

See entry under Small Ornamental Evergreen. Medium and large abies are suitable for specimen or group planting in large gardens, parks and estates.

● *A. cephalonica* (Grecian fir)
Greece ⑥ ⌖
Height up to 27m (90ft). Shoots red-brown and shiny. Leaves 2.5cm (1in) in length, sharply pointed, shiny and deep green on the upper surface, silvery undersides. Cones cylindrical, 15cm (6in) in length, brown. Thrives in alkaline soils.

● *A. concolor* (White fir, Colorado white fir)
North America ④ ⌖
Height up to 30m (100ft). Leaves 5cm (2in) in length, blue-green on the upper surface. Cylindrical cones about 15cm (6in) in length, green or purple. Bark smooth and grey. Timber used commercially. The cultivar 'Violacea' has grey-blue leaves and 'Wattezii' has light yellow foliage which turns silvery-white.

● *A. homolepis* (Nikko fir) Japan ⑤ ⌖
Height up to 30m (100ft). Leaves 2.5cm (1in) in length, the upper surface deep shiny green, banded white on the undersides. Cones cylindrical, 10cm (4in) in length, purple.

● *A. koreana* (Korean fir) Korea ⑤ ⌖
Height 18m (60ft), but a slow grower. Leaves up to 2.5cm (1in) in length, shiny green on the upper surface with white undersides. Cones cylindrical, 8cm (3in) in length, deep blue-purple, produced by young specimens. A pleasing specimen tree, thoroughly recommended.

● *A. nordmanniana* (Caucasian fir)
Caucasus, Greece, Asia Minor ⑤ ⌖
Height up to 45m (150ft). Leaves about 3.8cm (1½in) in length, deep shiny green above with white bands below. Cones cylindrical, 15cm (6in) in length, red-brown.

● *A. pinsapo* (Spanish fir, Hedgehog fir)
Spain ⑦ ⌖
Height up to 23m (75ft). Leaves under 2.5cm (1in) in length, rigid, arranged around the shoots, deep green on the upper surface. Cones cylindrical, over 10cm (4in) in length, purple-brown. The cultivar 'Glauca' has beautiful blue-grey, very glaucous foliage. Excellent for alkaline soils.

● *A. procera* (*A. nobilis*) (Noble fir)
North America ⑥ ⌖
Height at least 45m (150ft). Leaves up to 3.8cm (1½in) in length, blue-green. Cones cylindrical, up to 25cm (10in) in length, purple-brown. Bark silver-grey. The cultivar 'Glauca' has very glaucous leaves. Grow both in acid soils.

Cultivation

☼ ☽ ☉ A AL ▨

It is best to plant small trees, approximately 30cm (1ft) high, with a strong leading shoot, as it can be difficult to establish older ones. New growth may be damaged by frosts late in the spring. The ideal site is shaded from early morning sun to avoid frost damage. Mulch young trees with organic matter. Train a strong leading shoot to a stake, removing competing side shoots or forking shoots if necessary in early to mid-spring.

Problems

Adelgids, die-back (fungal diseases).

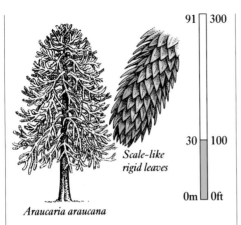

91 ┌ 300

30 ┤ 100

0m └ 0ft

Scale-like rigid leaves

Araucaria araucana

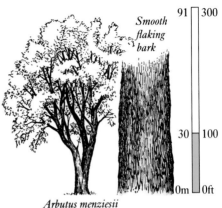

Smooth flaking bark

91 ┌ 300

30 ┤ 100

0m └ 0ft

Arbutus menziesii

ARAUCARIA

Araucaria

Araucariaceae

A genus of tall coniferous trees from the southern hemisphere, few being hardy enough for outdoor cultivation in cool temperate climates. However, the monkey puzzle, described here, is sufficiently hardy. Araucaria provides an exotic effect and should be planted with discretion.

● *A. araucana* (Monkey puzzle, Chilean pine) Chile ⑦ ♀

Height up to 30m (100ft). Habit is variable: in some trees the branches reach the ground, in others branching starts quite high up. Leaves scale-like, rigid, tipped with a sharp spine, overlapping, dark green, carried on long branches. Globe-shaped cones produced at the tops of female trees.

Cultivation

☼ ☽ A AL ▨

Easy-going tree, being wind resistant, but does not tolerate poorly drained soils. Suitable for towns and cities. Plant seedlings no more than 30cm (1ft) in height.

Problems

Honey fungus.

ARBUTUS

Strawberry tree, Madrone

Ericaceae

S ee entry under Small Ornamental Evergreen. The species described here makes a fine specimen tree in lawns or shrub borders.

● *A. menziesii* (Madrona, Pacific madrone) North America ⑦ ♀

Height up to 30m (100ft) in the wild but may be less, perhaps half this, under cultivation. Leaves elliptic, about 15cm (6in) in length, deep green and shiny on the upper surface with grey-green undersides. Flowers carried in upright panicles, urn-shaped, white, late spring. Fruits globular, red or orange. Bark smooth, but flaking off, orange. Does not tolerate cold, drying winds.

Cultivation

☼ ⊙ A ▨

Young plants are tender, needing protection in winter, but become hardier as they age. No regular pruning required.

Problems

Leaf spot.

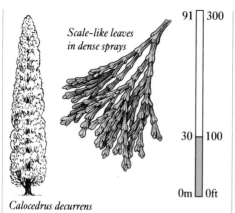

Scale-like leaves in dense sprays

91 | 300

30 | 100

0m | 0ft

Calocedrus decurrens

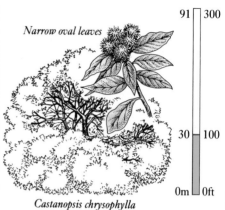

Narrow oval leaves

91 | 300

30 | 100

0m | 0ft

Castanopsis chrysophylla

CALOCEDRUS

Incense cedar

Cupressaceae

A small genus of coniferous trees from western North America and Asia. The species described here, which is the most popular, is a tall, broadly columnar tree that makes a marvellous single specimen, or a group, in a large lawn; excellent for creating a focal point.

• *C. decurrens* (*Libocedrus decurrens*) (California incense cedar) western North America ⑥ ☿
Height up to 30m (100ft). Leaves scale-like and deep green, carried in dense sprays on flattened branchlets. This species has fragrant timber.

Cultivation

Best growth is obtained in a deep fertile soil although the tree is adaptable. No regular pruning needed. No particular problems, although the foliage and branches of older trees subjected to atmospheric pollution may die, creating an unsightly appearance, and will need to be pruned out.

CASTANOPSIS

Chinquapin

Fagaceae

A fairly large genus of trees and shrubs, all evergreen, from western North America and Asia, producing fruits like those of the sweet chestnut or castanea. The species described is one of the hardiest and makes a good lawn specimen in large gardens.

• *C. chrysophylla* (*Chrysolepis chrysophylla*) (Giant castanopsis, Golden chinkapin) western North America ⑧ ♀
Height 30m (100ft) or more in the wild but may be less under cultivation. Leaves oval, narrow, up to 10cm (4in) in length, deep shiny green with golden-yellow scaly undersides. The nuts are enclosed in spiny ball-shaped capsules.

Cultivation

Will not grow on alkaline soils. No regular pruning needed. With a well-grown specimen the canopy may reach down to the ground. Sometimes an odd branch may die back, in which case prune it out. New growth may be produced to fill the gap.

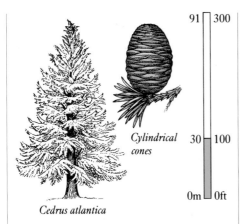

Cylindrical
cones

91 | 300

30 | 100

0m | 0ft

Cedrus atlantica

CEDRUS

Cedar

Pinaceae

*T*his small genus contains some giant trees which make superb lawn specimens in the largest gardens, parks and estates. These wide-spreading coniferous trees, conical when young, are native to mountainous areas of north Africa and Asia. They have rigid needle-like leaves carried in clusters. Mature trees bear cylindrical cones.

● *C. atlantica* (Atlas cedar)
north Africa ⑦ ♠
Height at least 30m (100ft). Leaves under 2.5cm (1in) in length and grey-green. Cones cylindrical and about 8cm (3in) in length. More familiar cultivars include 'Fastigiata', of fastigiate or narrow conical habit, with blue-green foliage; and 'Glauca' (blue Atlas cedar), with grey-blue foliage. Of these, 'Glauca' is the most commonly grown cultivar.

● *C. deodara* (Deodar) Himalayas ⑦ ♠
Height up to 45m (150ft). The branchlets are pendulous, creating a very distinctive habit. A truly superb specimen tree. Leaves about 5cm (2in) in length, deep blue-green. Cones up to 12.5cm (5in) in length. Timber used commercially in India. Cultivars include 'Aurea' (golden deodar), whose new leaves are yellow in spring.

● *C. libani* (Cedar of Lebanon)
Asia Minor ⑥ ♠
Height 30m (100ft). Young trees are conical but gradually the tiers of branches form a flat-topped tree. Leaves about 2.5cm (1in) in length and deep green. Cones about 10cm (4in) in length.

Cultivation

☼ A AL ▦

Specially recommended for coastal gardens. Plant small specimens no more than 45cm (18in) in height. Make sure a single leading shoot is maintained. If a double leader occurs, remove the weakest. Eventually lower branches will start to deteriorate, when they should be cut off flush with the trunk.

Problems
Honey fungus.

KEY TO SYMBOLS

Shape		Aspect		Soils	
♠	Conical	☼	Full sun	A	Acid
♀	Spreading	◓	Partial shade	AL	Alkaline
♭	Broad columnar	●	Shade	A-N	Acid to neutral
◊	Fastigiate	⊙	Sheltered from cold winds	▪	Rich in humus
♈	Weeping			▦	Well drained

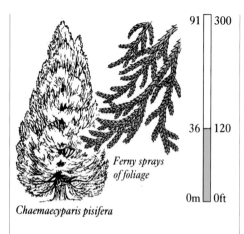

91 / 300

36 / 120

0m / 0ft

Ferny sprays of foliage

Chaemaecyparis pisifera

CHAMAECYPARIS

False cypress, White cedar

Cupressaceae

*F*or additional details, see entry under Small Ornamental Evergreen.

• *C. lawsoniana* (Lawson cypress, Lawson false cypress, Port Orford cedar) North America (6) ◊

Height up to 30m (100ft) but many cultivars shorter. The species is not often grown in gardens. Leaves deep green, greyish beneath, aromatic. Peeling bark. Together with its cultivars this species is suitable for specimen planting, hedges and tall screens. Cultivars that form medium-size trees, growing up to 18m (60ft) in height, include 'Allumii', soft bluish-grey foliage; 'Erecta', narrow columnar habit, bright green foliage; 'Hillieri', bright deep yellow feathery foliage, best grown in partial shade; 'Intertexa', deep glaucous foliage, the branchlets pendulous; 'Lane' ('Lanei'), golden-yellow foliage, very popular; 'Lutea', broad columnar habit, golden yellow feathery foliage; 'Pendula', drooping branches, deep green foliage, pleasing habit; 'Pottenii', broad columnar habit, very dense feathery glaucous foliage, slow grower; 'Stewartii', deep yellow foliage in large flat sprays; 'Westermanii', broad conical habit, pale yellow young foliage, later turning yellow-green;

and 'Wisellii', fast-growing and with glaucous ferny foliage.

• *C. nootkatensis* (Nootka cypress, Alaska cedar, Yellow cypress) North America, Alaska (5) ◊

Height at least 30m (100ft). The branchlets are pendulous. Leaves deep green, carried in long flat sprays which have a rough texture. Flowers yellow. An important timber tree in its natural habitats. Cultivars include 'Glauca', deep grey-green foliage; and 'Pendula', with upward-growing branches and drooping branchlets rather like streamers, making a most attractive specimen tree.

• *C. obtusa* (Hinoki cypress, White cedar) Japan (5) ◊

Height up to 36m (120ft). Leaves bright green, aromatic. Bark reddish-brown. The timber is used commercially in Japan. Makes a pleasing large-lawn specimen with its flattened, rather frond-like pendulous branchlets. It is also an excellent subject for bonsai and ideal for Japanese-style gardens.

• *C. pisifera* (Sawara cypress) Japan (5) ◊

Height up to 36m (120ft). Ferny sprays of bright green aromatic foliage. Attractive brown bark. Try to avoid exposed positions for this species, which makes an attractive lawn specimen or member of a group of conifers.

• *C. thyoides* (Atlantic white cypress, White cypress) North America (5) ◊

Height up to 27m (90ft). Flattened branches. Leaves pale green or pale grey-green. In its natural habitat it grows in acid bogs. Grows only in acid soil. Timber used commercially.

Cultivation

☼ ☻ A AL ▨

Golden cultivars generally need to be grown in full sun for best colour. Prune only to maintain single leading shoot.

Problems

Honey fungus.

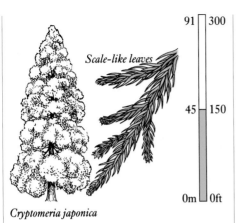

91 ⌐ 300

Scale-like leaves

45 ⊢ 150

0m ⌐ 0ft

Cryptomeria japonica

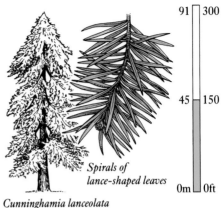

91 ⌐ 300

45 ⊢ 150

*Spirals of
lance-shaped leaves*

0m ⌐ 0ft

Cunninghamia lanceolata

CRYPTOMERIA

Japanese cedar

Taxodiaceae

*T*here is only one species in this genus, a Japanese coniferous tree that makes an imposing specimen in lawns and is good as a focal point in the garden to draw the eye to a particular part.
• *C. japonica* (Japanese cedar)
Japan ⑦ ⚲
Height 45m (150ft). A massive fast-growing forest tree with scale-like dark green leaves. Bark soft and shredding, orange-brown; a distinctive feature.
Cultivation

☼ ⊙ A-N ▦

Plant small specimens as they establish better than larger ones: maximum height 60cm (2ft). Young plants benefit from feeding with a general-purpose fertilizer in late spring. Do not let the soil dry out as this can be fatal for young plants. Moisture-retentive soil is desirable. No regular pruning required and no particular problems.

CUNNINGHAMIA

Cunninghamia

Taxodiaceae

A small genus of coniferous trees from eastern Asia, reminiscent of *Araucaria*. The trees carry whorls of branches and make pleasing if rather exotic-looking lawn specimens.
• *C. lanceolata* (Chinese fir) China ⑦ ⚲
Height up to 45m (150ft). Leaves lance-shaped, curved, sharp, pointed, almost 8cm (3in) in length, arranged in spirals, leathery texture, bright green above with white bands beneath, turning bronze in autumn. The leaves, which live for about five years, generally remain for quite a long period before they are shed with the branchlets, which creates a rather unsightly appearance. The light fragrant timber is widely used in China.
Cultivation

☼ ⊙ A AL ▦

They thrive in fertile soil. No regular pruning needed, but it is worthwhile noting that cunninghamias will produce new growth from cut-down specimens, unlike most other conifers.

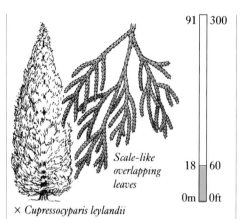

Scale-like overlapping leaves

91 | 300
18 | 60
0m | 0ft

× *Cupressocyparis leylandii*

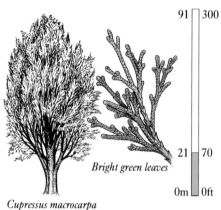

Bright green leaves

91 | 300
21 | 70
0m | 0ft

Cupressus macrocarpa

× CUPRESSOCYPARIS

(Cupressus × chamaecyparis)

Cupressaceae

*F*ast-growing coniferous trees that can be used as specimens or tall screens. The species described is also widely used for creating formal hedges.
- × *C. leylandii* (*Chamaecyparis nootkatensis* × *Cupressus macrocarpa*) (Leyland cypress)
Great Britain ⑤ ⵗ
Height over 18m (60ft). Very fast-growing. Leaves scale-like, overlapping, grey-green, carried on flattened branches. Can be grown as a specimen but more often used as a tall screen or planted as a formal hedge. Cultivars include 'Castlewellan', yellow foliage; 'Leighton Green', grey-green young foliage, deepening with age; 'Haggerston Grey', leaves green above with light grey-green undersides; and 'Naylor's Blue', leaves grey-blue above with light grey-green undersides.

Cultivation

☼ ☽ A AL ▨

Best results in a deep fertile soil. After some years trees may become loose in shallow soils, in which case they will need guying. The best planting size is 45–60cm (18–24in).

CUPRESSUS

Cypress

Cupressaceae

*T*his genus from North America, Europe and Asia contains some of the most popular coniferous trees. Rather similar and closely related to *Chamaecyparis* (False cypress, White cedar), generally with a conical or broad columnar habit, in mild climates they make fine lawn specimens or may be incorporated into mixed groups of conifers. Some species can also be used to form tall screens or windbreaks in mild coastal areas.

The adult foliage is scale-like and pressed closely to the shoots, the juvenile leaves being needle-like. Most trees freely produce small globe-shaped cones at an early age.
- *C. arizonica* (Arizona cypress)
North America ⑥ ⵗ
Height up to 21m (70ft). Branches upright. Leaves pale grey-green, emitting an unpleasant odour when crushed. Cultivars include 'Pyramidalis', of pyramidal habit with very glaucous foliage.
- *C. cashmeriana* (Kashmir cypress)
Kashmir, Tibet ⑨ ⵗ
Height at least 18m (60ft). Long, flattened, pendulous branchlets make this a most attractive and graceful tree. Leaves very glaucous. In areas

with hardiness zone numbers lower than 9 it is often grown in conservatories.

● *C. glabra* (Smooth-barked Arizona cypress) North America ⑦ ⚕
Height up to 21m (70ft). Confused with and similar to *C. arizonica*. Leaves glaucous. Male flowers yellow and conspicuous. Cones purple-brown, 2.5cm (1in) in diameter. Bark smooth, flaking to reveal very smooth reddish underbark.

● *C. lusitanica* (Mexican cypress, Cedar of Goa) Mexico, Guatemala, Costa Rica
Suitable only for mild climate ♀
Height up to 23m (75ft). Pendulous branchlets. Leaves glaucous. Female cones glaucous. Bark peeling, deep brown.

● *C. macrocarpa* (Monterey cypress) Monterey, California ⑧ ⚲
Height up to 21m (70ft). Fast grower. Leaves bright green. Makes a very good windbreak in mild coastal areas. Often used as a formal hedge, but not recommended for this purpose as it will not tolerate hard pruning, which can result in plants dying. Cultivars include 'Golden Pillar', leaves golden yellow; and 'Lutea', leaves light yellow, turning green.

● *C. sempervirens* (Mediterranean cypress, Italian cypress) southern Europe, western Asia ⑧ ♀
Height up to 24m (80ft). Very narrow habit. Leaves dark green. A familiar sight in the Mediterranean and superb species for creating a focal point. The fragrant timber is used commercially in southern Europe.

Cultivation

☼ ☉ A AL ▦

Best planting size is under 60cm (2ft) in height. No regular pruning needed, but any double leaders should be reduced to one. Young trees should be well staked until established and the leading shoot trained vertically.

Problems
Aphids, honey fungus.

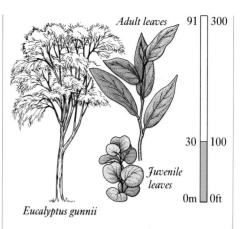

Eucalyptus gunnii

Adult leaves 91 300
30 100
Juvenile leaves
0m 0ft

EUCALYPTUS

Gum tree

Myrtaceae

*F*or additional details, see entry under Small Ornamental Evergreen.

● *E. coccifera* (Tasmanian snow gum, Mount Wellington peppermint) Tasmania ⑨ ♀
Height up to 21m (70ft). Leaves: juvenile round or oval, glaucous; adult lance-shaped, about 10cm (4in) long, glaucous. Flowers conspicuous, white, and appearing in late spring/early summer. Bark a patchwork of grey and white. Good wind resistance so suitable for forming windbreaks and screens.

● *E. dalrympleana* (Mountain gum) New South Wales, Victoria ⑨ ⚲
Height up to 30m (100ft). Juvenile leaves oval, blue-green or deep green; adult lanceolate, sickle-shaped, pale green, drooping. Flowers white, mid- to late autumn. New shoots have orange or red bark. Patchwork bark on trunk is cream, pinkish and light brown; a most attractive feature.

● *E. gunnii* (Cider gum) Tasmania ⑨ ♀
Height up to 30m (100ft). Very fast-growing and a good tree to plant where shade is desirable. Juvenile leaves rounded, blue-green to silver; adult lance-shaped, blue-green or deep green.

Flowers white, mid- to late summer. New shoots may be glaucous. Bark on trunk cream or light green, changing to grey-brown.

● *E. johnstonii* (*E. subcrenulata*) (Johnston's gum) Tasmania ⑨ ♀
Height up to 60m (200ft). Juvenile leaves rounded, opposite, slightly over 5cm (2in) in diameter, the thick, shiny, dark green adult leaves being alternate and oval to lance-shaped. At the base of the trunk the bark is scaly, while higher up it is smooth and grey-green. This species has proved quite hardy in Zone 9 and is growing in a number of mild gardens on the west coast of Britain.

● *E. nitens* (Silver top) Victoria, New South Wales ⑨ ♀
Height up to 91m (300ft). The opposite grey-green juvenile leaves are broadly lance-shaped and about 10cm (4in) in length. The alternate adult leaves are also lance-shaped but much narrower, grey-green and have a smooth shiny surface. Although they are on the tender side they are capable of surviving in Zone 9, and grow well in several mild west-coast gardens in Britain.

● *E. urnigera* (Urn-fruited gum) Tasmania ⑨ ♀
Height 15m (50ft) or more. Juvenile leaves rounded, adult lanceolate; both deep green and shiny. Flowers cream, and appearing in mid- to late summer. The shiny green fruits are urn-shaped, hence the popular name. Bark cream or light green, eventually with brown patches forming. A vigorous species.

Cultivation

For further cultivation details see entry under Small Ornamental Evergreen.

Problems

Few problems encountered, perhaps silver leaf occasionally.

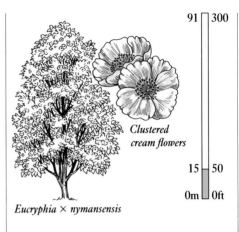

Clustered cream flowers

Eucryphia × nymansensis

EUCRYPHIA
Eucryphia
Eucryphiaceae

*F*or additional details, see entry under Small Ornamental Evergreen.

● *E. × nymansensis* (*E. cordifolia × E. glutinosa*) Europe ⑧ ♀
Height 15m (50ft). A fast-growing tree with upright branches. Leaves are both simple and pinnate, deep green. Flowers almost 8cm (3in) in diameter, cream, carried singly and in clusters, late summer and early autumn. The cultivar 'Nymansay' is similar and a fast grower.

Cultivation

The ideal soil is light and cool. Young plants are best protected from severe frosts over winter with a surround of straw. No regular pruning required; indeed, these trees do not tolerate any form of training. However, any dead wood should be removed as necessary. No particular problems.

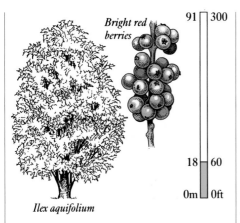

Bright red berries

91 | 300

18 | 60

0m | 0ft

Ilex aquifolium

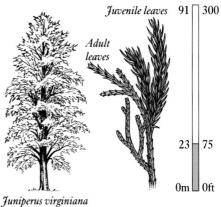

Juvenile leaves

Adult leaves

91 | 300

23 | 75

0m | 0ft

Juniperus virginiana

ILEX

Holly

Aquifoliaceae

*F*or additional details, see entry under Small Ornamental Evergreen.

● *I. aquifolium* (English or European holly)
Europe, north Africa, western Asia ⑦ ♀
Height up to 18m (60ft) or more. Slow-growing. Leaves oval with very spiny edges, dark glossy green. Clusters of bright red berries produced by female trees, autumn and winter; both male and female trees needed for berry production. The species and its cultivars make imposing formal-looking specimens for lawns and other large areas. Cultivars of tree form include 'Pyramidalis' with bright green foliage and heavy crops of red berries; and 'Pyramidalis Fructuluteo' which freely produces bright yellow berries.

Cultivation

☼ ◐ ☉ A AL ▦

For further details of cultivation refer to entry under Small Ornamental Evergreen.

Problems

Holly leaf miner, birds (they eat the berries), honey fungus.

JUNIPERUS

Juniper

Cupressaceae

*F*or additional details, see entry under Small Ornamental Evergreen.

● *J. chinensis* (Chinese juniper)
China, Mongolia, Japan ④ ♀
Height 18m (60ft). Leaves deep green, often a combination of juvenile (needle-like) and adult (scale-like). Bark brown and shredding.

● *J. virginiana* (Pencil cedar, Red cedar)
North America ③ ♢
Height up to 23m (75ft). Leaves a combination of juvenile (needle-like) and adult (scale-like), light to medium green. Bark red-brown. The fragrant timber is used commercially in North America.

Cultivation

☼ ◐ A AL ▦

An excellent choice for alkaline and/or dry soils.

Problems

Juniper webber moth caterpillars, scale insects.

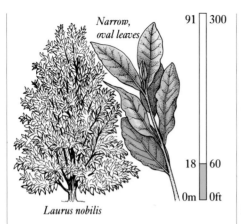

Narrow, oval leaves

91 | 300

18 | 60

0m | 0ft

Laurus nobilis

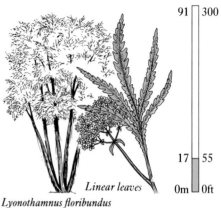

91 | 300

17 | 55

0m | 0ft

Linear leaves

Lyonothamnus floribundus

LAURUS

Sweet bay, Bay laurel

Lauraceae

*T*here are two species in this genus, native to southern Europe and the Atlantic Islands. They have aromatic evergreen foliage and small, insignificant greenish flowers. The species described below can be used as a lawn specimen in a sheltered spot as it grows into quite an attractive pyramidal tree.

● *L. nobilis* (Sweet bay, Bay laurel, Grecian laurel) southern Europe ⑥ ⚘
Height up to 18m (60ft). Leaves narrowly oval, up to 10cm (4in) in length, aromatic, dark green and glossy, used for culinary purposes. This species is the true laurel of antiquity, whose shoots and leaves were made into garlands to symbolize accomplishment, especially by the Romans. It is also used for hedging, and as clipped tub specimens, as it responds well to pruning.

Cultivation

☼ ☉ A AL ▦

When grown as a tree no regular pruning required, but if suckers are produced these should be removed at their source.

Problems
Scale insects.

LYONOTHAMNUS

Catalina ironwood, Lyon tree

Rosaceae

*T*here is only one species in this genus and it grows naturally in the islands off the coast of southern California. It has attractive shredding bark and spiraea-like flowers in early summer. Best grown in a sheltered situation and recommended only for mild areas.

● *L. floribundus* (Catalina ironwood, Lyon tree) islands off southern California ⑧ ⚘
Height up to 17m (55ft). Leaves linear, to 20cm (8in) in length. Conspicuous clusters of white flowers produced between late spring and midsummer. Bark rich brown, shredding off in strips; a distinctive feature. The sub-species *asplenifolius*, a superb foliage tree, has pinnate leaves consisting of up to seven finely lobed leaflets and creating a ferny effect.

Cultivation

☼ ☉ A ▦

No regular pruning needed and no particular problems, but should be grown only in mild areas.

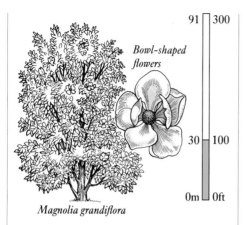

Bowl-shaped flowers

91 | 300

30 | 100

0m | 0ft

Magnolia grandiflora

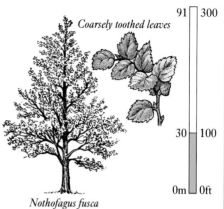

Coarsely toothed leaves

91 | 300

30 | 100

0m | 0ft

Nothofagus fusca

MAGNOLIA

Magnolia

Magnoliaceae

Magnolias are popular flowering trees and shrubs. The evergreen species described below is noted for its magnificent large leaves and huge flowers. It makes an imposing lawn specimen given a suitable climate but in Britain it is traditionally grown as a wall shrub.

• *M. grandiflora* (Southern magnolia, Bull bay) North America ⑦ ♀
Height up to 30m (100ft). Leaves obovate-oblong, up to 20cm (8in) in length, with a very thick leathery texture, medium to deep green, shiny, often with rust-coloured undersides. Flowers bowl-shaped, up to 20cm (8in) in diameter, white, fragrant, mid-summer to early autumn. These are followed by cone-shaped fruits. This species is, however, variable in habit. Cultivars include 'Exmouth', which starts flowering at an earlier age than the species; and 'Goliath', with flowers up to 30cm (1ft) in diameter, produced from an early age.

Cultivation

See entry under Small Ornamental Deciduous.

NOTHOFAGUS

Nothofagus

Fagaceae

Nothofagus are native to Australia, New Zealand, Tasmania and South America and are related to the true beeches or fagus, although they have smaller leaves. They make fine specimens on large estates and in parks, although they are not suitable for very cold regions.

• *N. fusca* New Zealand ⑧ ♀
Height up to 30m (100ft). Leaves rounded or broadly oval, coarsely toothed, sometimes becoming flushed with copper in autumn. An important timber tree in its native country. The old bark flakes off.

• *N. solandri* New Zealand ⑧ ♀
Height up to 24m (80ft). Leaves oval, under 2.5cm (1in) in length, toothless, with smooth and shiny upper surface and greyish downy undersides.

Cultivation

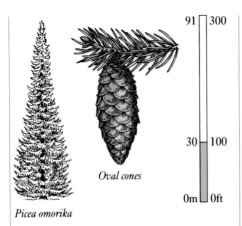

91 ⌐ 300

30 ⊢ 100

0m ⌐ 0ft

Oval cones

Picea omorika

PICEA

Spruce, Fir

Pinaceae

For additional details, see entry under Small Ornamental Evergreen.

● *P. abies* (*P. excelsa*) (Norway spruce, Common spruce) central and northern Europe ③ ♦

Height up to 45m (150ft). Leaves dark green, glossy. Cones cylindrical, about 15cm (6in) in length. Flaking orange-brown bark. An important timber tree. Also the traditional 'Christmas tree' and widely grown commercially for this purpose. Cultivars include 'Pyramidata', of narrow fastigiate habit. Many others are dwarf shrubs.

● *P. brewerana* (Brewer's weeping spruce) North America ⑥ ♦

Height up to 30m (100ft). Although the outline is conical, the spreading branches carry "curtains" of pendulous branchlets making this a highly distinctive conifer and one of the best lawn specimens. Leaves flattened, deep glossy blue-green above with white undersides. Cones oblong, 12.5cm (5in) in length, pale orange-brown. Bark grey, flaking. Must have moisture-retentive soil.

● *P. glauca* (*P. alba*) (White spruce) Canada, USA ③ ♦

Height up to 30m (100ft) but often less. Pendu-

lous branchlets. Leaves blue-green, giving off an unpleasant odour when bruised. Cones cylindrical, light brown, about 5cm (2in) in length, bark scaly, grey-brown. An important timber tree in Canada and the USA. Would also make a good windbreak. Cultivars include 'Caerulea' with glaucous foliage.

● *P. likiangensis* western China ⑥ ♦

Height up to 27m (90ft). Young shoots light brown or red-brown. Leaves flattened, green or blue-green on upper surface and with grey-green undersides. Conspicuous bright red flowers, mid- to late spring. Cones oval, more than 8cm (3in) in length. Bark light grey.

● *P. mariana* (*P. nigra*) (Black spruce) Alaska, North America ② ♦

Height up to 18m (60ft). Leaves overlapping, dull green or blue-green, emitting a menthol aroma when crushed. Cones about 3.8cm (1½in) in length, deep purple.

● *P. omorika* (Serbian spruce) southern Europe ④ ♦

Height up to 30m (100ft). Branches short, drooping, but the tips turn upwards. Leaves flattened, white-banded below, shiny deep green above. Cones oval, almost 8cm (3in) in length, blue-black, then turning deep brown. Bark red-brown. The cultivar 'Pendula' has drooping branches. Provide shelter from cold winds.

● *P. pungens* (Colorado spruce, Blue spruce) North America ④ ♦

Height at least 30m (100ft). Leaves stiff, spine-tipped, radiating from the shoots, often blue-green. Cones cylindrical, up to 10cm (4in) in length, maturing pale brown.

● *P. sitchensis* (Sitka spruce) Alaska, North America ⑥ ♦

Height at least 36m (120ft). Leaves flattened, stiff, spine-tipped, shiny green with silver-banded undersides. Cones cylindrical, up to 10cm (4in) in length, pale brown. This species forms a massive trunk. Bark scaling. An important timber tree that prefers a humid, cool climate.

Cultivation

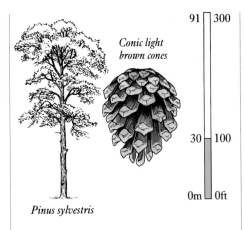

91 300

*Conic light
brown cones*

30 100

0m 0ft

Pinus sylvestris

PINUS

Pine

Pinaceae

*F*or additional details, see entry under Small Ornamental Evergreen.

● *P. ayacahuite* (Mexican white pine)
Mexico, Guatemala ⑧ ♀
Height up to 30m (100ft). Branches borne horizontally. Leaves carried in groups of five, about 15cm (6in) in length, somewhat drooping, blue-green. Cones cylindrical, up to 15cm (6in) in length, pendulous, deep brown, producing much resin. It grows in mountainous areas in its native countries. An extremely attractive and moderately hardy species that makes an excellent lawn specimen.

● *P. cembra* (Arolla pine, Swiss stone pine)
central Europe, north-east USSR,
Siberia ③ ◬
Height 23m (75ft) or more. A slow-growing species. Leaves carried in groups of five, about 12.5cm (5in) in length, stiff and deep green. Oval cones more than 8cm (3in) in length, maturing to purplish brown. The seeds are edible.

● *P. contorta latifolia* (Lodgepole pine)
Alaska, North America ④ ◬
Height 21–45m (70–150ft). Leaves in pairs, over 5cm (2in) in length, stiff, twisted, medium green. Bark scaling, deep red-brown. Must be grown in acid soils.

● *P. densiflora* (Japanese red pine)
Japan ⑤ ♀
Height 30m (100ft) or more. Leaves in pairs, up to 12.5cm (5in) in length, soft to the touch, sharply pointed tips, blue-green. Cones oval to oblong, 5cm (2in) in length, brown. Bark peeling, reddish brown; a distinctive feature. Plant only in acid soils.

● *P. montezumae* (Rough-barked Mexican pine, Montezuma pine) Mexico, North America ⑥ ♀
Height 21m (70ft) or more. Leaves usually in clusters of five, pendulous but stiff, up to 30cm (12in) in length, blue-green. Cones cylindrical, up to 20cm (8in) in length, of variable colour, from yellow-brown to almost black. Bark rough, red-brown. An important timber tree in its native countries. Grow in sheltered conditions, such as on the edge of a woodland area. One of the most beautiful pines with a huge domed head and striking foliage creating a marvellous textural effect.

● *P. nigra* (Austrian pine, Black pine)
Europe, Asia ④ ◬
Height 30m (100ft) or more. Leaves in pairs, slightly over 15cm (6in) in length, stiff and deep green. Heavy branches and very dense foliage are characteristic. Cones oval, in excess of 8cm (3in) in length, yellow-brown. Bark dark brown. Particularly recommended for forming windbreaks. Excellent for alkaline soils and maritime areas. The variety *maritima* (*calabrica*) (Corsican pine) has a straighter trunk and less stiff grey-green foliage. Grows well in any soil and situation.

● *P. parviflora* (Japanese white pine)
Japan ⑥ ◬ to ♀
Height 15m (50ft) or more, but slow-growing. Starting conical, but eventually becoming flat-topped. Leaves in clusters of five, carried in tufts at the tips of the branchlets, 3.8cm (1½in) in length, blue-green. Cones oval, 8cm (3in) in length, light brown. Bark purple-brown. It also makes an excellent subject for bonsai. The cultivar 'Glauca' has glaucous foliage.

● *P. pinaster* (Maritime pine, Cluster pine)
Mediterranean ⑦ ◬
Height 30m (100ft) or more. A fast-growing

species that thrives in light sandy soils and maritime conditions. Few branches are produced. Leaves carried in pairs, up to 25cm (10in) in length, rigid, shiny green. Cones oval, up to 25cm (10in) in length, produced in clusters, brown and shiny, persisting on the tree for several years. They are produced at an early age. Red, brown and purple patchwork bark in older trees.

● *P. pinea* (Stone pine, Umbrella pine)
Mediterranean ⑧ ♀
Height up to 24m (80ft). It has a distinctive flat-topped crown. Leaves carried in pairs, about 15cm (6in) in length, rigid and spine-tipped, bright green. The oval pale brown cones attain a length of almost 15cm (6in) and produce edible seeds. These are available as pine kernels. This species thrives in maritime areas and light sandy soils and is very tolerant of drought. Old trees have rugged orange- or red-brown bark.

● *P. ponderosa* (Western yellow pine, Ponderosa pine) North America ⑥ ♈
Height 61m (200ft) but generally less. Spreading and drooping branches. Leaves carried in groups of three, 15cm (6in) to almost 30cm (1ft) in length, rigid with sharply pointed tips, deep green. Cones oval, to 20cm (8in) in length. In North America it is grown as a very important timber tree.

● *P. radiata* (Monterey pine)
California ⑦ ♀
Height 23m (75ft) or more., A fast-growing species. Leaves carried in groups of three, up to 15cm (6in) in length, bright green, creating extremely dense foliage. From a distance the tree has a very dark appearance. The long male flowers are conspicuous in the spring. Cones oval, about 15cm (6in) in length, carried in clusters, deep brown and remaining on the tree for many years. Bark rugged, deep grey-brown. Widely planted in mild climates for timber and also makes a good windbreak, especially in mild coastal regions.

● *P. strobus* (White pine, Southern white pine)
eastern North America ③ ♈ to ♀
Height 36m (120ft) or more. Fast-growing, eventually forming a round crown. Leaves carried in groups of five, 12.5cm (5in) in length, blue-green. Cylindrical cones about 15cm (6in)

in length, carried in clusters, dark brown and covered in resin. Young trees produce cones. In North America it is cultivated as an important timber tree.

● *P. sylvestris* (Scots pine)
Europe, Asia ③ ♈
Height 30m (100ft) or more. Leaves carried in pairs, 8cm (3in) in length, rigid, twisted, grey-green. Cones conic, about 6cm (2½in) in length, light brown. Bark red-brown. Extremely hardy and adaptable. The cultivar 'Argentea' has silver blue-green foliage. Although widely grown as an important timber tree, this species is also an attractive ornamental and can be used to good effect as a lawn specimen or to help form ornamental woodland.

● *P. wallichiana* (*P. excelsa*, *P. griffithii*)
(Bhutan pine, Himalayan white pine)
Himalayas ⑥ ♀
Height up to 45m (150ft). A species of vigorous habit with heavy branches and a wide-spreading crown. Leaves carried in clusters of five, about 20cm (8in) in length, pendulous, grey-green. Cones cylindrical, up to 30cm (1ft) in length, producing large quantities of resin. The bark is smooth, but eventually becomes fissured and orange-brown. It makes an attractive specimen tree or can be effectively included in groups of conifers.

Cultivation

☼ A AL A-N ▨

Do not plant large specimens of pine: plants up to 60cm (2ft) in height establish much better. No regular pruning needed. If leading shoot is damaged or killed, resulting in several apical shoots, reduce these to the strongest one to form a new leader.

Problems
Adelgids, caterpillars (pine-shoot moth), sawfly larvae, honey fungus.

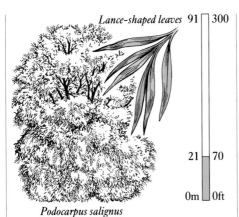

Lance-shaped leaves 91 | 300

21 | 70

0m | 0ft

Podocarpus salignus

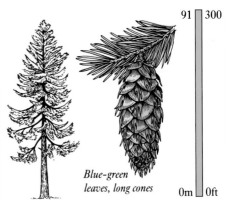

91 | 300

Blue-green leaves, long cones 0m | 0ft

Pseudotsuga menziesii

PODOCARPUS

Podocarpus

Podocarpaceae

This genus of coniferous trees and shrubs is found mainly in the southern hemisphere. Many species are ornamental and some are important timber trees. The flat, usually narrow leaves are arranged in spirals. Male flowers are catkin-like and the seeds are produced in fleshy receptacles. Most species are not hardy in cool temperate climates. The species described below is quite well known and will thrive given a mild climate and sheltered conditions.

● *P. salignus* Chile ⑧ ♤

Height up to 21m (70ft). In some climates it may grow as a large shrub. It has slender pendulous branches. Leaves narrow, lance-shaped, up to 12.5cm (5in) in length, generally curved, the upper surface being deep green and shiny, the undersides lighter in colour. Seed receptacles deep purple. Bark peeling in strips, orange- or red-brown.

Cultivation

☼ ☉ A AL 🏵

No regular pruning needed and no particular problems.

PSEUDOTSUGA

Pseudotsuga ·

Pinaceae

A small genus of coniferous trees from west-ern North America and eastern Asia. The massive species described here is an important timber tree in its native countries but also makes an impressive lawn specimen in parks and large estates.

● *P. menziesii* (*P. taxifolia*) (Douglas fir)
North America ⑥ ♤

Height can be up to 91m (300ft) but is generally less. A very vigorous species with downward-sweeping lower branches. Leaves about 2.5cm (1in) in length, deep or blue-green, pleasantly aromatic. Cones almost 12.5cm (5in) in length. Bark thick, fissured and deep brown on older trees.

Cultivation

☼ A 🏵

Best results in a deep, rich, loamy, moisture-retentive soil. Excellent for regions that are subjected to high rainfall. Plant small specimens up to 60cm (2ft) in height.

Problems

Adelgids.

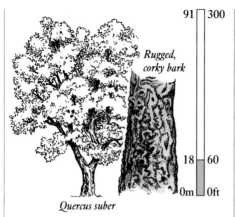

91 ⌐ 300

18 ⊢ 60

0m └ 0ft

Rugged, corky bark

Quercus suber

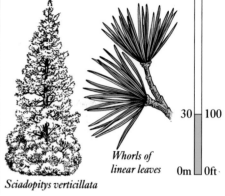

91 ⌐ 300

30 ⊢ 100

0m └ 0ft

Whorls of linear leaves

Sciadopitys verticillata

QUERCUS

Oak

Fagaceae

*F*or additional details, see entry under Medium to Large Deciduous.

● *Q. ilex* (Holm oak, Evergreen oak)
Mediterranean ⑧ ♀
Height 18m (60ft). Leaves oval to lance-shaped, 8cm (3in) in length, toothed or toothless, leathery texture, deep green and shiny on the upper surface, with white-felted undersides. Dense foliage. Acorns very freely produced. Bark almost black. Makes an excellent windbreak in coastal regions and also recommended as a specimen tree in lawns. Grows particularly well in alkaline soils but also suitable for acid conditions.

● *Q. suber* (Cork oak)
southern Europe, North Africa ⑧ ♀
Height 18m (60ft). Leaves oval, about 8cm (3in) in length, edges toothed, leathery texture, the upper surface deep green and glossy, the undersides covered with grey felt. The extremely thick bark is rugged and corky. This tree provides commercial cork.

Cultivation

☼ ☕ A AL ▦

SCIADOPITYS

Sciadopitys

Taxodiaceae

*T*his genus contains only one species, an attractive medium to tall conifer which makes a fine lawn specimen, although it is slow growing.

● *S. verticillata* (Umbrella pine)
central and south-west Japan ⑥ ⚬
Height 30m (100ft) or more but generally less under cultivation. The branches are carried horizontally in whorls and turn up at the ends. There are two types of leaves: small scale-like ones arranged in spirals on shoots, and linear ones in whorls, up to 12.5cm (5in) in length, deep green or yellow-green and shiny above with two white bands on the undersides. These long leaves are arranged like the spokes of an umbrella, hence the common name.

Cultivation

☼ ☕ ⊙ A ■ ▦

Thrives in a deep, fertile, moisture-retentive, loamy soil. Small specimens establish much better than larger ones. Appreciates a permanent mulch of leafmould or peat.

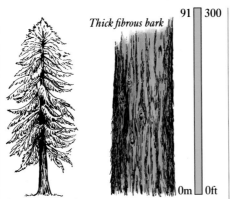

Thick fibrous bark

91 | 300

0m | 0ft

Sequoia sempervirens

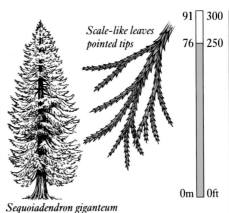

Scale-like leaves pointed tips

91 | 300
76 | 250

0m | 0ft

Sequoiadendron giganteum

SEQUOIA

Redwood

Taxodiaceae

There is only one species in this genus, a huge conifer from western North America. It makes an impressive lawn specimen in parks and large estates with its red-brown trunk and contrasting dark green foliage.

• *S. sempervirens* (Redwood, Coast redwood, Californian redwood) California and Oregon ⑦ ♦
Height 91m (300ft) or more. There are two types of leaves: scale-like and linear, the latter about 2.5cm (1in) in length. They are dark green. The huge trunk is covered with thick, soft, fibrous, red-brown bark; a most attractive feature.

Cultivation

☼ ☉ A AL ▣

Best results in a deep moisture-retentive soil. Plant small specimens, up to 45cm (18in) in height, as these establish better than larger plants. Young trees should be kept moist and mulched. No regular pruning needed, but double leaders should be reduced to one.

Problems
Honey fungus.

SEQUOIADENDRON

Sequoiadendron

Taxodiaceae

There is only one species in this genus, a huge coniferous tree from California. Like the sequoia, it makes an impressive lawn specimen in parks and large estates and also has distinctive red-brown bark.

• *S. giganteum* (*Sequoia gigantea,
Sequoia wellingtonia*) (Giant sequoia, Big tree, Giant redwood, Sierra redwood) California ⑦ ♦
Height 76m (250ft) or more. Forms a very thick trunk and has branches that sweep down to the ground. Leaves scale-like and bright green, with pointed tips. Bark red-brown, spongy and fibrous, up to 50cm (20in) thick and furrowed.

Cultivation

☼ ☉ A AL ▣

A vigorous tree that grows best in a deep moisture-retentive soil. Plant small specimens, up to 45cm (18in) in height, as these establish better than larger ones. Young trees should be kept moist and given a permanent mulch. No regular pruning needed but double leaders should be reduced to one.

Problems
Honey fungus.

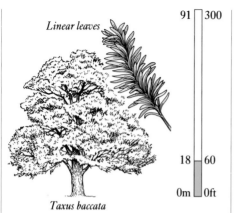

91 ⎡ 300

18 ⎣ 60

0m ⎣ 0ft

Linear leaves

Taxus baccata

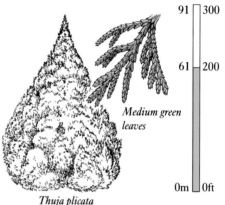

91 ⎡ 300

61 ⎣ 200

Medium green leaves

0m ⎣ 0ft

Thuja plicata

TAXUS

Yew

Taxaceae

A small genus of coniferous trees and shrubs native to Europe, Asia Minor, eastern Asia and North America. Of bushy habit, the species described here makes an excellent focal point in a garden and also looks good when planted in groups with other conifers. It is often used for hedging and topiary and is extremely long-lived. In Britain many large, ancient specimens are to be found in churchyards. Also an excellent conifer for planting in woodland as it takes shade.

• *T. baccata* (English yew)
Europe, North Africa, western Asia ⑦ ♀
Height up to 18m (60ft). Very wide spreading with age. Leaves linear, dark green, shiny, paler below. The leaves are poisonous so livestock should be kept away.

Cultivation

 ☼ ☻ ● A AL 🏠

Extremely adaptable and grows particularly well in alkaline soils. It tolerates exposure and atmospheric pollution. No regular pruning needed when grown as a tree.

Problems
Scale insects, honey fungus.

THUJA

Arbor-vitae

Cupressaceae

A small genus of conifers native to North America and eastern Asia. They have flat branches clothed with aromatic scale-like leaves and are mainly of broadly columnar habit. This makes them ideally suited to creating focal points in gardens or for use as lawn specimens. The thujas are also frequently included in mixed groups of conifers. Some species are important timber trees.

• *T. occidentalis* (American arbor-vitae, White cedar, Eastern white cedar, Northern white cedar)
Canada and USA ③ 🬂
Height 18m (60ft). Leaves deep green on the upper surface with yellow-green undersides. Bark red-brown, peeling. An important timber tree in its native countries.

• *T. plicata* (*T. lobbii*) (Western red cedar, Giant arbor-vitae) Alaska, North America ⑤ 🬂
Height up to 61m (200ft). A vigorous, fast-growing species. Leaves medium green and shiny above, with lighter undersides marked with white. The foliage has a strong, pleasant, fruity fragrance when crushed. Bark pale brown, peeling off in strips. This species is frequently

used for hedging and is also an important timber tree. Cultivars include 'Aurea', with deep golden foliage; 'Fastigiata', with very upright branches, making an excellent focal point in a garden; and 'Zebrina', whose green foliage is banded with cream. The latter is an extremely popular ornamental conifer.

Cultivation

☼ ☉ A AL ▦

Best growth is achieved in a deep moisture-retentive soil with plenty of shelter from strong winds. Plant small specimens, no more than 60cm (24in) in height, as these establish better than larger trees. The soil should be kept moist around young trees and they appreciate a permanent mulch of organic matter. No regular pruning required.

Problems

Honey fungus.

CLIMATIC ZONES

1. Below −45°C (−50°F)
2. −45 to −39°C (−50 to −40°F)
3. −39 to −35°C (−40 to −30°F)
4. −35 to −29°C (−30 to −20°F)
5. −29 to −23°C (−20 to −10°F)
6. −23 to −18°C (−10 to 0°F)
7. −18 to −12°C (0 to 10°F)
8. −12 to −6°C (10 to 20°F)
9. −6 to −1°C (20 to 30°F)
10. −1 to 4°C (30 to 40°F)

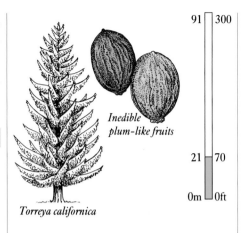

Inedible plum-like fruits

Torreya californica

91 | 300

21 | 70

0m | 0ft

TORREYA

Torreya

Taxaceae

A small genus of coniferous trees from Asia and North America with linear leaves rather like those of yew, with two grey bands on the undersides, and fleshy plum-like fruits each containing one seed. The torreyas make attractive specimen trees in large gardens.

● *T. californica* (California nutmeg, California torreya) California ⑥ ۵
Height 21m (70ft) or more. Branching starts virtually at ground level. The bark of the branchlets is reddish-brown. Leaves linear, over 5cm (2in) in length, deep green and shiny on the upper surface. Fruits oval, nearly 5cm (2in) long, green, streaked with purple.

Cultivation

☼ ☉ A AL ▦

Grows especially well in alkaline soils but is also suitable for acid conditions. Generally recommended for Zone 7 and above; when grown in Zone 6 it should be given sheltered conditions and may be deciduous. No regular pruning required and no particular problems. For the best-shaped tree it is important to maintain a strong leading shoot.

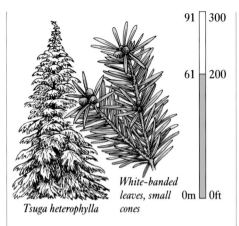

91 | 300

61 | 200

White-banded leaves, small cones

0m | 0ft

Tsuga heterophylla

TSUGA

Hemlock

Pinaceae

*T*he hemlocks are coniferous trees from temperate areas and are found in the USA, Canada and eastern Asia. The rather thin branches are carried horizontally and the leaves are linear, the undersides having two conspicuous white bands. Some species are important timber trees in their native countries. They are also highly attractive trees and should be considered for specimen or group planting on estates and in large gardens. They make superb lawn specimens and are also good for hedging. They should be sheltered from strong winds but will tolerate shade.

● *T. canadensis* (Canada hemlock, Eastern hemlock) Canada, Alaska ③ ☖
Height 24m (80ft) or more. Leaves deep green, with conspicuous white-banded undersides. Myriad small brown cones produced. Bark rough textured, deep greyish-brown. Cultivars include the slow-growing 'Lutea', with brilliant yellow leaves.

● *T. caroliniana* (Carolina hemlock)
North America ⑤ ☖
Height up to 21m (70ft). The young shoots are variable in colour: they may be red-brown, yellow-brown or grey. The deep green leaves,

with white bands on the undersides, are just under 2.5cm (1in) in length and generally the tips are slightly notched. The cones are approximately 3.8cm (1½in) in length. This species is not suitable for alkaline soils.

● *T. heterophylla* (Western hemlock)
Alaska, North America ③ ☖
Height 61m (200ft) or more. A fast-growing species. Shoots hairy. Leaves deep green on the upper surface, the undersides having two conspicuous white bands. Produces many small light brown cones. The bark is corrugated and deep brown. This species can be used for forming hedges. It also makes a most attractive lawn specimen and is cultivated as an important timber tree.

● *T. mertensiana* (Mountain hemlock)
North America ⑥ ☖
Height 45m (150ft). This species has downy grey-brown branchlets. Leaves about 2.5cm (1in) in length and blue-green in colour. Cones about 8cm (3in) in length and quite conspicuous. A very handsome and desirable tree, making an imposing lawn specimen. In the cultivar 'Argentea' the leaves are blue-white. The cultivar 'Glauca' has grey-green foliage and is extremely attractive. The species and its cultivars are best given a site sheltered from high winds.

Cultivation

☀ ☉ A AL A-N ▦

It is not recommended that tsugas be grown in very alkaline soils. Ideally suited to areas of high rainfall. If the soil is poor, and especially if inclined to dry out rapidly, it is recommended that a copious amount of bulky organic matter is incorporated into the site before planting. Young trees can, with advantage, be permanently mulched with organic matter. Plant small specimens, about 60cm (2ft) in height, as these establish better. No regular pruning needed and no particular problems.

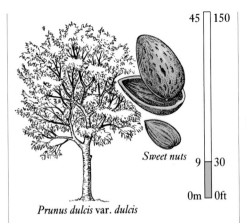

45 | 150

Sweet nuts 9 | 30

0m | 0ft

Prunus dulcis var. *dulcis*

Large rounded fruits

45 | 150

6 | 20

0m | 0ft

Malus pumila

ALMOND	APPLE
Prunus	Malus
Rosaceae	*Rosaceae*

The almonds are valued for their nuts; but these may not be produced in areas subject to spring frosts as early flowers may be killed.
● *P. dulcis* var. *dulcis* (Sweet almond)
western Asia ⑧ to ⑩ ♀
Height 9m (30ft). Leaves lance-shaped, up to 12.5cm (5in) in length, deciduous. Flowers pink, produced in early spring. Produces sweet nuts.
● *P. dulcis* var. *amara* (Bitter almond)
western Asia ⑧ to ⑩ ♀
Similar to var. *dulcis* but the nuts are bitter and inedible; they produce oil of bitter almond.

Cultivation

☼ ☉ A AL ▣

Almonds make fine standard trees but can be obtained as bush trees or half-standards. Plant several together to ensure cross-pollination of flowers and good nut crop. Avoid frost pockets. Regular pruning not necessary. Feed in late winter with a balanced fertilizer. Mulch well with organic matter. Keep soil 'moist in dry weather. Nuts are harvested in mid-autumn.

Problems
Aphids, bacterial canker, red spider mite, peach leaf curl, silver leaf.

Apples rank among the most important fruits in cool temperate climates. Numerous large commercial orchards worldwide supply the huge consumer demand and countless private gardeners grow them. There are many thousands of cultivars produced for both dessert and culinary use, and each apple-growing country has its particular favourites. Since there are so many cultivars, it is relatively easy to choose a variety to suit your climate. If you live in an area prone to late frosts which may damage blossoms, for example, choose a variety that flowers later in the year. A mature, standard apple tree, which may well have a gnarled trunk and branches, is very attractive, especially in the spring when laden with blossom. It makes a fine lawn specimen, where its shade can also be enjoyed on a hot summer's day. Apples can be trained to numerous shapes and the trend today is for very small or restricted trained forms. However, it is the large tree form (standard or half-standard tree) that is discussed here.
● *M. pumila* (*M. domestica*) (Apple)
Europe, western Asia ⑥ to ⑧ ♀
Apple cultivars are of complex hybrid origin but are descended from the above and other species

Apple blossom

such as *M. sylvestris* and *M. prunifolia*. Standard trees reach a height of 6m (20ft) or more. Leaves oval or elliptic, grey-green or dark green, deciduous. Flowers carried in clusters during spring, opening white from pink buds. Large rounded fruits produced in summer and autumn, varying greatly in flavour, sweetness, colour and texture. There are very early varieties, which can be kept in good condition for only a few weeks; mid-season, which may be stored for a few months; and late cultivars, which can be stored throughout winter in cool, slightly humid conditions.

Cultivation

☼ ⊙ **A AL A-N**

Plant several different cultivars together to ensure cross-pollination; they must be compatible and flower at the same time. For best results, plant in deep loamy soil. Avoid planting in frost pockets. Pruning is necessary, carried out annually in winter. The centre of standard apple trees should be kept open so prune out any branches growing inwards.

Many varieties form fruit buds on spurs, which are produced on two-year-old and older shoots. Other varieties form fruit buds at the tips of previous year's shoots.

With spur bearers, unpruned lateral shoots growing from branches are pruned back to four buds so that they form spurs. Shoots produced by existing spurs are cut back to one bud. If spurs become too long they can be reduced by half, provided they contain plenty of fruit buds.

Tip-bearing cultivars are pruned more lightly, mainly to remove crowded and crossing branches and ensure the centre of the tree is kept open. Aim for well-spaced branches and lateral shoots. Leading shoots can be pruned as this encourages the production of fruit-bearing lateral shoots.

Feed annually in spring by applying a fertilizer containing nitrogen, phosphorus and potash, and apply a mulch of bulky organic matter. In mid-summer, after trees have naturally shed surplus fruitlets, further thinning may be needed to ensure fruits are spaced approximately 15cm (6in) apart.

Apples are ready for picking if they leave the spur easily when gently lifted in the palm of one hand. Those suitable for storing should first be dried if necessary and then kept in a temperature of 4–7°C (40–45°F). The storage area should be airy and have a slightly humid atmosphere.

Problems

Aphids, canker, caterpillars, codling moth larvae, mildew, sawfly larvae, scab.

KEY TO SYMBOLS

Shape	Aspect	Soils
Conical	☼ Full sun	A Acid
Spreading	Partial shade	AL Alkaline
Broad columnar	● Shade	A-N Acid to neutral
Fastigiate	⊙ Sheltered from cold winds	■ Rich in humus
Weeping		Well drained

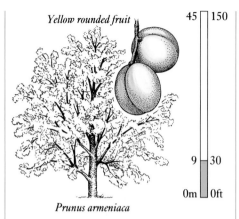

Yellow rounded fruit

45 — 150

9 — 30

0m — 0ft

Prunus armeniaca

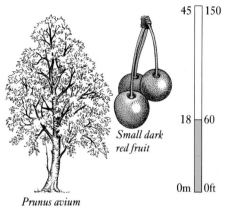

45 — 150

18 — 60

Small dark
red fruit

0m — 0ft

Prunus avium

APRICOT
Prunus
Rosaceae

*I*n areas where the flowers are not likely to be killed by late-spring frosts, apricots are worthwhile fruiting trees.

● *P. armeniaca* (Apricot) China ⑥ to ⑩ ♀
Height up to 9m (30ft). Amateurs may wish to grow bush trees on dwarfing rootstocks, with a height in the region of 3m (10ft). Clusters of white or pink flowers produced in early spring. Fruits round, over 2.5cm (1in) in diameter, yellow, flushed red, ripening mid-summer to early autumn. Numerous cultivars.

Cultivation

☼ ⊙ **AL** ▣

It is self-fertile so only one tree need be grown for fruit production. Best growth in moisture-retentive soil. Prune out weak or dead shoots or branches in winter; very old shoots can be pruned out as necessary.

Apply a balanced fertilizer in spring and mulch the tree with bulky organic matter. Maintain pH range between 6.5 and 8.

Problems
Aphids, bacterial canker, red spider mite, silver leaf.

CHERRY
Prunus
Rosaceae

*T*here are three types of edible cherry: sweet, duke and acid. Sweet and duke cherries are very vigorous trees, acid cherries less so and therefore more suitable for small gardens. They are generally grown as standards or half-standards. All produce clusters of small, rounded, single-seeded fruits in summer.

● *P. avium* (Sweet cherry)
Europe, Asia ⑥ to ⑨ ♀
Height up to 18m (60ft). Leaves oval, up to 12.5cm (5in) long, toothed, medium green,

P. avium

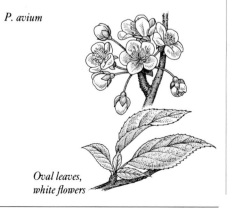

Oval leaves,
white flowers

deciduous. Flowers white, mid-spring. Fruits round, under 2.5cm (1in) in diameter, sweet, generally dark red. Numerous cultivars are available but it is necessary to grow several compatible cultivars together to ensure cross-pollination and good fruit crops.

● *P. cerasus* (Acid cherry, Sour cherry)
Europe, Asia ⑥ to ⑨ ♀
Height 6m (20ft). Leaves oval or elliptic, 8cm (3in) long, finely toothed, mid-green and shiny, deciduous. Clusters of white or pink flowers in spring. Fruits round, under 2.5cm (1in) in diameter, red, acid, summer. A well-known acid cherry is Morello. Acid cherries are self-compatible so can be planted singly.

● *P. × effusus* (Duke cherry)
(*P. avium × P. cerasus*) ⑥ to ⑨ ♀
In habit like the sweet cherry, but with acid fruits.

Cultivation

☼ ☉ A AL A-N ▦

Best growth in a deep fertile soil. Avoid planting in frost pockets. Little pruning is needed for sweet and duke cherries and if required should be carried out in spring. Remove dead, crossing or overcrowded branches. Acid cherries are best pruned annually in early spring to encourage new shoots that will crop the following year. Prune back shoots that are at least two years old to young lateral shoots. Apply a balanced fertilizer in spring and mulch young trees with bulky organic matter. Pick fruits with the stalk when fully ripe.

Problems
Aphids, bacterial canker, caterpillars, silver leaf.

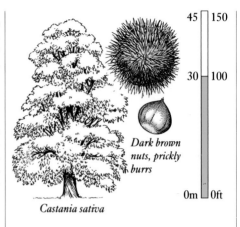

Dark brown
nuts, prickly
burrs

Castania sativa

45	150
30	100
0m	0ft

CHESTNUT

Castania

Fagaceae

Chestnuts are large deciduous trees from temperate areas of the northern hemisphere, grown for nuts and for ornamental purposes. They make impressive lawn specimens in very large gardens and estates. Some are also valuable timber trees.

● *C. sativa* (Sweet chestnut, Spanish chestnut)
southern Europe, north Africa,
western Asia ⑥ ♀
Height up to 30m (100ft). Leaves lance-shaped, up to 20cm (8in) in length, coarsely toothed, medium green, deciduous. Flowers are light yellow catkins produced in mid-summer. The nuts are about 2.5cm (1in) in diameter, dark brown and contained in prickly burrs. Bark formed into spiralling grooves on older trees.

Cultivation

☼ A A-N ▦

Grows well in light, sandy, dry soils. Unsuitable for chalk and wet conditions. No regular pruning required and no particular problems.

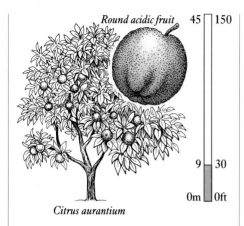

Round acidic fruit

45 | 150

9 | 30

0m | 0ft

Citrus aurantium

CITRUS FRUITS

Citrus

Rutaceae

Citrus fruits such as oranges, limes, lemons and grapefruit originate from southern and south-east Asia and the Malay Peninsula. They will withstand light frosts but are grown permanently outdoors only in favoured parts of Zones 9 and 10. In other areas they can be grown in tubs in a conservatory or greenhouse and stood outside for the summer. Citrus need a minimum temperature of 13–16°C (55–61°F) for six months after flowering for fruits to ripen. The hardiest citrus are oranges, followed (in order of increasing tenderness) by grapefruit, lemon and lime. They are attractive evergreen trees and are grown to a limited extent by home gardeners. Commercially they are extremely important fruits and grown extensively for the consumer market, especially in California and Florida.

● *C. aurantiifolia* (Lime) south-east Asia, India ⑩ ♀
Height up to 4.5m (15ft). Densely branched and spiny. Sometimes grows as a shrub. Leaves elliptic, about 8cm (3in) in length, thick and leathery, light green. Flowers white, fragrant, in clusters. Fruits oval, about 8cm (3in) in length, green-yellow, skin very thin and smooth, extremely acid flesh although there are sweet

types. A very tender species, young shoots being killed by even a slight frost. Numerous cultivars.
● *C. aurantium* (Seville orange, Bitter orange, Sour orange) south-east Asia ⑨ to ⑩ ♀
Height 6–9m (20–30ft). Branches spiny. Leaves oval, 10cm (4in) in length, dark green. Flowers in clusters, white, fragrant, spring. Fruits round, approximately 8cm (3in) in diameter, orange skin, acid flesh. Used for making marmalade thus important commercially. One of the hardiest citrus. Numerous cultivars.

Seville orange blossom

● *C. limon* (Lemon) south-east Asia ⑩ ♀
Height 6m (20ft). Spiny branches. Leaves elliptic or oval, 10cm (4in) in length, dark green. Flowers white, tinted red, fragrant, produced in spring. Fruits oval, up to 12.5cm (5in) in length, bright yellow, flesh extremely acid. Many culinary uses. An important commercial fruit. Numerous cultivars, including 'Meyer', popular with amateur gardeners.

Lemon, and blossom

- *C. × paradisi* (*C. maxima* × *C. sinensis*) (Grapefruit) West Indies ⑨ to ⑩ ♀
Height 9–15m (30–50ft). Leaves oval, 15cm (6in) in length, dark green and shiny. Flowers white, spring. Fruit round, large, pale yellow or orange-yellow, flesh moderately acid. Grown commercially for the production of grapefruit juice and dessert fruits, especially in the USA.
- *C. sinensis* (Sweet orange) China, South Vietnam ⑩ ♀
Height 12m (40ft). Spiny branches. Leaves elliptic, 10cm (4in) in length, deep green. Flowers white, fragrant, produced in spring. Fruits round, orange in colour, sweet flesh. This is the most important citrus fruit, grown commercially for orange-juice production and dessert fruits. There are many cultivars, an important commercial one being 'Valencia'.

Cultivation

☼ ☉ A AL ▣

They are self-fertile so a single tree can be grown if desired. Adaptable regarding soil types. Feed annually with a balanced fertilizer. Regular pruning is not required. If shoots become too crowded, thin them out. Remove dead growth.

In areas with unsuitable climates citrus can be grown in tubs of soil-based compost or soil beds in frost-free greenhouses or conservatories. Try to provide a minimum winter temperature of 7–10°C (45–50°F). Trees can be placed outdoors from early summer to early autumn. Feed annually with a balanced fertilizer; or liquid-feed fortnightly for container-grown trees. No regular pruning needed.

Problems

There are serious problems in commercial plantations, but these do not concern the amateur grower. The home gardener may come across aphids, mealybugs, scale insects and whitefly.

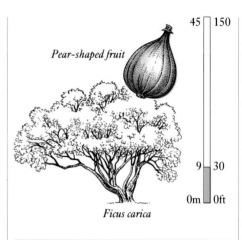

Pear-shaped fruit

45 — 150

9 — 30

0m — 0ft

Ficus carica

FIG

Ficus

Moraceae

This is a large genus of mainly tropical evergreen trees and shrubs. Some are familiar as house or conservatory plants, while the common fig is grown in Mediterranean-type climates for its fruits.

- *F. carica* (Common fig) Mediterranean ⑧ ♀
Height 9m (30ft) with a wide-spreading habit. Leaves large, with three to five lobes, of thick texture, medium green, deciduous. Fruits variable in shape and colour, but roughly pear-shaped, flushed with purple or brown, summer and autumn.

Cultivation

☼ ☉ A AL ▣

They are self-fertile and flourish in any well-drained soil. Under glass, figs can be grown in 45cm (18in) wide tubs with a similar depth. Little pruning is needed for trees grown in the open. With tub-grown plants thin out on a regular basis shoots which have fruited: after harvesting prune back to two leaves about half the old fruited shoots. Pick fruits when fully ripe and soft, and eat soon after harvesting.

Problems

Mealybug, red spider mite, scale insects.

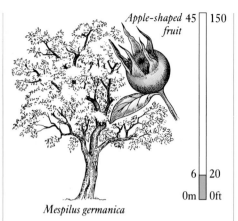

Apple-shaped fruit 45 150

6 20

0m 0ft

Mespilus germanica

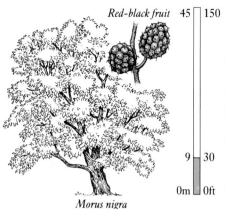

Red-black fruit 45 150

9 30

0m 0ft

Morus nigra

MEDLAR

Mespilus

Rosaceae

*T*here is only one species in this genus, a small deciduous tree which is sufficiently attractive to be grown in the ornamental part of the garden, perhaps as a lawn specimen.
• *M. germanica* (Medlar) south-east Europe, Asia Minor ⑥ ♀
Height up to 6m (20ft). Branches are sometimes spiny. Leaves oblong, up to 12.5cm (5in) in length, dull green, turning brown and yellow in the autumn. Flowers bowl-shaped, white, late spring and early summer. Fruits somewhat apple-shaped, up to 5cm (2in) in diameter, brown when fully ripe.

Cultivation

It is self-fertile so a single tree can be grown. Best results in soil well supplied with bulky organic matter. Mulch young trees. Harvest fruits in autumn while still hard and store for several weeks until very soft.

Problems
Aphids, caterpillars, mildew.

MULBERRY

Morus

Moraceae

A small genus of deciduous trees, native to Asia, Africa and North and South America. The species described here is an extremely attractive tree, becoming gnarled as it matures, and ideally suited to specimen planting in lawns. It is self-fertile and bears very dark red fruits, sharp yet sweet, in shape like those of loganberries.
• *M. nigra* (Black mulberry) western Asia ⑤ ♀
Height 9m (30ft). Slow-growing. Leaves oval, rather broad, up to 20cm (8in) in length, sometimes lobed, margins coarsely toothed, dull green. Fruits very dark red, almost black, about 2.5cm (1in) in length, late summer and early autumn.

Cultivation

☼ ☉ A AL 🛡

Best growth in a deep fertile soil that retains moisture. No pruning required, except for the removal in winter of dead or crossing branches. No particular problems apart from birds, which relish the fruits. Harvest fruits when fully ripe.

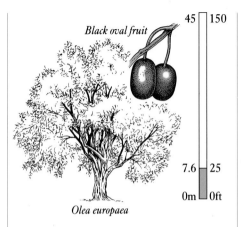

Olea europaea

45 ⌐ 150

7.6 ⌐ 25

0m ⌐ 0ft

Black oval fruit

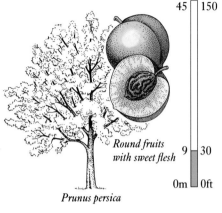

Prunus persica

45 ⌐ 150

9 ⌐ 30

0m ⌐ 0ft

Round fruits
with sweet flesh

OLIVE	PEACH AND NECTARINE
Olea	Prunus
Oleaceae	*Rosaceae*

*T*he olives are evergreen trees and shrubs widely distributed in the northern hemisphere. The species described here is grown commercially in mild climates such as California and the Mediterranean region for the production of fruits, which yield olive oil and are also used as a food and relish. An extremely attractive tree that makes a fine lawn specimen in a suitable climate.

● *O. europaea* (Common olive)
Mediterranean ⑨ ♀
Height 7.6m (25ft) or more. Leaves elliptic or lance-shaped, about 8cm (3in) in length, leathery texture, grey-green with silvery undersides, evergreen. Small white flowers in spring. Fruits oval, just over 2.5cm (1in) in length, ripening black, autumn. A lengthy hot growing season is needed for fruit to be produced.

Cultivation

☼ ☉ A AL ▦

Growth improved by annual feeding in spring and watering in summer. Trees are resistant to drought and intense heat. No regular pruning needed and no problems with single trees in private gardens.

*T*he peach is widely grown commercially in temperate zones and is also popular with private gardeners. The standard tree makes an attractive lawn specimen decked with blossoms in spring, but needs a warm climate to fruit. The nectarine is a smooth-skinned mutation and generally has smaller, better-flavoured fruits.

● *P. persica* (Peach, Nectarine)
China ⑧ to ⑩ ♀
Height up to 9m (30ft). Leaves lance-shaped, up to 15cm (6in) in length, mid-green, deciduous. Flowers pink, produced in spring before leaves. Fruits round, up to 8cm (3in) in diameter, with downy skins in peaches and smooth in nectarines, sweet, juicy, yellow flesh, summer.

Cultivation

☼ ☉ A AL ▦

Self-fertile so single trees can be grown. Avoid frost pockets. Prune annually in early spring to encourage new growth for fruit the following year. Apply a balanced fertilizer each year in early spring. Thin fruits to 20cm (8in) apart.

Problems

Aphids, bacterial canker, peach leaf curl, red spider mite, silver leaf.

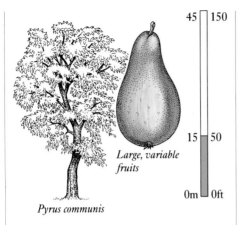

Large, variable fruits

45 — 150

15 — 50

0m — 0ft

Pyrus communis

PEAR

Pyrus

Rosaceae

*P*ears are important commercial fruits in cool temperate climates, being used mainly in the canning industry, although fresh fruits are also marketed. Pears are popular with home gardeners, too, and a mature tree makes an attractive specimen in the ornamental garden, especially when in flower during the spring. Many cultivars are available for both dessert and culinary use. Each country has its particular range of favourite varieties. In addition, pears can be trained to various restricted shapes, which makes pear growing feasible even in very small gardens, but it is the large tree form (standard or half-standard) that is discussed here.

● *P. communis* (Common pear)
Europe, western Asia ⑥ to ⑧ ⚇
Many cultivars have been derived from this species. Height 12–15m (40–50ft). Leaves oval to circular, up to 8cm (3in) in length. Flowers in clusters, white, produced during mid-spring. The large fruits of the cultivars are produced in summer and vary tremendously in flavour, sweetness, colour and texture. Early and mid-season cultivars cannot be kept for long once they are ripe but late kinds can be stored for use during the winter.

Cultivation

☼ ⊙ A AL A-N ⬛

Plant two or more different cultivars together to ensure cross-pollination; it is essential they flower at the same time and be compatible. Best results in deep loamy soil. Avoid planting in frost pockets.

Pruning is necessary, annually in winter. Most cultivars form fruit buds on spurs, which are produced on two-year-old and older shoots. Other cultivars form fruits buds at the tips of previous year's shoots. For pruning and other cultural details see the entry for Apple.

Pears are ready for picking when they part readily from the tree; lift a fruit and give it a slight twist and gentle pull. Pick early and mid-season cultivars before fully ripe and allow to finish indoors. In a temperature of 7°C (45°F) they will keep longer. Late cultivars will be hard when picked. They will keep in a cold storage area of 4–7°C (40–45°F) and can be ripened as required in warmer conditions. The storage area should be airy and have a slightly humid atmosphere.

Problems

Aphids, caterpillars, fireblight, scab.

CLIMATIC ZONES

①	Below −45°C (−50°F)
②	−45 to −39°C (−50 to −40°F)
③	−39 to −35°C (−40 to −30°F)
④	−35 to −29°C (−30 to −20°F)
⑤	−29 to −23°C (−20 to −10°F)
⑥	−23 to −18°C (−10 to 0°F)
⑦	−18 to −12°C (0 to 10°F)
⑧	−12 to −6°C (10 to 20°F)
⑨	−6 to −1°C (20 to 30°F)
⑩	−1 to 4°C (30 to 40°F)

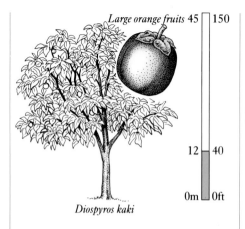

Large orange fruits 45 | 150

12 | 40

0m | 0ft

Diospyros kaki

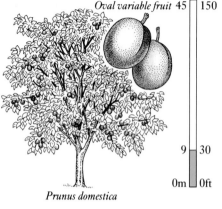

Oval variable fruit 45 | 150

9 | 30

0m | 0ft

Prunus domestica

PERSIMMON
Diospyros
Ebenaceae

Some persimmons are quite tender fruits but can be grown outdoors in suitable temperate climates. In late summer small fruits are produced that look rather like tomatoes.

● *D. kaki* (*D. chinensis*) (Chinese or Japanese persimmon) China, Japan ⑧ ♀
Height up to 12m (40ft). Leaves oval or obovate, about 15cm (6in) in length, glossy green on the upper surface with downy undersides, turning orange or red in the autumn, deciduous. Flowers yellow-white. Fruits 8cm (3in) in diameter, orange.

● *D. virginiana* (Common or North American persimmon) North America ⑤ ♀
Height 12m (40ft). Leaves oval or elliptic, 15cm (6in) in length, shiny and deep green above, with pale undersides, producing colourful autumn tints, deciduous. Flowers green-yellow. Fruits 5cm (2in) in diameter, varying from yellow to orange.

Cultivation

☼ ☉ **A AL** ▣

Best results in deep, fertile, loamy soils. Easily grown. No regular pruning needed.

PLUM
Prunus
Rosaceae

Plums are popular fruits with private gardeners and are also grown commercially, especially for canning and drying.

● *P. domestica* (European, garden or common plum) Europe, Asia ④ to ⑧ ♀
Height up to 9m (30ft). Leaves oval or obovate, about 10cm (4in) in length, dull green, deciduous. Flowers white, often before the leaves appear. Fruits oval, up to 8cm (3in) in length, produced in summer. Many cultivars.

Cultivation

☼ ☉ **A AL** ▣

Some cultivars are self-compatible so can be planted singly; others need to be cross-pollinated. Best results in deep fertile soil that retains moisture. Not too alkaline. Avoid planting in frost pockets.

Apply a balanced fertilizer in early spring. Young trees can be mulched with bulky organic matter. Thin fruits while small to 5–8cm (2–3in) apart if necessary.

Problems

Aphids, bacterial canker, birds (which damage buds and fruits), honey fungus, plum sawfly, red spider mite, silver leaf.

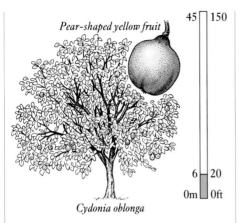

Pear-shaped yellow fruit

45 | 150

6 | 20

0m | 0ft

Cydonia oblonga

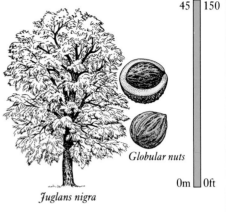

45 | 150

Globular nuts

0m | 0ft

Juglans nigra

QUINCE

Cydonia

Rosaceae

The quince is an attractive deciduous tree producing pear-shaped, aromatic, very acid fruits in summer which are often used for preserves. Old trees are frequently crooked and of irregular form, making attractive lawn specimens.

● *C. oblonga* (Common quince) western Asia ⑤ ♀
Height 6m (20ft). Slow-growing. Leaves oval or oblong, about 10cm (4in) in length, deep green above, with downy undersides, turning yellow in autumn. Flowers white or light pink, late spring. Fruits pear-shaped, about 10cm (4in) in length, yellow skin and flesh, aromatic, hard flesh.

Cultivation

☼ A AL 🛡

Self-fertile so a single tree can be grown. Best results in a deep, fertile, moisture-retentive soil. Harvest fruits when mature, when the skin is yellow. Best to use fruits soon after gathering. Can be stored for short periods in very cool conditions. No regular pruning needed.

Problems
Aphids, caterpillars, codling moth, fireblight, mildew.

WALNUT

Juglans

Juglandaceae

The walnuts are large deciduous trees grown not only for their nuts but for ornamental purposes and for their high-quality timber. Grown commercially in the south of the USA. The leaves are pinnate.

● *J. nigra* (Black walnut) North America ⑤ ♀
Height 45m (150ft). Leaves consist of 15–23 leaflets. The nuts are globular, about 5cm (2in) in diameter. High-quality timber.

● *J. regia* (Common, English or Persian walnut) south-east Europe, western Asia ⑦ ♀
Height 30m (100ft). Leaves composed of 7–9 leaflets. Nuts globular, about 5cm (2in) in diameter. Bark silver-grey. High-quality timber. Numerous cultivars including 'Laciniata' (cut-leaved walnut), with leaflets deeply divided.

Cultivation

☼ A AL 🛡

Best results in deep, fertile, loamy soil with protection from spring frosts. No regular pruning required. Remove dead or crossing branches in late summer.

Problems
Honey fungus.

INDEX

Figures in italics refer to illustrations

D

E

F

G

H

T

U V

ulex europaeus 31
ulmus (elm) *75*, 88, *88*, 182–3
  americana (American, white, water) 182
  carpinifolia (smooth-leaved, Cornish, Wheatly, Jersey) 182–3
  glabra (wych, Scotch, Camperdown) 109, 183
  × *hollandica* (Dutch, Huntingdon) 183
  procera (campestris) (English) 183
variegated trees, reversion 69
varnish tree 123

W

walnut *see juglans*
water shoots 68, *68*
watering 39, 60–1
weather problems 56–7
weedkillers 49, 60
  see also spraying
weevils 85, *85*
  see also pests
wet areas 31, *31*
whitebeam *see sorbus*
whitefly 85, *85*, 95
willow *see salix*
wind scorch 92
windbreak netting 56, 92

winds 48, 56–7, 92
wingnut 175
winter temperatures 111·
wires 53, *53*, 70
witch hazel, Chinese 36
woodland gardens 30
wounds 69

Y Z

yellow wood *see cladrastis*
yew *see taxus*
zelkova 183
  carpinifolia 183
  serrata (Japanese) 183

ACKNOWLEDGEMENTS

Swallow Publishing wish to thank the following individuals and organizations for their help in the preparation of this book. We apologize to anyone we may have omitted to mention.

A-Z Botanical Collection 10, 12, 23, 24, 28, 45, 50, 72/73, 80bl, 81tl, 84bl, 91r, 94, 102/103, 106/107; Bruce Coleman 9, 59, 67, 76tr, 82bl, 84tl, 85tl and bl, 86r, 88tr, 90, 92, 95; Liz Eddison 37, 70/71; Ron and Christine Foord 74, 75bl and r, 76br, 77tl and bl, 80tr, 81bl, 82tl, 88l; Jerry Harpur 80br; Peter McHoy 21, 26/27, 29b, 32, 33, 53, 77r, 78/79, 82r, 87, 89l, 108; Tania Midgley 2/3, 6/7, 8, 14/15, 17, 20/21, 47, 54/55, 62/63, 96/97; Oxford Scientific Films 58/59, 81r; RHS Wisley 79, 84r, 86l; Harry Smith Collection 25, 30/31, 34/35, 38, 40/41, 42/43, 46, 56, 68, 75tl, 83, 88br, 89r, 911, 98/99; Smith/Polunin Collection 29t, 103; Michael Warren 76l, 80tl

The map on pages 112/113 of the plant hardiness zones of the USA and southern Canada was devised by the US Department of Agriculture, Agricultural Research Service.

The map on pages 114/115 of the plant hardiness zones of Europe is © Mitchell Beazley Publishers Inc., reproduced by permission.